Adieu to God

Adieu to God

Why Psychology Leads to Atheism

Mick Power

WILEY-BLACKWELL

A John Wiley & Sons, Ltd., Publication

This edition first published 2012
© 2012 Mick Power

Wiley-Blackwell is an imprint of John Wiley & Sons, formed by the merger of Wiley's global
Scientific, Technical and Medical business with Blackwell Publishing.

Registered Office
John Wiley & Sons Ltd, The Atrium, Southern Gate, Chichester, West Sussex, PO19 8SQ, UK

Editorial Offices
The Atrium, Southern Gate, Chichester, West Sussex, PO19 8SQ, UK
350 Main Street, Malden, MA 02148-5020, USA
9600 Garsington Road, Oxford, OX4 2DQ, UK

For details of our global editorial offices, for customer services, and for information about how to
apply for permission to reuse the copyright material in this book please see our website at
www.wiley.com/wiley-blackwell.

The right of Mick Power to be identified as the author of this work has been asserted in
accordance with the UK Copyright, Designs and Patents Act 1988.

Wiley also publishes its books in a variety of electronic formats. Some content that appears in
print may not be available in electronic books.

Designations used by companies to distinguish their products are often claimed as trademarks. All
brand names and product names used in this book are trade names, service marks, trademarks or
registered trademarks of their respective owners. The publisher is not associated with any product
or vendor mentioned in this book. This publication is designed to provide accurate and
authoritative information in regard to the subject matter covered. It is sold on the understanding
that the publisher is not engaged in rendering professional services. If professional advice or other
expert assistance is required, the services of a competent professional should be sought.

Library of Congress Cataloging-in-Publication Data

Power, Michael J.
    Adieu to God : why psychology leads to atheism / Mick Power.
        p. cm.
    Includes bibliographical references and indexes.
    ISBN 978-0-470-66993-8 (cloth) – ISBN 978-0-470-66994-5 (pbk.)
    1. Psychology, Religious.   2. Psychology and religion.   I. Title.
    BL53.P69 2012
    200.1'9–dc22

                                                    2011015219

A catalogue record for this book is available from the British Library.

This book is published in the following electronic formats: ePDFs 9781119950875;
Wiley Online Library 9781119950868; ePub 9781119979951; eMobi 9781119979968

Set in 10.5/13pt Minion by Aptara Inc., New Delhi, India.
Printed in Singapore by Ho Printing Singapore Pte Ltd

1   2012

To Irina

Contents

Preface   ix

1. A Short History of Religion   1

2. The Psychology of Religion—The Varieties of
    Normal Experience   33

3. The Psychology of Religion—The Varieties of
    Abnormal Experience   61

4. Social Structures and Religion   89

5. Religion, Power, and Control   113

6. Religion and Health   141

7. How to Be a Healthy Atheist   167

References   181

Author Index   191

Subject Index   195

Preface

The release of Stephen Hawking's book *The Grand Design* in 2010 witnessed the expected reactions from the religious community. As the world's greatest living scientist, and probably the only one to have been given a starring role in an episode of *The Simpsons,* Stephen Hawking had previously seemed to play dice with the public and with whether or not God was necessary. Hawking had finally declared, about the Big Bang at the beginning of the (current) Universe, "It is not necessary to invoke God to light the blue touch paper and set the Universe going." The United Kingdom's Chief Rabbi, Lord Sacks, responded by stating that science is about explanation, but religion is about interpretation. This distinction between the magisterium of science and the magisterium of religion, as the great evolutionist Stephen Jay Gould referred to them, is of course nonsense. Absolute nonsense. To propose that science is about the how, but religion is about the why, is to misunderstand science completely. Psychology is a science, which we can define as follows: "The science of psychology is the how and why of mental life and behaviour." Psychology and adjoining areas such as anthropology, philosophy, psychiatry, and sociology have much to say about the *how* and *why* of religion. These magisteria are not "non-overlapping" in any sense. From the Copernican revolution onwards, the Christian Church has been fighting a losing rearguard action against the major advances in science, enough to have led many major sociologists to predict its death. However, from a psychological perspective religions offer far more than science does, because the promise of eternity, paradise, and damnation for your enemies is guaranteed to win over a lot of people, especially on a bad day. As a psychologist, therefore, I believe it essential to understand why all cultures in all epochs have created religious systems and beliefs in the supernatural, in order to understand why in many parts of the world, including the United States, religion is gaining in strength and in followers, despite the advances in the physical and biological sciences. How can the majority of Americans believe in creationism and intelligent design instead of evolution?

Religions are social systems that have been developed by people. These systems are typically based on the reported religious experiences of charismatic leaders, and are therefore ultimately about universal psychological experiences that have become incorporated into the 30 000 or so known religions, plus the other 100 000 that have yet to be invented in response to the special experiences of future charismatic leaders. Each religious system will of course have you think that it is the one true religion and that you are to forget the tens of thousands of other religions as if they did not exist. But the existence of so many contradictory religious systems can only be explained by psychological and social explanations that offer interpretations as to why we, as a human species, are so vulnerable to giving reality to the spectres in our minds.

In writing a book about the psychology of religion, I think it important to declare that although I became an atheist when I was 16 I was in fact attending a Catholic grammar school at the time, Saint Phillip's, in Birmingham. I was a disputatious student that the governing Catholic Oratorian Fathers must have tired of regularly. Some people would say that nothing has changed. However, I look back now with some gratitude that at least the Oratorians in these modern times allowed discussion and dispute, rather than handing me over to the Dominicans of the Middle Ages when I would have been put through the full Inquisition with torture followed by being burnt at the stake. Anyway, I always suspected that there were one or two latent atheists in their midst, not to mention those who had reached their own conclusions about Catholic vows of celibacy. However, I am not the "aggressive atheist" type that frightened off poor Cardinal Karl Jasper from joining Pope Benedict XVI on his recent visit to the United Kingdom. My mother is a devout Catholic, my wife believes in a spiritual world, and I have many friends, students, and clients who practice a wide range of different religions. In fact, when I read the "aggressive atheists" like Richard Dawkins and Christopher Hitchens, sometimes I agree that they can sound too aggressive even to a fellow atheist. I have an empathy with most (though not all) religious belief and with most (though not all) religious believers. My intention in writing this book is to convey something of this empathy through an understanding of religious experience and belief but without ever sounding patronizing or sneering, even though my belief is that psychology (with help from philosophy, anthropology, sociology, physics, biology . . .) offers a far more powerful explanation than any religious system ever will.

Well, it is not just the Oratorians who ran Saint Phillip's that I need to acknowledge and thank in the writing of this book, but also the many school friends who, both at that time and in the many years since, have been astute sparring partners. So thank you, Tony Manville, Paul Shobrook (and your brother Tony, now an Anglican monk), Mick Quille, Mick Drury, and Mick Garvey. From university days I would especially like to thank Charlie Sharp, Andy MacLeod, Lorna Champion, Tim Dalgleish, and Jonathan Cavanagh for their inspiring discussions. My son Liam, now studying philosophy at St Andrew's University, is an able match for all of us. I would especially like to thank Charlie Sharp, Andy MacLeod and Kate Loewenthal who read and commented on an earlier draft of the book. I would also like to thank Andrew Peart, my editor at Wiley, who responded with unbelievable enthusiasm the same day I sent him the proposal for the book. We share an atheist's love of Iona, so I discovered. Finally, my thanks to Irina, who also loves Iona, for being challenging from start to finish, who has thrown every argument for the existence of god and God at me regularly, and who, once she accepted that she had escaped Soviet atheism only to marry a Western atheist, has been totally supportive of this endeavour throughout.

Mick Power
Christmas (or should I say
Sol Invictus and Saturnalia?), 2010

1

A Short History of Religion

Ancestor worship must be an appealing idea to those who are about to become ancestors.

Stephen Pinker

Introduction

Karol Józef Wojtyła was a frail 84-year-old who could barely walk because of his osteoarthritis. He suffered from Parkinson's disease, which left his speech slurred and his memory failing. His increasing deafness made it difficult for him to understand others. He had experienced a cardiac arrest and a near-fatal shooting, and had had a colostomy. He eventually suffered multiple organ failure and sepsis, and died on April 2, 2005. At the time of his death, Karol Józef, otherwise known as Pope John Paul II, was the leader of an estimated one billion Catholics worldwide (the world's largest religion) and had spent nearly 27 years viewed by those Catholics as "God's representative on Earth." An estimated four million people attended his funeral, which included a record number of heads of state ever to attend such an event.

At the age of two years, Llamo Thondup's family received a visit from a Buddhist delegation in their tiny village of Takster in Tibet. Llamo was the fifth of 16 children born to a farming and horse-trading family. On being shown items belonging to the Thirteenth Yellow Hat Dalai Lama the two-year-old evidently exclaimed "They are mine! They are mine!" at which point he was declared to be the Fourteenth Dalai Lama and, therefore, the

Adieu to God: Why Psychology Leads to Atheism, First Edition. Mick Power.
© 2012 Mick Power. Published 2012 by John Wiley & Sons, Ltd.

reincarnation of the Buddhist god of compassion. At the age of four he was taken to the Potala Palace in Lhasa and began his studies of Buddhism, though a meeting at age 11 with an Austrian mountaineer (played by Brad Pitt in the Hollywood film, *Seven Years in Tibet*) clearly broadened the young boy's knowledge of the outside world.

Emperor Hirohito of Japan was born with what many might consider to be a definite advantage in life. Because of his divine descent from the goddess Amaterasu Omikami, Hirohito was an absolute deity within the beliefs of the Shinto religion. His declaration of war against the USA was therefore viewed as the act of a god against a secular power, such that the Japanese could not envisage defeat. However, a few days after the dropping of the atomic bombs Little Boy on Hiroshima and Fat Man on Nagasaki on August 15, 1945, the Americans forced Hirohito to make a radio announcement in which he had to reject the Shinto claim that he was an incarnate deity. Many Japanese did not believe the announcement and continued to believe that the Emperor was a deity until his death in 1989, even though supernatural power clearly lost out to atomic power on this occasion.

These three short case studies are presented to illustrate that even in the present age of reason and science there are those who believe that there are deities or near-deities who walk among us. Many people in the West, even those who are strongly religious, tend to think that beliefs in incarnate deities are quaint and archaic, like the medieval kings who presented themselves as gods to their peoples. Yet the Dalai Lama, who seems to have become a superstar in the West, regularly visits presidents and prime ministers and appears on television chat shows while believing that he is a deity. Charm and a very disarming smile do not, however, make the Dalai Lama a deity.

What we will examine in this book is how beliefs such as these arise in the first place and what allows the beliefs to be sustained in the face of possible disproof. If they were gods, a mere secular power would not be expected to be able to overcome them, yet both Emperor Hirohito at the hands of the Americans and the Dalai Lama at the hands of the Chinese have suffered major and unexpected defeats during their lifetimes to mere secular powers. Surely these defeats should have persuaded their followers that perhaps they are not deities after all?

Whatever protects their followers' beliefs from evident disproof is a question that psychology must address. Moreover, the question of current and recent human deities gives us access to possible tests of religious beliefs in a manner that is not available for most religions, because many of these are based on long-past deities and prophets who now exist only in memory or, in some cases, only in fantasy. We might try to put to the test the Catholic religion's belief that the Pope is God's representative on Earth. The Pope, however, is unlikely to subject himself to such proof or disproof because of his belief that ultimately *faith* is stronger than reason. Furthermore, the apparent disproofs that do not fit with existing beliefs seem to be easily rejected. As psychologists such as George Kelly and philosophers such as Karl Popper have emphasized, we are all too good at collecting evidence *for* our beliefs, but extremely poor at seeking out evidence *against* our beliefs. We will examine these powerful confirmation biases in later chapters, but in the remainder of this chapter we will try to understand something of the history and cultural context for the different types of religious belief and examine why some religious systems have come to be predominant over others.

The overall structure of this book will first begin with a very brief skim over the history of religion from the earliest animistic religions to the polytheistic and then to the monotheistic. This summary will include brief points about the challenges presented to world religions by advances in the sciences. A reader who is familiar with or even an expert in this history may wish to jump straight to Chapter 2, where we begin an examination of everyday psychological experiences that often lead people towards religious explanations for such experiences. When these are added to the more unusual experiences of some religious mystics that we detail in Chapter 3, we have to conclude that there is a considerable body of common and uncommon experiences for which religions provide often very comforting explanations, especially when those experiences might be frightening or overwhelming. In Chapters 4 and 5 we will examine some of the social structures that are present both in religious institutions and in beliefs about the gods. As William James did in 1902, we will consider some of the more negative features of religious institutions, but we will not forget the many positive benefits that membership of such institutions can also provide. These positive benefits for health and well-being come more to the fore in Chapter 6, when we examine exactly what the evidence shows for such health and longevity benefits from religion. The conclusion of the review is that religion is the ultimate curate's egg. There can be many benefits, such that the poor honest atheist may well be disadvantaged by comparison, but there can be many disadvantages too. In the final chapter, Chapter 7, we therefore attempt to summarize the key benefits of religion and spirituality, and consider what the atheist might do in order to achieve benefits of a similar nature. In the remainder of the present chapter we provide a very brief summary of the history of religions to set the appropriate context for subsequent discussion for those readers who may not be familiar with all aspects of this history.

The Gods of Thunder

All cultures at all times in recorded history have developed complex belief systems that involve one or more supernatural powers that need to be worshipped through religious rituals. Freud (1927) famously referred to these developments as the *universal obsessional neurosis* in his essay *The Future of an Illusion*. Freud's analysis will be considered in more detail later, and, as we will see, although it may have some applicability to the role of the father in the monotheistic religions, it has much less relevance to the polytheistic and animistic religions. The Victorian anthropologist Edward Tylor was a strong proponent of animism as the origin of religious beliefs. He interpreted primitive religion as being based on the belief that everything in the Paleolithic period possessed a soul. The sociologist Emile Durkheim had considered totemism (a word derived from an Ojibwa Algonquin tribal word *ototeman,* which indicates a blood relationship) as the likely origin, in which the totem animal is considered to be the ancestor of the group. Later anthropologists, however, such as Edward Evans-Pritchard and Claude Levi-Strauss, strongly disputed totemism as an explanation of the development of religion. Levi-Strauss's classic work *The Savage Mind* (first published in French in 1962) emphasized the continuity between the "primitive" mind and the "modern" mind. We will emphasize this continuity throughout the book as we consider historical, cross-cultural, and developmental clues to religious belief.

One of our great evolutionary advances is the human capacity to seek to understand and find meaning and repeating patterns in the world around us. But this capacity can sometimes lead us to be easily fooled into finding patterns and associations where none in fact exists. The development of superstitious behaviors is a classic example: most people have superstitious beliefs which may be more evident under times of stress. If, when a child hears thunder, she repeats the words, "Mother save me, Mother save me," to herself and then she survives the storm, she may come to believe that the words have a magical and protective power and that she must repeat these words whenever she hears the sound of thunder. These superstitious learned associations are very common in childhood, and developmental psychology demonstrates to us that children have many such magical and animistic beliefs. Harry Potter is not popular because he is a fictional character, but rather because children identify with him and wish to have his powers in order to defeat the evil around them. The earliest animistic belief systems seem to share much with the beliefs of children in that they hold that supernatural forces exist in any animate or inanimate object and that beliefs in these forces help people to understand and ultimately to control and protect themselves against them.

In her excellent overview of early belief systems, Karen Armstrong (2005) in *A Short History of Myth* organizes myths into three periods: the Paleolithic period (20 000 to 8000 BCE) when myths were focused on hunting, the Neolithic period (8000 to 4000 BCE) in which myths related to farming, and the Early Civilizations (4000 to 800 BCE) when the large state religions came into being. Archeological excavations have shown that the Paleolithic hunter-gatherers made animal sacrifices; the cave paintings in Lascaux and in Altamira highlight the significance of the hunt in the Paleolithic period with depictions not only of the hunted animals but also of their hunters wearing animal head-dresses. The hunt was an especially dangerous time, and the emergence of individuals with special powers, the priest-shamans, seems to have occurred partly as a result of the desire to bring good fortune to the hunters and to protect them from danger. The myths of this period also focus on difficult-to-understand natural forces, among them the cycles of regeneration for plant life, the "regeneration" of the heavenly bodies such as the sun and the moon, also on regular cycles, and the experience of powerful natural phenomena such as lightning, thunder, volcanoes, and hot springs. All of these external natural phenomena required explanation. The sky was a source of particular fascination and incomprehension, and most of these early groups seem to have developed myths about one or more sky gods.

In addition to the puzzlement with the external, Karen Armstrong also points to the importance of the *internal* even for these early Paleolithic groups. Anthropologists point to societies such as the Australian aborigines, who still live as hunter-gatherers and who have not developed agriculture, as providing possible insights into the belief systems of earlier Paleolithic groups. Australian aborigines believe that, in addition to the day-to-day reality in which we live, there is a parallel reality or "Dreamtime" in which the ancestors live and out of which all cycles of creation emerge. Some living individuals are believed to have special powers to communicate between the two, though all people experience both realities through dreaming. Interestingly, it is believed that the child's eternal spirit enters the fetus around the fifth month of pregnancy when the pregnant woman first experiences the child's movements in the womb. We will of course consider the importance of internal experience in religious belief in much more detail in later chapters.

These early Paleolithic animistic belief systems already present us with a repeating structure and an attempt to explain a combination of phenomena external to the individual and a set of phenomena internal to the individual. The external phenomena include repeating cycles such as the daily movement of the sun, the monthly changes in the moon, and the seasonal changes in plant and animal life. In addition to these cycles of creation, of birth, death, and re-birth, there are also one-off and unpredictable external events such as storms, droughts, volcanoes, and earthquakes. Predictable cycles also occur in the internal psychological experiences such as in waking, sleeping, and dreaming, but internal experiences also include one-off and unpredictable events that can cause pain and that warrant explanation. These unpredictable experiences include injuries, diseases, and the deaths of loved ones. The pain of grief at the loss of a loved one, especially the loss of one's child, can be overwhelming for the individual, so it would be normal to seek solace and explanation from someone with special powers in the group, such as a priest-shaman, who can offer a system of explanation and even a continuing connection to the lost significant other.

The priest-shaman has clearly played an important role through all religions, even in the earliest animistic ones. Although the term "shaman" arises from a word used by a nomadic Siberian group, the term is now generally used to describe a whole range of witch-doctors, medicine men, sorcerers, and so on. They are people with special powers and experiences, which can include trance states, drug-induced hallucinations, and dream-like phenomena that are used as evidence that they can communicate from everyday reality to a supernatural reality such as in the Australian Aboriginal Dreamtime. Shamans became the holders of oral knowledge and tradition, such that in some societies the special knowledge would be passed from father to son. In whatever form the knowledge is retained and passed on from generation to generation, these oral traditions were the beginnings of our modern religious institutions and the claims of prophets and preachers that they have insight into the eternal and supernatural truths.

The Neolithic Period (c. 8000 to 4000 BCE)

The first agricultural communities were faced with different problems and demands than were the early hunter-gatherers, such that religious beliefs and practices began to change. About 10 000 years ago the first farming communities developed and began to replace the smaller nomadic hunter-gatherer groups with larger communities in settled locations. Awareness developed of the cyclical nature of farming, and a belief arose that there was a spiritual power that was locked in seeds and fruits that allowed them to burst into life, a process typically accompanied by appropriate spiritual and practical rituals. The generative power of the earth was recognized and therefore its power was replenished both with fertility rituals and, in some societies, with human sacrifice. For example, ritual fertility orgies could accompany the planting of seeds in springtime, in which the earth (which in many cultures came to be seen as mother earth and subsequently begat mother-goddesses) was considered to be implanted with the sacred seeds or semen and the same process of generation and birth occurred for both. As Karen Armstrong (2005) notes, interestingly the Bible presents evidence of these early fertility orgies in ancient Israel because the prophets implore their people to stop practicing them:

> Then shall ye know that I am the Lord, when their slain men shall be among their idols round about their altars, upon every high hill . . . and under every green tree, and under every thick oak, the place where they did offer sweet savour to all their idols. (Ezekiel 6:13)

> Thou hast moreover multiplied thy fornication in the land of Canaan unto Chaldea; and yet thou wast not satisfied herewith. (Ezekiel 16:29)

> Thus I will cause lewdness to cease out of the land, that all women may be taught not to do after your lewdness. (Ezekiel 23:48)

You just have to read the whole of the book of Ezekiel to learn how the early Israelites seem to have combined adulterous fornication with the extensive worship of false idols and from this to get a sense of the pre-Abrahamic fertility cults and practices that the monotheistic religions have gone to great lengths to eliminate.

The early creation myths see humans as originating from the earth in the same manner as plants and trees, which, given modern evolutionary theory, is a view not as wide of the mark as the monotheistic religions might originally have had us believe. Farming was therefore a *spiritual* activity in which earth and sky (in particular through rain and sun from the sky) combine to create all forms of life. This marriage of earth and sky can be seen in the Assyrian earth-mother goddess Asherah (the Hebrew name for

Athirat) who was the wife of El, the High Almighty sky god, who himself seems to have been the key predecessor of the Jewish Yahweh and whose name was even incorporated into the name Isra-*el*. The god Baal, who was worshipped by many early Israelites and by the Canaanites, was a fertility god also called the god of rain. From these we can see the practical nature of many of the early polytheistic religions, with their crucial links to cycles of farming and survival and the constant battles against death and the gods of destruction.

In terms of social structures, these early agrarian societies typically came to be organized as "chiefdoms." Widespread examples of such social organization have been studied by anthropologists in agrarian societies in Polynesia, Africa, and the Americas. Explorations of the Pacific Islands during the eighteenth and nineteenth centuries were illustrated by numerous accounts of the power of the chiefs in such chiefdoms, who in many cases held a near god-like status among their citizens (see, for example, Wright, 2009). These chiefs were imbued with special *mana*, a supernatural-type power that gave them rights and ownership and allowed them to set the *tabus* (the origin of the word taboo) for the groups that they ruled. In many cases, the chiefs were both the religious and political leaders of the group and thereby developed the power of the shaman into that of political and social power also. However, in groups where the chief was not the leading shaman, the two worked closely together to invest power in each other.

The Early Civilizations (c. 4000–800 BCE)

There are few ancient civilizations that retain the fascination of the Ancient Egyptians. The pyramids at Giza are one of the most highly visited tourist sites on Earth with an estimated three million visitors each year. Rosalie David's book *The Ancient Egyptians* (1998) provides one among many overviews of the growth of religious beliefs in Ancient Egypt through its Predynastic, Old Kingdom, Middle Kingdom, and New Kingdom phases. The Predynastic period begins around 5000 BCE with Neolithic farming communities beginning to settle along the banks of the Nile. The river's annual cycle of inundation and retreat provided a rich source of fertile land along its banks in a country that otherwise had too low a rainfall to sustain such farming communities. This dependence on the cycle of the river Nile therefore became central to Egyptian myth and religious belief. These Neolithic communities seem to have been organized in the form of the chiefdoms typical of agricultural communities until around 3100 BCE following a possible new group of arrivals, the so-called "Dynastic Race," into

Egypt, probably from Mesopotamia. From this period on there is a flourishing of art, architecture, and writing within Egypt. The Upper (Southern) and Lower (Northern) areas eventually came to be unified initially under the Upper Egyptian king, Scorpion, and were completed by his successor, Narmer (also known as King Menes). The first dynasty of the Old Kingdom therefore begins with Narmer. As part of the unification, Narmer moved his capital from the city of This in Upper Egypt to Memphis in Lower Egypt, though the city of This continued as an important religious centre.

The Predynastic and Early Dynastic Egyptian burial practices provide most information about the religious beliefs of this period. The fact that the dead were carefully buried with a variety of personal possessions and food points to a belief in life after death. The inclusion of amulets for magical protection with the bodies became increasingly common. These were shaped as animals such as the crocodile, the snake, and the falcon. The body was buried with the head to the south and looking to the west. Initially, chieftains were given similar graves to their subjects, but with the appearance of the Dynastic Race more elaborate tombs came to be built for the ruling classes. The style that emerged for the noble burials in the early period continued the burial below ground, but increasingly elaborate buildings were built above ground in which the initial funerary practices were carried out. The careful burial of certain animals such as cows and jackals also indicates the development of animal cults in these early communities.

Like many Neolithic farming communities, mother earth and the mother goddess came to be worshipped, the early Egyptian goddess taking the form of a cow and early painted pottery depicting her with a human head and cow's horns. Some of the graves indicate that the leaders were considered to be possessed of magical powers because special implements were included that were used in ritual magical fertility practices. By the time of Scorpion and Narmer's unification of Upper and Lower Egypt, the god of fertility, Min, was one of the key gods. He was typically represented as black (the colour of the fertile mud of the Nile) and ithyphallic (having an erect and uncovered penis), such that early Christian explorers often defaced his monuments and, with the introduction of photography, he would only be photographed from the waist upwards. Worship of the sun god, Ra, also seems to have started in the Predynastic period. His form and importance continued to develop throughout Egyptian history, and Ra (or, in the later form, Aton) became the major god in the Egyptian pantheon. His main cult centre was Heliopolis (originally "Iunu"), close to modern Cairo. Other well-known gods from the Old Kingdom period include Osiris, Seth, Isis, and Horus, who are linked together in a death and regeneration myth that reflected the annual inundation and retreat of the Nile and the growth of crops. In this myth, Osiris was originally a human king who was murdered by his brother Seth and his body was scattered throughout Egypt. Isis, who was both Osiris's wife and his sister, collected the pieces of his body together and restored them by magic, with which she conceived their son Horus. Eventually, Osiris became the king of the Underworld, with Horus identified with the living king of Egypt, and Seth came to represent all that is evil in the world.

The Old Kingdom (dynasties III to VI, from 2686 to 2181 BCE) sees the king become a near-divine being who is the son of a god but born to a human royal mother (here one already sees echoes of the "virgin birth" in the Christian mythology of Jesus as the son of a human mother and a divine archangel). This unique birth gave the king the central role as the intermediary between the gods and humans. However, in order to maintain the succession, the eldest daughter of the ruling king and queen normally became the wife of the next heir, which was usually her brother or half-brother. The king, as a divine being, owned all the land and the people of Egypt, and the successful passage of the dead to the afterlife came to be seen as dependent on the good will of the king. The Old Kingdom also saw the building of the pyramids, with the first step pyramid at Saqqara being designed by Imhotep, vizier to King Djoser. Imhotep was also known as a great healer. Under his Greek name, Asclepius, he became the god of medicine, and he is the likely origin of the "Great Architect of the Universe," which is the name given to the god of the Freemasons. He became the only non-royal to be elevated to divine status in later Egyptian history. The famous step pyramid at Saqqara was the first of the great pyramids; it stands 62 metres high, it is oriented east–west, and it consists of six giant steps, which are believed to permit the ascension of the king to join the sun god Ra in the celestial barque as he makes his daily journey across the sky. Although the later pyramids at Giza did not have the step structure, the builder of the Great Pyramid, King Cheops, covered his pyramid in white limestone which was believed to focus a ray of sunshine along which the king could travel back and forth between the heavens and his burial place. The original Egyptian name for pyramid ("pyramid" is the later Greek name now in common parlance) was "Mer," which has been translated as a "place of ascension" (again one can note resonances with the ascension of Jesus into heaven from the Mount of Olives near Jerusalem). While on the subject of the etymology of well-known Egyptian words, subsequent kings of Egypt came to be known as pharaohs because the royal residence in Memphis or "Great House" was called the "Per Wer" in Egyptian, a name that was eventually applied to the king himself.

The Egyptian Middle Kingdom and the preceding "First Intermediate Period" ran from about 2181 BCE to 1786 BCE and covered dynasties VII to XII. The decline of the power of the pharaohs at the end of the Old Kingdom changed religious beliefs and practices in that successful passage to the afterlife was no longer considered to be dependent on the gift of the pharaoh but instead came to be considered as based on the actions of individuals themselves such as in the observation of appropriate rituals and worship of the gods. Because of the significance of Osiris, in that he was murdered but then resurrected, his cult became of increasing importance in the Middle Kingdom period. Abydos, near to This in Upper Egypt, became a pilgrimage centre for the Osiris cult because Osiris' body was believed to have been buried there and therefore his resurrection would increase the likelihood of the resurrection of the pilgrims to his cult centre. An annual cycle of mystery plays that presented the birth, death, and resurrection of Osiris were enacted at Abydos by the priests. The eternal paradise, which now became the dream of all, was known as the "Field of Reeds," in which there was permanent springtime with lush and abundant harvests that never failed. It is remarkable how the conceptualization of paradise simply represented an easier version of life on Earth. As someone who hates gardening (presumably in common with many later theologians of the afterlife), the idea of having to grow and harvest crops for the rest of time would, I have to confess, come closer to hell than to heaven for me.

The Egyptian New Kingdom and its preceding "Second Intermediate Period" ran from about 1786 BCE to 1085 BCE and included dynasties XIII to XX. Thebes in Upper Egypt became an important centre of power, and the local god Amun had been worshipped there since at least Dynasty XII. In fact, Amun incorporated the older sun god Ra and thereby acquired the sun god's powers. The priests at Thebes further developed the power and the cult of Amun, who was now presented as the "king of gods" in that he ruled all other gods. Thebes therefore became Egypt's most important city in this period, and the associated temple complex at Karnak still stands as one of the greatest engineering achievements of all time. The development of the priesthood at Thebes and Karnak saw the increasing power of the priests in comparison with that of the pharaohs. This led to growing conflict in the reign of the pharaoh Amenhotep III in the eighteenth dynasty, the climax of this conflict occurring in the reign of his son Amenhotep IV. In fact, the religious crisis that occurred during the reign of Amenhotep IV could lay claim to being one of the most significant events in the history and development of religion.

Amenhotep IV suffered the ignominy of being struck out of the Egyptian chronology by his successors, hence little was known about him until the discovery in the nineteenth century of his new city of Amarna, excavated by Flinders Petrie. Amenhotep's chief wife, Nefertiti, was famed for her beauty. Recent DNA testing has confirmed that he was the father of one of the most famous of the pharaohs in modern times, Tutankhamun (who was named Tutankhaten at birth but, with the subsequent rejection of his father's Aten-based religion, changed his name to Tutankhamun to indicate his endorsement of the older Amun-based religion). Within a few years of becoming pharaoh, Amenhotep IV changed his name to Akhenaten, he developed a monotheistic religion that rejected Amun and other Egyptian gods, and he replaced these with the Aten (his new name Akhenaten means "Servant of the Aten"), who was a single sun god and who also incorporated the older sun god Ra. Historians and anthropologists have referred to Akhenaten as the "first individual in history" because of the range of reforms that he brought about not only in religion but also in the arts. We will return to the importance of Akhenaten in the development of the monotheistic religions in the next section. For Egypt, subsequent notable events include the Greek conquest of Egypt under Alexander the Great in 332 BCE, with the establishment of the Greek Ptolemaic pharaohs. Cleopatra was the last of the Ptolemaic pharaohs, following the Roman conquest of Egypt in 30 BCE.

The focus in this section has been placed on the Ancient Egyptians, but of course there were many other significant religions that developed in the period of the early civilizations. One such key religion that, unlike the Egyptian religion, still exists today is Zoroastrianism, which has an estimated 200 000 followers, the majority of whom live in India and are known as Parsis ("the people of Persia"). The founding leader, Zoroaster (the Latin version of Zarathrustra in the original language), is believed to have lived at about 1400 to 1200 BCE (see, for example, Mary Boyce's 2001 book *Zoroastrians*) and he may have lived near the Caspian Sea in North Western Kazakhstan. One warning for would-be modern-day gurus though is that, apart from his wife and children who clearly had little choice, Zoroaster is said to have converted only one person in his own village to his new religion, and that was his cousin—hence the saying, "You are never a prophet in your own town" (though we must note that Jesus of Nazareth had a similar problem in failing to convert people in his home town of Nazareth, and that Muhammad did not convert the people of his hometown Mecca until he returned from

Medina with an army that forced the Meccans to listen to him). Fortunately for the spread of Zoroastrianism, Zoroaster eventually began to travel and Zoroastrianism became the main religion of Iran and surrounding areas until the later spread of Islam almost led to the extinction of the religion.

Zoroastrianism provides an interesting intermediate religion between early animism plus polytheism and the later development of the monotheistic religions. Following a divine revelation at the age of 30, Zoroaster composed a set of holy songs, the "Gathas," which are the earliest surviving scriptures, though later scriptures have been collected into the "Avesta." The main god is "Ahura Mazda" ("The God of Wisdom"), whom Zoroaster saw or heard the voice of many times in divine revelation. Ahura Mazda declared himself to be the divine creator of all that is good and of the other good deities. There is, however, an equally powerful leader of the bad deities, Angra Mainyu, who presides over hell. It is the purpose of all humans to choose between these two equally powerful forces of good and evil. This split between good and evil is an important one psychologically, and is a theme that recurs in Judaism, Christianity and the dualistic Manichaeism of the followers of the religious leader Mani in the third century CE. The links in Zoroastrianism to earlier animistic beliefs are represented in the importance of fire, sun, and water for the religion, to the extent that Zoroastrians are sometimes referred to as "fire worshippers." The Zoroastrian temples came to have sacred fires that were kept permanently burning in them; these fires are attended to by the priests and it is estimated that some of the oldest extant fires have been kept burning continually for many hundreds of years. The religion also has important beliefs about purity, such that dead bodies cannot be buried in the earth for fear of contamination and are typically left exposed in funerary towers, nor is washing allowed in rivers or lakes because it would contaminate the sacred water. Any flow of blood was also seen as impure, therefore women were segregated and not allowed to engage in daily activities during their menstrual blood flow.

The Rise of Monotheism

Origins

The development of monotheism under the Pharaoh Akhenaten, who reigned from about 1353 to 1336 BCE, provides one of the key turning points in the development of religious belief. Akhenaten abandoned the previous Egyptian gods such as the powerful Amun-Ra and destroyed their temples. He moved his capital city from Thebes, where the priests of Amun-Ra were extremely powerful, and founded a new capital city at Amarna (Akhetaten) on the *east* bank of the Nile (in contrast to the preferred use of the west bank for most earlier Egyptian cities). The Aten had originally been considered as a minor god who had represented one aspect of the sun god Amun-Ra, that is, of the sun disk itself, but now Aten was elevated to being the sole creative force. Akhenaten wrote, in his Great Hymn to the Aten, "O sole God beside whom there is none," which many scholars have seen as the origin of Psalm 104 in the Bible ("Who coverest thyself with light as with a garment: who stretchest out the heavens like a curtain: . . . who maketh the clouds his chariot: . . . who maketh his ministers a flaming fire" Psalms 104:2–4). Of course, there were certain personal advantages to Akhenaten's declaration that the Aten was the one and only god: not only did he eliminate the powerful priesthood of Amun-Ra in Thebes, but he reasserted his own divinity in that he was the sole intermediary between the Aten and mankind.

The significance of the Egyptian Pharaoh Akhenaten in the rise of monotheism seems to have been underplayed by many commentators on the history of religion. However, commentators with a Judaeo-Christian background can perhaps be understood to have taken the view from the Book of Exodus in The Bible that the Egyptians were the bad guys and that nothing good could have come from them. The prophet Moses is seen as the good guy who led the Israelites out of slavery in Egypt to the "promised land," who gave them their new monotheistic religion after conversations with Yahweh on Mount Sinai, but who died before he made it to the promised land himself. As an aside, there is an interesting link here to animism and polytheism, with Yahweh originating as a volcano god, and the translation as "Jove" in the Roman pantheon of gods, who, among other things, was the Roman god of thunder.

The problem with the biblical account of the Exodus from Egypt is that there is little or no historical or archeological evidence to support the idea that Moses led 600 000 men plus women and children out of Egypt into Sinai where they wandered for 40 years. Sigmund Freud in his book *Moses and Monotheism* (1937) made the interesting proposal that Moses was actually an Egyptian and had been a priest or other senior figure within Akhenaten's loyal supporters. When Akhenaten died, the brief reign of Smenkhkare, quickly followed by the reign of the 9-year-old Tutankhamun, led to the re-establishment of the previous gods and the persecution and attempted

elimination of the monotheistic Atenism. Freud proposed that Moses managed to escape persecution and then led a small group of Atenists into
Canaan, where eventually the Aten religion provided the foundations for
biblical monotheism, and the sun god joined forces with the god of volcanoes to become the all powerful Yahweh. Freud's proposal has of course
been disputed by many historians and archeologists because, for example,
the earliest settlements of the Israelites seem to date from just after the reign
of Rameses II (who ruled 1279–1213 BCE). If there were any truth in the
Exodus, the period that has better support from the evidence is at least
a hundred years after Akhenaten's death. However, it seems a mistake to
think that Atenism simply died out after Akhenaten's death and its subsequent rejection by his son Tutankhamun. There may well have been secret
worshippers and priests of Aten, especially in the sun god's temples in Heliopolis, whose teachings spread northwards through Sinai and into Canaan
at around the time of the first Israelite settlements. Freud also makes the
interesting observation that circumcision, which is an obligatory practice
for both Jewish and Islamic believers (though it did not catch on in Christianity because the Greek and Roman "gentiles," who were the targets of
St Paul's proselytizing, found the practice repulsive, not to mention painful
and dangerous), originated as an ancient Egyptian custom, though the Bible
for obvious reasons avoids any mention of this link. However, the fact that
Judaism took the practice of circumcision from the ancient Egyptians lends
weight to the proposal that they took other practices from the Egyptians
such as monotheism too. A further point that Freud and others have noted
is that the name "Moses" is an Egyptian rather than Hebrew name, though
its closest links in the eighteenth and nineteenth dynasties seem to be to
"Rameses," which would strengthen the interpretation that Moses and the
Exodus were linked to this later period. We might also note the speculative
origin of the "Amen" proclamation that is made during prayers and religious
services, with its possible links to the Egyptian god Amen.

The Abrahamic Monotheisms

Whether or not it was Atenism that was the catalyst for the growth of
monotheism among the Israelites from 1200 BCE onwards, we must ask
the question as to why the polytheist Israelites of the early Bible eventually
abandoned their polytheism in favour of the monotheism based on the
creator god, Jehovah. Moreover, this monotheism provided the foundation
for the other two great monotheistic religions, Christianity and Islam, who

also accept the Old Testament as part of their holy scriptures. All three of these monotheisms are referred to as the Abrahamic religions. Abraham is considered as the founding patriarch of the Israelites, who trace their lineage through his son Isaac by his wife Sarah, and therefore Christians also take Abraham as the founding patriarch because Jesus was a Jew. In contrast, Muhammad traced the origin of Islam through Abraham's other son, Ishmael, by his wife Hagar, and of whom Muslims claim that Muhammad was a direct descendant. Abraham is famous in the Book of Genesis for the story in which he makes his son Isaac carry a stack of wood up to the top of a mountain and then ties Isaac to the wood and is about to burn him because God told him to do so. Fortunately for Isaac and the future Israelites an angel intervened at the last moment and provided Abraham with a ram to sacrifice instead. The Muslim belief is that Abraham founded Mecca and built the Muslim centre of worship, the Kaaba. This is now a pillar of Islam, with the expectation that all Muslims will make a pilgrimage, or *hajj*, to visit it. The Islamic festival of Eid is a re-enactment of Abraham's near-sacrifice of his son, though again Islamic sons, fortunately for them, are replaced by sheep or goats for ritual sacrifice and consumption.

One of the first problems to arise with the Abrahamic account of monotheism is that the Jewish traditional dating for Abraham is somewhere between the nineteenth and seventeenth centuries BCE. However, the writing of the first five books of the Bible, the Pentateuch (Genesis, Exodus, Leviticus, Numbers, and Deuteronomy) is thought to have begun in the eighth century BCE under King Hezekiah and in the seventh century BCE under King Josiah, then not completed until the Israelites returned from exile in Persia somewhere between 500 and 450 BCE. By the time of the completion of the first five books of the Bible, therefore, Jewish monotheism had been long established, so the biblical accounts of the rise of monotheism include a substantial rewriting of Jewish history in which the polytheism of the early Israelites is minimized and the role of the great prophets Abraham and Moses is maximized, especially in their mythical conversations with the one god, Yahweh. What we must ask, however, is, if we trace the origins of monotheism to Egypt and to Akhenaten instead, what were the psychological, social, and political advantages for a shift to monotheism in a minor tribe such as the Israelites, and why did monotheism develop and flourish with this minor tribe when it failed to develop in the powerful Egyptian civilization?

The question of the development of monotheism from polytheism is not therefore one of truth versus myth, but of psychological, social, and political advantage. The Egyptians were a powerful, long-established, complex civilization, and were feared by all small surrounding tribes such as the Israelites. As noted earlier, whether or not the Israelites were taken into slavery in Egypt and Moses led them out during the Exodus, the influence of Egyptian ideas was extremely powerful and it is clear that many of the Judaeo-Christian beliefs such as those relating to Paradise, resurrection, the afterlife, the soul, and, we argue, of monotheism itself originate in Egyptian beliefs. What the monotheism of Yahweh offered the Israelites was a rejection of other non-Israelite gods as false gods, the knowledge that they believed in the one true god, and the certainty that they were God's chosen people. A small, weak, and inferior tribe was thereby able to elevate itself above all the great civilizations that had threatened or conquered it in the past, as well as those great civilizations that were to conquer it in the future, and to assume a position of superiority both psychologically and socially. Robert Wright in his book *The Evolution of God* (2009) and other writers have argued that the Babylonian conquest of Israel in the sixth century BCE with the destruction of the Temple of Solomon in Jerusalem was a cataclysmic experience for the Israelites that pushed them completely into monotheism as a way of coping with the ignominy of defeat and of exile and subordination in Babylon, while believing that they were the chosen people of the one true god. One can understand how such beliefs can be sustaining on a long cold night in Baghdad when you are far from home and waiting for God's messiah to defeat your enemies and lead you back to the promised land. As Robert Wright notes about the later chapters in the Book of Isaiah, which were written in exile in Babylon:

> And so it is in Second Isaiah: God is promising that the various peoples who have tormented and enslaved Israel over the centuries will eventually get their just deserts; they'll be forced to acknowledge Israel's superiority on both a political and a theological plane. (p.173)

The problem with polytheisms is that they are typically god-tolerant religions; polytheistic cultures accept the existence of gods from other cultures and often even incorporate them into their own pantheons. In contrast to polytheisms, therefore, monotheism is intolerant but offers a sense of superiority and chosen-ness to its believers. To give a later example, when Muhammad and his followers eventually captured the holy site of the Kaaba in Mecca, Muhammad is reported to have removed the 360 gods from many polytheistic religions (including Jesus and his mother Mary) that were present in the Kaaba in pre-Islamic times. Indeed the Koran criticizes Christianity for not being a truly monotheistic religion because of its concept of the "trinity," which was established following the Council of Nicaea (in 325 CE) to deal with the decision at the Council that Jesus was also divine even though many Christians had disputed this until that time. Taking Muhammad and the Koran's point even further, we might ask whether any religious system that includes angels, devils, the mother of god, and so on can truly be labelled "monotheistic."

The period of time that the Israelites spent in exile in Babylon can also allow one to trace influences of the Babylonian religion, Zoroastrianism, on Jewish theology, in particular the "dualistic" split between the god of goodness (Ahura Mazda in Zoroastrianism, see above) and the evilness of Satan (or Angra Mainyu as he was known in Zorostrianism). These lesser deities seem to have been a way of incorporating the lesser deities of polytheism into so-called monotheism. Nevertheless, despite Muhammad's criticisms of Christianity and our criticisms of them all, we can acknowledge how the biblical inferiority of the Israelites in this world over hundreds of years was compensated for by their belief in a supernatural world in which they and their god dominated all others, especially their enemies. It is hard to escape the psychological function of a belief in their own supernatural superiority over their enemies during the Israelites' long periods of subjugation.

Theism and Deism

We have to be careful, therefore, not to fall into a trap that the monotheistic religions set for us, which is somehow to make us believe that monotheism is superior to "earlier" pagan polytheisms, and that it was merely a matter of time for the one true god to emerge from among all of the false idols. The emergence of monolatry (that is, the worship of one god even though other gods are believed to exist) and subsequently monotheism among the Israelites and its heritage for Christian and Muslim religions can lead to a false psychological perspective of progress and advancement. This is perhaps analogous to the way in which democracy as a sociopolitical system is considered to be superior to absolute monarchy or dictatorships. In order to countermand this false impression, we will briefly consider two other leading world religions, that is, Hinduism and Buddhism, which in their complexity do not permit any easy categorization as polytheistic, monotheistic, or deistic.

Hinduism is the world's third-largest religion after Christianity and Islam and has an estimated one billion followers worldwide, though the majority of practitioners are in India. The earliest texts, the *Vedas*, were recorded about 1500 BCE and have been attributed to a group of invaders into north-west India, the so-called Aryan people. However, Victorian ideas of a super-race, and their unfortunate repercussions in Nazi Germany, have been complicated by more recent archeological evidence for the existence of cities that developed in the Indus Valley region (in present-day Pakistan) around 2500 BCE and possibly even earlier. The continuity with this early civilization has led many Hindus to claim that Hinduism is the world's oldest surviving religion. The pantheon of gods worshipped in Hinduism includes the male gods Vishnu and Shiva and the female deity Devi, but other gods that are familiar in the West include the elephant-god Ganesha, the murderous Kali (considered to be a manifestation of Devi), the monkey-god Hanuman, Brahman who is the supreme spirit, and Krishna who is an avatar or earthly incarnation of Vishnu. In non-dualist versions of monotheistic Hinduism such as the followers of the guru Shankara (788–820 CE), the self and the absolute spiritual reality of Brahman are seen as one; in dualist versions such as that to which the followers of the philosopher Madhva adhere, the self (*atman*) is considered distinct from the spiritual god Brahman.

Hindus consider that Buddha was one of the avatars of Vishnu. The founder of Buddhism, Siddhartha Gotama, was born in north-east India in about the fifth century BCE. Like the Hinduism out of which it developed, Buddhism defies easy categorization in terms of the categories of animism, polytheism, and monotheism that we have discussed so far. The term "Buddha" that is applied to Siddhartha Gotama simply means "enlightened one" even though it is often used as if it were a proper name. The process of enlightenment within Buddhism is an attempt to escape from the ego and the desires of the self, and thereby escape the birth–death–rebirth cycle or karma that was already an important belief within Hinduism. Different traditions have emerged in Buddhism, the two main divisions being Theravada and Mahayana Buddhism, the former being prevalent in countries such as Sri Lanka, Thailand and Myanmar, whereas the latter is prevalent in China, Japan and Tibet. Only in Tibet, however, did the feudal theocracy that seems to be so beloved of Western romantics develop from the twelfth century onwards, to be replaced by the Chinese liberation in the 1950s. (This is not the normal Western view of the Dalai Lama and Tibet, but the question for Westerners has to be, how many would like to live in a feudal theocracy in which the Archbishop of Canterbury were president for life in the United Kingdom, or Pastor Pat Robertson were president for life in the United States? The proposal usually leaves Westerners perplexed.)

The well-known Zen version of Buddhism began in China in the sixth century CE and subsequently became the dominant form in Japan from the twelfth century CE onwards. Zen Buddhism emphasizes the importance of meditation, for example on paradoxical statements or koans such as the famous "the sound of one hand clapping." Meditation on these paradoxical statements is meant to lead to a state of intellectual exhaustion in which the ego is eventually abandoned on the route to enlightenment. There is clearly something of a fatal attraction for those steeped in the logical–rational traditions of the West for such challenges to rationality within approaches such as Zen and other forms of Buddhism. An interesting phenomenon that highlights some of the tolerance and attractiveness of Buddhism is its increasing appeal for Hindu low-caste individuals known as "dalits" or "untouchables," whose plight within Hinduism has been very problematic. Because Buddhism rejects the caste system, there have been many millions of dalit converts to Buddhism in the past century. In fact, the majority of Christians in India are also converts from the Hindu untouchable caste, with very few converts from higher castes such as Brahmins.

The alert reader at this point may say, "Hang on a minute. You have not mentioned anything about a god or gods in your discussion of Buddhism." Well, that is why we have saved Buddhism till last in our overview of world religions. The fact that there is a cycle of reincarnation in which the individual can return as any living human or other animal indicates that there is a sphere of what are called "gods" (devas), though these are more like "angels" in the monotheistic religions. These gods or spirits are still subject to karma and will be reborn again. The ultimate aim in Buddhism is that of "nirvana," which is a state of pure mental energy beyond nothingness in which there are no longer any gods. However, it is a mistake to label Buddhism "atheistic," as some commentators have done, because its ultimate state is beyond nothingness, and it may be preferable to extend the term "deism" to include this energy state. As a term "deism" originally referred to the beliefs of a British group who, under the influence of advances in the scientific descriptions of the universe, believed that God had created the universe but then stepped back and allowed it to function according to scientific laws without any further intervention. There are also a number of modern physicists such as Paul Davies whose arguments for the supernatural come close to the Buddhist notions of energy, and for whom, therefore, deism in this altered definition would also be appropriate as a label. From the psychological viewpoint, the most interesting thing about Buddhist cosmology is that it derives from meditation-based alterations in consciousness, in which there is an experience of a loss of sense of self and an experience of oneness with the universe: this labelling of a psychological experience as an insight into the structure of the universe is obviously open to question, though we will wait until Chapters 2 and 3 to examine the psychology of religious experience in detail.

The Mammon of Science (or "Thank God for the Enlightenment")

Science is both a process or method and an accumulation of facts and theories. The scientific process itself leads to an examination of religious beliefs and practices in a way that many religious individuals find contrary to prescriptions of *faith*, which, they argue, are givens that cannot and should not be examined by such means. Perhaps, though, if the early scientific investigations had supported the idea that the Earth was flat, that it was at the centre of the universe, and that God had created the Earth and all creatures in six days in 4004 BCE (the date declared by Archbishop Ussher in 1650 to be the age of the universe based on the genealogies within the Old Testament), then religions might have been a lot happier with science. The problem, however, is that the Earth is round, that we are nowhere near the centre of the universe, and that your mother really was an ape. We will examine briefly how Christianity has tried to deny these facts, has persecuted those that dared to put forward such ideas, and has now had to play catch-up with the extraordinary developments in science over the last few hundred years. Some claim that religion and science are different domains and that science has no relevance for the domain of religion, but such claims are disingenuous nonsense because religions are testable with the methods of science as we will show.

The Position of the Earth in the Universe

The mediaeval Christian Church held the view that the Earth was at the centre of a universe that had been created by God in six days, as recounted in the Book of Genesis. This view of the universe followed the proposals by Aristotle in the fourth century BCE that the universe is centred around the

Earth (that it is "geocentric"), that it has existed unchanged throughout time, and that there is a set of nested concentric celestial spheres that rotate around the Earth and that contain the sun, the planets, and the stars. Aristotle's ideas were further developed by the Alexandrian Claudius Ptolemaeus (known simply as "Ptolemy" in the West, though he is not thought to be related to the Egyptian Greek Ptolemy dynasty that ended with Cleopatra). Ptolemy's great work, *The Almagest*, elaborated on Aristotle's geocentric universe with the proposals that the Earth is stationary, and, more usefully, he provided detailed mathematical tables that predicted positions of planets, stars, and times of eclipses.

The most significant initial challenge to the Biblical and Ptolemaic geocentric cosmologies came from Nicolaus Copernicus in the sixteenth century, a challenge that was subsequently developed by Galileo, Kepler, and Newton in the seventeenth century. Although, as we will discuss, Galileo is celebrated because of the Roman Inquisition that set out to discredit his work, Copernicus (1473–1543) has to be one of the most extraordinary individuals in the history of science. To begin with, Copernicus was a Catholic cleric for whom astronomy was a part-time hobby rather than a professional activity. Nevertheless, his accumulation of observations of the moon, the sun, and the planets led him to conclude by around 1514 that the geocentric cosmology of Ptolemy was in error, and that it needed to be replaced by a heliocentric cosmology in which the apparent motion of the sun and the stars is a consequence of the daily rotation of the Earth on its axis. Although Copernicus wrote a short unpublished pamphlet sometime around 1514, he continually delayed publication of his great book *On The Revolutions of the Celestial Spheres* until near his death in 1543 because he knew that there were errors in his mathematical calculations. In fact, the apocryphal story is that he awoke from a coma to be given the first printed copy of his book and then died the same day! (See, for example, the Irish novelist John Banville's (1999) *Doctor Copernicus.*)

The Catholic Church had been aware of Copernicus's heliocentric proposals even during his lifetime, and Copernicus had been one of the experts involved in the revision of the Julian calendar by Pope Gregory XIII on the strength of his reputation. Hence, why it took until 1616 before the Church officially declared Copernicus to be wrong is an interesting question. In his majestic *A History of Christianity*, Diarmaid MacCulloch (2009) suggests that, by the beginning of the seventeenth century, the long onslaught of Protestantism on Roman Catholicism had left the Catholic Church in a precarious and insecure state. In this precarious position, the outright challenge presented by Galileo in his support of Copernicanism was greeted not with tolerance but instead with the infamous Inquisition. Galileo Galilei (1564–1642) discovered the moons of Jupiter and the orbit of the planet Venus around the sun, all of which contradicted the geocentric views of the Catholic Church: "[The Lord] laid the foundation of the earth, that it should not be removed for ever" (Psalms 104:5). Galileo had been denounced to the Roman Inquisition in 1615 and instructed to abandon his heliocentric heresy. However, the subsequent publication in 1632 of his heliocentric proposals in the "Dialogue Concerning the Two Chief World Systems" led to the Catholic Church placing him under house arrest for the rest of his life. Still, at least he was spared the fate of Giordano Bruno, the former Dominican monk and supporter of Copernicanism, who was burned at the stake for his heretical views. The Catholic Inquisition continues to this day, though as far as we know it no longer practices torture and burns people at the stake; and it now has the more homely title of the "Congregation for the Doctrine of Faith," which was headed by Cardinal Joseph Ratzinger, "The Enforcer," until his promotion in 2005 when he became Pope Benedict XVI.

The Position of Man in the Universe

The climax of the challenges to the Catholic Church from science came with Charles Darwin's publication of *On the Origin of Species* in 1859. Darwin's momentous work must, however, be considered in the context of an accumulation of questions about the biblical timescales and creation story, such as the claim in 1650 by Archbishop Ussher that the Earth had been created at midday on Monday October 23, 4004 BCE. Prior to Darwin, the evidence from geology and paleontology was already leading to widespread questioning of the biblical account. James Hutton (1726–1797), known as the Father of Geology, had observed a range of "unconformities" in East Lothian near Edinburgh including at Siccar Point, which necessitated geological cycles of seabed deposition, uplift, and erosion in order to explain some of the geological structures that he observed. In 1795, in his famously unreadable *A Theory of the Earth with Proofs and Illustrations,* Hutton noted that "we find no vestige of a beginning and no prospect of an end." Charles Lyell (1797–1875) was the great Victorian geologist who became a close friend of Darwin, and whose *The Principles of Geology* was taken by the young Darwin on the voyage of *The Beagle.* Darwin wrote about Lyell's book, "it altered the whole tone of one's mind . . . when seeing a thing never seen by Lyell, one yet saw it partially through his eyes." During the nineteenth century the estimated age of the Earth increased into the millions of years, Lord Kelvin estimating it to be in the order of 20 million years old. Darwin himself had estimated that the area near his house at Down in Kent had taken over 300 million years to have formed. More recent estimations from radio isotope dating put the Earth's age at over 4.5 *billion* years, which, to put it mildly, is just a little beyond the biblical estimate.

The impact of Darwin's work on the theory of evolution, as it eventually came to be called, must therefore be understood in the context of the accumulation of geological and paleontological evidence that was a direct challenge to the biblical account. The geological evidence had begun to accumulate to show that the Earth was at least millions of years old rather than the 6000 or so proposed by biblical scholars; paleontological evidence demonstrated that there were creatures such as the famous dinosaurs (the name first given to them in 1841 by the paleontologist Richard Owen, which means "terrible lizard") that were long extinct and that therefore disproved biblical statements about the permanence of all species. Darwin's work was therefore the climax of the Victorian attack on the Bible because it demonstrated that, over sufficiently long periods of time, species evolved or died out through processes such as natural selection; that all species did not exist from the beginning of creation:

> And God created great whales, and every living creature that moveth . . . and the evening and the morning were the fifth day. (Genesis 1:21–23)

Darwin did not discuss the origin of mankind in 1859 in *On the Origin of Species*, but the implications for the evolution of humans were soon apparent. It was not, however, until *The Descent of Man,* first published in 1871, that Darwin clearly stated that humans had developed from earlier primates.

In the past 150 years the reactions of different religious groups to Darwin's proposals have been extreme. It is well known that all biblical religions vehemently rejected evolution to begin with. Subsequently, during his tenure of the papacy from 1878 to 1903, Pope Leo XIII proposed a compromise with Darwinian evolution with the suggestion that the human *body* might have evolved from earlier animals but the human *soul* was created by God. The creationist movement in the USA, however, has been far less compromising than the Roman Catholic Church, which had perhaps learned something from its medieval mistakes with the likes of Galileo. The infamous Scopes Trial in Dayton, Tennessee, in 1925 set the scene for the American creationists' attacks on the teaching of evolution in schools, when the teacher, John T.

Scopes, was found "guilty" of teaching evolutionary theory, a trial that was brilliantly captured in the Stanley Kramer film *Inherit the Wind* in 1960 with Spencer Tracy and Fredric Marsh playing the combative lawyers. In 1961 the Americans Henry Morris and John Whitcomb published *The Genesis Flood* in which, on the basis of so-called scientific evidence, they claimed that the world really was created in six days and therefore that humans had lived concurrently with dinosaurs. Following from the Morris and Whitcomb book there are now intelligent design and creation institutes and museums springing up all over the USA. Take a look, for example, at the website for the Creation Museum in Petersburg, Kentucky (at www.creationmuseum.org), and you can see displays of dinosaurs roaming around the Garden of Eden next to Adam and Eve. You might have thought that, instead of just highlighting whales, Genesis would have mentioned dinosaurs had they been known to be wandering around the Jurassic Park version of the Garden of Eden.

The puzzle for psychology is how people maintain views of the world that are contrary to the evidence. Why, for example, is the USA both a powerhouse of science and scientific discovery, while at the same time it demonstrates a rapid growth in fundamentalist religious sects that deny or distort the very evidence that science presents? In subsequent chapters, we will examine the range of psychological mechanisms by which belief systems are maintained, and how reasoning processes can be biased in support of false beliefs. Psychology demonstrates that distortions in memory, belief, reasoning, and perception are commonplace. Such distortions can be mildly amusing and entertaining when it comes to visual illusions such as the Müller-Lyer. However, recent debates and arguments over so-called repressed and false memories, which have, for example, led to bitter court cases in alleged child abuse cases, show that even in the secular world our psychological faculties place restrictions and limitations on us. Some of the consequences of these will be examined in subsequent chapters.

The Anthropic Principle

In order to illustrate that all is not fixed in science but that everything is open to debate, we will briefly discuss the so-called "Anthropic Principle" (for a much fuller discussion see Richard Dawkins' (2006) excellent discussion in *The God Delusion*). The idea was first proposed by Brandon Carter (1974), then followed up with a book-length account by John Barrow and Frank Tipler (1988) in *The Anthropic Cosmological Principle*. The original argument refers to the fact that our universe exists because of a number of very fine-tuned physical constants. If even one of these constants were to deviate by a small fraction, life and the universe as we know it would not be possible. These physical constants include the gravitational constant, the mass of the proton, and the fine structure constant, for which the smallest of variations in value could have meant that the universe consisted only of hydrogen, or only of helium, and that no heavier elements such as carbon would ever have been formed, so carbon-based life-forms such as ourselves would have been impossible. One possible conclusion therefore is that there must have been a deistic "fine tuner" who set these physical constants at exactly the right values in order for life to have developed in this universe, though there could be other universes where the fine tuner did actually set other values for the physical constants just for the fun of it. The Anthropic Principle and similar arguments are of course based on fallacious reasoning; namely, the false conclusion that because we are here, therefore we are *necessarily* here, that is, we are predestined to be here. Unfortunately, such arguments still try to present humankind as the centre of the universe, in the way that the Book of Genesis places us at the centre of a God-created universe. The history of our universe and the history of our planet do not place us at the centre of anything, but this psychological fact seems to be extremely difficult for our species to accept. We will examine the sources of our species' narcissistic problem in the next chapter.

A related issue to the Anthropic Principle is the so-called "god-of-the-gaps" in which theists argue that the (shrinking) number of issues that science has not yet explained require the existence of a god. For example, science has not (yet) been able to demonstrate the creation of a primitive life-form in the laboratory from non-living material (though US geneticist Craig Venter's recent demonstration lays claim to having created such a laboratory synthetic life-form, the "Mycoplasma Laboratorium"). It is therefore concluded that a god is necessary to account for this step because of the "gap" in scientific knowledge. The issue of creating life in the laboratory (and other similar "gap" issues such as those in the fossil record) is reminiscent of other such "gaps" in the history of science that have since been bridged. For example, the laboratory synthesis of urea from inorganic materials by Friedrich Wöhler in 1828 at that time had nearly as much impact on religious believers as Copernicus's heliocentric universe proposal. From the time of the Ancient Egyptians, the doctrine of *vitalism* had been dominant. Vitalism argued that the functions of living organisms included a "vital force" and therefore were beyond the laws of physics and chemistry. Urea (carbamide) is a natural metabolite found in the urine of animals that had been widely used in agriculture as a fertilizer and in the production of phosphorus. However, Friedrich Wöhler was the first to demonstrate that a natural organic material could be synthesized from inorganic materials (a combination of silver isocyanate and ammonium chloride leads to urea as one of its products). The experiment led Wöhler famously to write to a fellow chemist that it was "the slaying of a beautiful hypothesis by an ugly fact," that is, the slaying of vitalism by urea in a Petri dish. In practice, it took more than just Wöhler's demonstration to slay vitalism as a scientific doctrine, but the synthesis of urea in the laboratory is one of the key advances in science in which the "gap" between the inorganic and the organic was finally bridged. And Wöhler certainly pissed on the doctrine of vitalism, if you will excuse a very bad joke.

Psychology and Religion: First Thoughts

We have so far resisted making too many psychological interpretations about religion except where these have been irresistible. The remainder of this book will examine in depth what it is about human psychology that has led to the invention of religion in all cultures. There are, however, a few pertinent issues that are worth picking up in this chapter that will set the scene for more detailed issues later. The issues that we will consider briefly are what we will term man-as-god, god-as-man, and Pascal's Wager, in order to illustrate the general approach that will be taken to religion and religious belief in the remainder of this book.

Man-as-God

We started the chapter with two examples of the man-as-god phenomenon with the Fourteenth Dalai Lama, Tenzin Gyatso, and Emperor Hirohito of Japan, both of whom serve as a reminder that we cannot simply dismiss the man-as-god phenomenon as a thing of the past. Nevertheless, it is worth reminding ourselves of previous divine humans because it has to be one of the best jobs around if you can get it. It may, however, be relatively easy for some people to persuade themselves that they are gods (both in the metaphorical sense, if you are a famous celebrity, and in the literal sense, if you are suffering from a delusional psychological disorder), but the catch is that you also have to persuade a large group of other people of your god-like status as well. Of course, if you have been lucky enough to have your ancestors establish these claims on your behalf, as with the Egyptian pharaohs and the medieval kings of Europe, then you are halfway there. Take, for example, King Jayavarman II who became king of the Khmer Empire with its capital at Angkor in Cambodia (see Higham, 2001). On his accession to the throne in 802 CE, he declared himself "king of the world" and "god-king." One of his many privileges as god-king was that any beautiful woman could be summoned to the royal court "to serve the king at his whim." Given that Angkor has been estimated from satellite mapping to have been the largest pre-industrial city in the world with a population of upwards of a million people, that was some choice of women that the god-king had. Again, very nice work if you can get it.

We will consider in detail in Chapter 3 how the impact of science in the West has led most Westerners to have at least some scepticism about anyone who claims to be a god. Indeed, most people in the West would now expect modern-day gods to be referred to psychiatry where they would be likely to be diagnosed with a delusional disorder and treated with major tranquilizers. Nevertheless, the majority of Christians in the West, despite the advances of modern-day science, hold the belief that Jesus was the "Son of God," born of a union between the divine God and an earthly virgin mother (as we noted earlier, a claim that is identical in all details to the Egyptian pharaohs' accounts of their own divine births). The advances of science therefore, as in the case of evolution and the rise of creationism in the USA, are relatively superficial in their impact on the religious beliefs of the majority of people: hence the tolerance of more recent claims of people in the East such as Emperor Hirohito and the Fourteenth Dalai Lama that they are reincarnated gods. As Claude Levi-Strauss emphasized, the primitive or savage mind is identical to the "modern" mind in terms of the range of belief systems, the processes of reasoning, and the capacity to distort or reject evidence that is contrary to these belief systems. In fact Levi-Strauss despaired of the "modern" mind with its capacity for denial and distortion, which led him to declare, "The world began without the human race and will certainly end without it." His conclusion certainly does not equate man with god but in fact the opposite.

God-as-Man

The Judaeo-Christian God is normally pictured as a wise old man with white hair and a beard in a long white tunic. In fact, he could even remind you of your local priest. And that is exactly the point. If there is a universal deity that is omniscient and omnipresent, that occupies the vast expanse of the universe(s), and that knows the past, present, and future position of every atom in the universe(s), it would be physically impossible for such a being to be an old man sitting on a cloud just above Planet Earth. This anthropomorphic view of the gods of course has a long and famous history: the animal, animal–human, and human gods evident from Paleolithic cave paintings onwards (see, for example, David Lewis-Williams' (2010) book, *Conceiving God*, in which he analyses the cave paintings from France and Spain, approximately 50 000 to 12 000 BCE) demonstrate how our visualizations of the gods are remarkably limited to what we see around us, that is, animals and other humans. The Judaeo-Christian biblical literalist will of course quote the Bible as the only necessary evidence:

> And God said, Let us make man in our image, after our likeness . . . So God created man in his own image, in the image of God created he him; male and female created he them. (Genesis 1:26–27)

The simple answer to the literalist is that the Bible was written by men with their own anthropomorphic view of what God would look like, to which the literalist would reply that the Bible is a scripture that was *revealed* to the writers and the prophets, therefore every word must be true. Although at this point it would be possible to conclude that the debate has reached an impasse, the problem for the literalist is that the Bible repeatedly contradicts itself. It is therefore absolutely impossible for the Bible to be literally true (see, for example, Jason Long's (2005) *Biblical Nonsense*). Even the story of the creation of man is contradicted within Genesis; thus, according to Genesis, Chapter 1 (cited above), males and females were both created at the same time on the sixth day of creation. However, by Chapter 2 of Genesis there is already the well-known alternative account:

> And the Lord God took the man, and put him into the Garden of Eden to dress it and to keep it . . . And the Lord God said, It is not good that the man should be alone; I will make him an help meet for him . . . And the Lord God caused a deep sleep to fall upon Adam, and he slept; and he took one of his ribs . . . and made he a woman, and brought her unto the man. (Genesis 2:15–22)

The best conclusion therefore is that *man* created God in his image and likeness, not the other way round.

We must also note that the other biblical religion, Islam, has a very different approach to the use of images to represent God or Muhammad, with such images being banned in mosques and many earlier portrayals even of Muhammad being defaced in more recent times because of Islamic iconophobia. A more positive view of the Islamic approach is that it suggests a more complex and less anthropomorphic view when it argues that its god cannot and should not be visualized. Negative consequences were threats to the life of the Danish cartoonist Kurt Westergaard in 2005 for drawing a cartoon of Muhammad, and, among many other appalling consequences, the banning of the Danish children's toy, Lego, in Saudi Arabia. Yes, that needs to be said twice: Lego was banned in Saudi Arabia because of a cartoon.

Pascal's Wager

Let us end this chapter with a bet. Not just any bet, but a bet that was placed by the French mathematician and philosopher Blaise Pascal (1623–1662), who also has the honour of having the computer programming language Pascal named after him. Pascal's Wager is that even if there is only a small probability of the existence of God, if he exists and we believe, then we would gain happiness for eternity (or infinity in mathematical terms). However, if we bet against his existence but he does exist, then we would have gained unhappiness (hell) for eternity. If however, there is no God, then the argument is that it does not matter. Table 1.1 presents a simplified summary of the Wager, which shows that if you were to decide your beliefs by gambling alone, then your best bet is that you should put your money on God's existence.

There has of course been much commentary and criticism of the Wager. As a number of commentators such as Richard Dawkins (2006) have pointed out, what happens if you believe in the *wrong* god? That it is Baal who turns out to be the true god rather than Yahweh? Perhaps out of jealousy Baal would be more punitive towards believers in the wrong gods than he would be towards an apologetic atheist who turned up and said "Wow! Forgive me—I got that one wrong!" An even worse outcome might be if you believed that God was a *He,* but he turned out to be a *She* who was absolutely fed up with thousands of years of misogynistic male-dominated religions. Now that would be some boost for feminism. Another problem, as others have pointed out, is that a *feigned* belief for the sake of betting on eternity might be viewed as worthy of even more eternal damnation by an omniscient god, akin to feigning love for someone when the genuine motive is not love but some other gain.

Table 1.1 Pascal's Wager: The possible consequences of getting wrong the existence or nonexistence of God.

	GOD EXISTS	GOD DOES NOT EXIST
BELIEF	ETERNAL HEAVEN	NO CONSEQUENCES
NON-BELIEF	ETERNAL HELL	NO CONSEQUENCES

As an addendum to Pascal's Wager, we might note that the worst consequence of being an atheist is that you will never know that you are right. Nor will you have the eternal schadenfreude of knowing that all those theists were wrong. A bit like your lottery ticket winning just after you have died. Perhaps we can call this Power's Misfortune Theory (and a very bad case of PMT it is). Atheists will never have the joy of gloating about being right, yet will have to suffer an eternity of humiliation if we are wrong. Coming to terms with this offers a psychological challenge, and choosing the option requires courage. But a belief in eternal existence cannot be based on cowardice, so in the next chapter we will examine closely the claims of proof based on religious experience.

2

The Psychology of Religion—The Varieties of Normal Experience

I do not fear death. I had been dead for billions of years before I was born.
Mark Twain

Introduction

William James, the philosopher and one of the founders of psychology, gave the Gifford Lectures in Edinburgh University in 1901 and 1902, lectures that came to be published under the title *The Varieties of Religious Experience*. James notoriously dismissed organized religion, and instead argued that the core of spirituality means "the feelings, acts, and experiences of individual men in their solitude, so far as they apprehend themselves to stand in relation to whatever they may consider the divine" and moreover that "We may lay it down as certain that in the distinctively religious sphere of experience, many persons . . . possess the objects of their belief, not in the form of mere conceptions which their intellect accepts as true, but rather in the form of quasi-sensible realities directly apprehended" (p. 64, 1902). We mentioned these internal experiences in the previous chapter with the proposal that they demand explanations equally as much as do unpredictable dramatic external events such as thunder, lightning, and volcanic eruptions. The range of such internal experiences, and the beliefs to which they have given rise, will be the focus of both this chapter and the next. In contrast to James, however, we will not be so dismissive of organized religion; although it is essential to understand what James poetically refers to as "quasi-sensible realities directly apprehended," it is also necessary to understand the social function of religions,

Adieu to God: Why Psychology Leads to Atheism, First Edition. Mick Power.
© 2012 Mick Power. Published 2012 by John Wiley & Sons, Ltd.

the importance of identification with such social organizations, the moral values that they offer their followers, and the promises of salvation that are also offered. In order to understand the purpose and function of organized religions, it is necessary that their psychological and social roles be examined, especially if, as seems extremely likely, religions will continue to survive and grow despite increasing scientific evidence against their basic tenets. In order to understand their survival, therefore, we must examine their psychological and social functions and how, given the universal need for meaning and purpose, their creeds will continue to be persuasive for many.

Religious Experience

There are many examples of unusual or pathological types of experience throughout the history of religion that have played a powerful role in the development of different religious systems. We will examine such unique or abnormal hallucinatory and related phenomena in detail in the next chapter, but here the focus will be more on the everyday types of experience that are universal but give rise to a sense of such puzzlement that they leave many people convinced of the divine or of the supernatural realm. The first and greatest of these everyday experiences has to be that of consciousness itself, scientific explanations of which have to date not been convincing. Consciousness therefore provides perhaps the remaining key arena for the "god-of the-gaps" type explanation. We will also consider other everyday phenomena such as the perception of causality, the function of dreaming, reactions to death and loss, how children view their parents, and our beliefs about good and evil.

The Problem of Consciousness

Consciousness has to sit in prime place as the most important and most puzzling question that remains to be answered. It puts the individual right at the centre of a personal universe, whose idiocentrism has clearly been the source of confusion and extravagant beliefs from both an individual and a social perspective. It is no surprise that our first human conceptions of the general universe were geocentric, given that consciousness provides an idiocentric or egocentric starting point for the personal universe that each of us inhabits. It also seems likely that the unique nowness and personal ownership of consciousness have led many of the owners to make extravagant but mistaken claims about its properties. These imagined properties include omnipotence, omniscience, invulnerability, and eternal existence, all of which have also been offered as descriptors of possible monotheistic and polytheistic beings. We will call this problem of consciousness the "immortality illusion." Such properties are not simply imagined from our historical past, but are evident in ordinary people, especially when they are pushed to their limits such as when they experience trauma (see Chapter 3), in certain personality disorders (especially of a more narcissistic type), and even during certain stages of development in childhood and adolescence.

So what is the function or purpose of consciousness? Within the dualistic philosophies such as that proposed by Descartes, the specialness of consciousness leads to either its equation with an eternal and supernatural soul, or at least to the view that it is the location of a soul or psyche. Like most philosophers, psychologists and neuroscientists in modern times, we reject the so-called "substance dualism" in which mind/soul and body are two completely different kinds of substances. At the other extreme, some modern philosophers, such as Daniel Dennett (1991) in his misleadingly titled book, *Consciousness Explained,* provide an eliminative reductionism, which ultimately dismisses consciousness as illusory. Dennett sees the distinction between the hardware and the software of the computer as providing a model of the distinction between the brain (hardware) and the mind (software). However, if consciousness were that simple, why do computers not display consciousness? When will my laptop on which I am writing this chapter turn around to me and say, "Look, I am having a bad day today, I feel like my world is falling to bits (or maybe even to bytes) and don't feel like typing words for you" or perhaps, "I have had enough of being a mere laptop. I want to be a mainframe! I want out!" There are clearly problems with both the dualistic consciousness as soul and the simple materialist computer model, otherwise Microsoft and Bill Gates are the new gods of consciousness. Many cognitive scientists believe that computers could come to display consciousness (for example, see Phil Johnson-Laird's (1988) *The Computer and the Mind*), but this seems unlikely because consciousness has arisen as a consequence of the evolution of neurological systems. Consciousness is located in the brain and it sleeps or dies when the brain sleeps or dies.

What is therefore clear from the little we know about consciousness is that it is an emergent property of our highly complex brains (see, for example, John Searle's (1997) *The Mystery of Consciousness*), features of which are present in lower animals, and disorders of which can occur in humans. For example, splits in consciousness can occur in dissociative states and dissociative identity disorders (previously known as multiple personality disorders). Such states show that the sense of unity and continuity in consciousness is something of a cognitive illusion, in the same way that we see a continuous visual field despite the break caused by the optic nerve on the retina. Our brains are good at adding in information or "joining the dots" at an automatic or unconscious level so that we experience continuities in consciousness. It is also clear that there are different states and varieties of consciousness, as emphasized in the Buddhist philosophies considered in Chapter 1. Being conscious of objects in the external world allows us to move beyond their simple physical or perceptual properties and can clearly offer new perspectives that simple data-driven perception would not permit.

It is clear that consciousness has many psychological and social functions. Explanations in cognitive psychology tend to emphasize the role that consciousness plays in the assignment and reassignment of goal priorities in the complex multi-goal systems that we are as humans (see, for example, our discussion in *Cognition and Emotion: From Order to Disorder*, Power and Dalgleish, 2008). Expressed more simply, at any point in time, consciousness acts as a central executive system that says, for example, of the many things that you could or should be doing at the moment, you can watch World Cup football for the next half-hour, but then you will need to get back to the exams you are supposed to be marking, and in between you will need to go to the toilet, eat a sandwich, and remember to put on the washing machine. Of course, just as you have sat down to watch England play Germany, the telephone rings but you decide to prioritize England's heavy need of your support, so leave the telephone to switch to the answering machine. It is clear that complex multi-goal systems such as ourselves require some form of overall executive system for setting and resetting currently active goals. However, such a system is implementable on a multi-tasking computer and does not necessitate that the computer's central executive also be conscious. Consciousness achieves all of these computational functions, but it offers something else besides. And, unfortunately, England lost so badly that I wished I had continued marking exams instead.

In the search for an understanding of consciousness, another interesting line of research has been the focus on the inter-individual functions of consciousness, not just its intra-individual functions. We might begin here with Robert Burns:

> O would some Power the gift to give us
> To see ourselves as others see us. (From "To a Louse")

Burns was clearly invoking the need for a *supernatural* power to help us. Evolutionary psychologists such as Nick Humphrey, however (see, for example, his enjoyable collection of essays, *The Mind Made Flesh: Essays From The Frontiers of Psychology and Evolution,* Humphrey, 2008), have argued that because we, like other higher primates, are fundamentally social animals, we have developed a capacity to understand other minds and thereby the capacity to understand how other minds see us. For example, the ability to lie is a highly evolved human capacity, though it is an example of deception that is used for individual advantage throughout nature. Richard Dawkins (1976) in *The Selfish Gene* goes so far as to speculate, "It is even possible that man's swollen brain . . . evolved as a mechanism of even more devious cheating, and ever more penetrating detection of cheating in others" (p. 188). But the capacity for lying requires awareness of your own true belief, the provision of false information to another, and, in skilled lying, the judgement that the false information has been believed, which then permits the liar to take full advantage of the successful lie. This capacity was developed into perhaps its highest art form in Machiavelli's *The Prince* (1532/2003), which provided an insight into the politics of the Florentine court in the fifteenth and sixteenth centuries, and which has given politics a bad name ever since, including famous modern lies of the form, "I did not have sexual relations with that woman," in which the then US President Clinton managed to redefine "sexual relations" in order to defend his presidency and which also included another of his much quoted defences that, "It depends on what the meaning of the word *is* is." Our purpose here is not to digress into endless though illustrative examples of famous lies in politics, or personal examples of how we have all suffered at the hands of skilled liars (though I have to confess that my own experience of academia is that many of my academic colleagues could outperform Machiavelli and Clinton any day of the week). The more general point is that consciousness allows us the capacity not only to reflect on ourselves but also to construe other people's mental states and thereby to construe how they construe us. In a social species the possession of such a capacity provides a major advantage, though it can be used for both good and bad.

To return to the starting question, however, we began this section with the proposal that the experience of consciousness has contributed to the dualism or split between body and soul, and that the "immortality illusion" permeates religious belief and earlier philosophical approaches. The major religion that has been most clearly based on a projection of experienced varieties of consciousness on to a model of the universe has been

Buddhism, as we summarized in Chapter 1. Indeed, Buddhist meditation practices encourage the training of skills in self-consciousness and reflectiveness as a route to spirituality. However, modern philosophy, psychology, and neuroscience mostly reject the "substance dualism" accounts that are beloved of most religions. In place of dualism, the consciousness and the mind more generally can be understood as emergent properties of a highly evolved complex neuronal system that are also evident in other social higher primates, but which have further evolved in humans because of the social and evolutionary advantage of such capacities. Of course, this line of explanation still does not answer fully the question of how consciousness can emerge from its albeit complex neuronal underpinnings. Although science does not have the complete answer, it is not necessary to equate consciousness with something akin to an immortal soul that can exist separately from those neuronal underpinnings; the immortality illusion is by definition an illusion. Furthermore, work in psychology from von Helmholtz and Freud onwards (e.g. Power, 1997) has emphasized that consciousness is just the tip of a mental iceberg in which so much of our waking and sleeping activity occurs at an unconscious or automatic level that is outside of our awareness. The importance of the unconscious and of unconscious processes will be considered further in their implications for religion and religious belief in later sections of this book.

The Search for Meaning

One of the perennial complaints made by religious believers about atheism is that it leaves people lost in a meaningless world in which all morality breaks down and chaos results; their fantasy is something along the lines of a world full of Viking raiders run amok. Such fantasies probably say more about the repressive nature of some religions and the restrictions that they place on their followers, especially in relation to sex and aggression. We will return to this issue later in the chapter. For now it is important to note, first, that there are plenty of atheists around the world who do not spend their time running amok, and, secondly, there have also been and still are vast areas of the world governed by atheistic ideologies. Two examples of these have been the Soviet Union and China in which the majority of people have been atheists. Now you might try to cite the Soviet Union as an atheistic system that collapsed, but you only need to read accounts such as Peter Kenez's (2006) excellent *A History of the Soviet Union from the Beginning to the End* to understand that it was the wayward internal economics of the

Soviet Union rather than the lack of religion that led to its collapse in 1991. In contrast, Chinese communism in the era after the death of Mao Zedong in 1976 reinvented itself so as to incorporate capitalist economics, and is set to become the world's major economy. Its primarily atheist ideology has not produced a nation of wayward Vikings, though its political restrictions sometimes seem as excessive as the religious restrictions it has come to replace. Still, given the choice between a feudal theocracy such as existed in Tibet and Chinese capitalist communism, there is no doubt which way I would choose if those were the only two choices. Fortunately, however, we live in pluralistic societies with democratically elected governments in which individual choice is respected.

But there are humble beginnings to which we must look in order to understand our search for meaning and purpose in life. To begin with, we need to understand how and when the search for meaning and cause develops in childhood and, therefore, what types of causal explanations are preponderant at different developmental stages. The best place to start with such a quest is with the work of the famous Swiss child psychologist Jean Piaget, who, despite never having any formal qualification in psychology, proved to be one of the most insightful observers ever of his own and other children's development. Piaget (see, for example, *The Construction of Reality in the Child,* 1954) proposed that there are four main developmental stages:

1. The sensori-motor period (roughly 0 to 2 years).
2. The pre-operational stage (roughly 2 to 7 years).
3. The concrete operations period (roughly 7 to 11 years).
4. The formal operations period (roughly 11 years upwards).

Piaget defined these stages in terms of the logical capacities of the child at the different stages, though more recent developmental psychologists would place less emphasis on logical development. The important point for our discussion is that a variety of different capacities develop across these stages, which impact on the child's ability to understand reality, including conservation (as illustrated in the famous study that showed that, when a liquid is poured into a taller glass, the child reports that there is now more liquid), object permanence, and egocentrism. Studies of the first two to three years show that babies already have a basic understanding of cause-and-effect outcomes in the physical world and display some basic understanding of human intentions. This capacity for causal reasoning matures considerably in later stages of development, but there is much use of animistic explanations of the form, "The rope is untwisting because it wants to," and magical thinking is seen to predominate up until about the age of seven years until the start of the concrete operations stage. Similarly, normal children develop so-called "theory of mind" at about four years of age as they move from the egocentrism of the sensori-motor period and begin to understand that other people have thoughts and feelings that are separate from their own. Problems arise for children with autism in whom this developmental step is extremely delayed or even absent and who therefore continue with the young child's egocentrism (see, for example, Leslie, 1994).

Piaget's developmental psychology therefore emphasizes the preponderance of egocentric, animistic, magical thinking until about seven years of age. Although, after age seven or thereabouts, thinking becomes more realistic, even in adulthood it can be animistic or magical. The difference is that normally adults can easily distinguish between animistic and magical thinking, such as knowing that the computer has not "deliberately" lost a morning's work even though they might shout and swear at it as if it had done it deliberately. While being mindful of Claude Levi-Strauss's (1962) warning in *The Savage Mind* that one must be careful when attributing child-like animistic thinking to early prehistoric human groups and to current nomadic tribes, we should note that a subtler version of the possibility arises from the observation that people with autism, schizophrenia, or some types of personality disorder have poor theory of mind and display more egocentrism and greater amounts of animistic and magical thinking. Given, as we have argued in Chapter 1, that the priest-shamans were more likely to suffer from such disorders, there is good reason to suspect, as have others, that the persistence of animistic and magical thinking into adulthood has been a source of much religious inspiration and belief. This is a topic that we will examine in detail in Chapter 3.

Dreaming

The most famous book ever written about dreams was Sigmund Freud's *The Interpretation of Dreams*, published in 1900. In Freud's account, dreams are typically a form of wish-fulfilment that incorporates residues of the previous day. He saw them as "the royal road to the unconscious." Freud however observes that one must be careful to distinguish between the *manifest* content of the dream, which can often seem bizarre and puzzling, and the *latent* content, which, although its meaning may be disguised from the dreamer, may become meaningful with careful analysis and reflection. So, you may well have dreamt that you were rising up fast through the air in a hot air balloon when suddenly the balloon burst and you fell rapidly back down to earth. As any psychoanalyst will tell you, however, what the dream means is that you clearly have considerable anxieties about your sexual performance.

Just as with the rest of Freud's work, there have been considerable criticisms of his dream theory, though one must acknowledge that some dreams can be of a Freudian nature. More recent dream theories have included Francis Crick's random neural activity theory (see *The Astonishing Hypothesis: The Scientific Search for the Soul,* Crick, 1994) in which dreams are simply a by-product of the random firing of neurones during sleep. Such a biologically reductionist theory is not appealing to a psychologist because it denies any possible function of the process of dreaming. A more interesting theory has been presented by Bill Domhoff (see, for example, *The Scientific Study of Dreams,* published in 2003), in which he argues that dreams are not significantly different from waking thoughts but reflect the activity of a top-down schematic or "conceptual" system that is active both during wakefulness and during sleep. Indeed, during wakefulness we often daydream and mind-wander in a manner that is akin to dreaming during sleep. According to Domhoff, therefore, the concerns and goals that drive our waking thoughts and activity are exactly those that provide the conceptual content of our dreams. If you enjoy listening to other people's dreams, then Domhoff and colleagues have a collection of over 23 000 dreams that you can search through on their website at http://dreambank.net/. Domhoff's approach certainly helps to account for the dreams of famous scientists in which dreaming provided the solution to scientific puzzles that had preoccupied their daytime activity. Examples are Kekulé's dream about the snake swallowing its tail, which provided him with the answer to the structure of the benzene molecule, and Einstein's dreams about travelling around the universe on a beam of light. (Interestingly, however, both of these famous dream sequences also have obvious Freudian interpretations.)

Dreams and daydreams have clearly played a significant role throughout the history and development of religion, whatever our modern understanding of their role and function might be. The most explicit use of dreams as the source of information about the supernatural is the Australian Aboriginal concept of the Dreamtime, discussed in Chapter 1, in which dreams are seen to connect this world with the world of the supernatural. The Dreamtime is the world of the ancestors and the world to which all living individuals will return after death. Other anthropological studies have shown that the Andaman Islanders believe that the soul wanders during sleep while it has dream adventures, such that if the sleeper is woken too soon there is a danger of illness that would result from the soul still being absent (Radcliffe-Brown, 1922). Examples of dreams within the Judaeo-Christian tradition are well known from the Bible. In Genesis (28:12–13) we read of Jacob's dream:

> And he dreamed, and behold a ladder set upon the earth, and the top of it reached to heaven: and behold the angels of God ascending and descending on it. And, behold, the LORD stood above it, and said, I *am* the LORD God of Abraham thy father . . . the land whereon thou liest, to thee will I give it, and to thy seed.

And so it came to pass and Jacob occupied the land that he dreamed that God had given him. Nice dreams if you can have them! Another famous biblical dream is that of Joseph, son of Jacob, he of the "coat of many colours" fame.

> And he said unto them, Hear, I Pray you, this dream which I have dreamed: For, behold, we *were* binding sheaves in the field, and, lo, my sheaf arose, and also stood upright; and, behold, your sheaves stood round about, and made obeisance to my sheaf. (Genesis 37:6–7)

Genesis goes on to tell us, "And they hated him yet more for his dreams, and for his words" (37:8). Joseph's dreams eventually led him to be sold into slavery to the Egyptians, where his capacity for dreaming and for dream interpretation see him interpret the Pharaoh's dreams to mean that Egypt will have seven years of plenty followed by seven years of famine. In gratitude Pharaoh gave Joseph "to wife Asenath the daughter of Potipherah priest of On," yet another possible Hebrew connection to the priests of the monotheistic religion of Akhenaten, which in Chapter 1 we considered a possible source of Abrahamic monotheism.

Dreams have played a significant role in most other religions, and along with visions (considered in Chapter 3) are often considered as a source of revelation. A final example of the role of dreams in religion comes from the dream of Queen Maya, the mother of Siddhartha Gautama (now simply referred to as the Buddha). On the night of the Buddha's conception, Queen Maya, who was named after the goddess of dreams, dreamt that a white elephant with six white tusks entered her right side, which was the first portent of the child's great future. The Buddha himself, at the age of 35 and after abandoning his life of royal privilege, spent 49 days sleeping, dreaming, and meditating under a sacred fig tree, the Bodhi, in Bodh Gaya, India, after which time he achieved enlightenment and began his teachings.

In summary, we can see that dreams have been important in almost all religions, either as a source of communication from the gods to humans, which humans with special powers such as the priest-shamans can interpret, or, as in the case of Australian Aboriginal tribes, the Dreaming or Dreamtime, *is* the supernatural reality in which there is eternal existence of the spirit. However, psychology and neuroscience now offer us very different accounts of the possible role of dreams. These accounts range from Freud's wish-fulfilment and protection of the ego, to Crick's random firing of neurones, to Domhoff's activity of the high-level conceptual system that is operating without sensory input. A small pinch of Freud with a large part of Domhoff would seem to provide the best current account of the role of dreaming.

Death, Loss, and Grief

The experience of our own consciousness, so we argued earlier, can mislead us into believing in our own permanence or immortality. It is no surprise, therefore, that we should hold similar beliefs about our close friends and family, or even the celebrities with whom we define our cultures. The death of such individuals is typically reacted to with disbelief, especially if the death has been sudden and unexpected, such as at the death of a child, or as a consequence of a dramatic event or disaster. John Bowlby (1980), in his highly influential three-volume work, *Attachment and Loss,* referred to this initial reaction to grief as the stage of "protest," which is then followed by the stage of "despair" when the loss finally begins to be accepted. Although it is clear from subsequent research that not all grief follows Bowlby's proposed stage sequence (see Stroebe *et al.*, 2001), when grief is characterized by a period of "protest," the intense longing and hope that the lost significant other will reappear can often be accompanied by waves of pain, feelings of tension and agitation, and hypervigilance. At the most extreme, visual, auditory, and other sensory hallucinations can also be experienced. We will consider the phenomena of hallucinations more generally in Chapter 3 when we look at rarer psychological phenomena, but, because of the relatively commonplace nature of such reactions following bereavement, we will consider this special category of hallucination in this section.

Agneta Grimby (1993) reported a study in Sweden of 50 older adults who had suffered a recent bereavement, whom she followed up for one year. Her results showed that, in the first month after the loss, 82% of the bereaved had experienced illusions or hallucinations of the dead spouse. Even after 12 months, 52% of the sample still reported such illusions or hallucinations. By illusions, Grimby meant that the person felt the presence of the dead spouse, whereas in hallucinations they reported seeing, hearing, and talking to the dead spouse. A more recent study by Field and Filanosky (2010) collected information over the internet from 502 bereaved participants, which included answers to questions about illusions and hallucinations as well as an assessment of the cause of death. Field and Filanosky found that the reported occurrence of illusions and hallucinations increased strongly if the spouse's death had been violent and sudden, and where someone was at least partly responsible for the death. In sum, these studies show that experiencing the presence of the lost person, and even seeing and hearing them, are commonplace, especially in the months after a sudden and unexpected death. We propose, therefore, that grief provides powerful information for sufferers that the spirit of the lost person continues to exist after death because the characteristic symptoms of grief can be interpreted in that way. Besides which, there are any number of spiritual mediums who will talk to the dead person on your behalf, given that the majority of people who visit a medium are attempting to communicate with a loved one who has died.

The alleged resurrection of Jesus after the crucifixion is not normally considered in the light of the possibly intense grief reactions of his followers. More mundane explanations that have been put forward have included his not actually having died on the cross, or even, in Philip Pullman's (2010) novel, *The Good Man Jesus and the Scoundrel Christ*, that Jesus had an identical twin brother who decided to make the most of his brother Jesus's death on the cross. What, however, of the possibility that the "visions" of Jesus were intense grief-related hallucinations in those closest to him? The earliest of the Gospels, that attributed to Mark and written in about 70 CE (see, for example, Karen Armstrong's *The Bible: The Biography*, published in 2007), presents the story following the crucifixion very briefly:

> And when the Sabbath was past, Mary Magdalene, and Mary the mother of Jesus, and Salome . . . [entered] into the sepulchre, they saw a young man sitting on the right side, clothed in a long white garment; and they were affrighted . . . And they went out quickly, and fled from the sepulchre . . . Now when Jesus was risen early the first day of the week, he appeared first to Mary Magdalene, out of whom he had cast seven devils. And she went and told them that had been with him, as they mourned and wept. (Mark 16:1–10)

Jesus's death was sudden and unexpected, and clearly caused intense suffering for his followers. It thus fulfils the criteria for the increased probability of the occurrence of illusions and hallucinations. The fact that the Gospel of Mark tells us that the first person to whom he appeared was Mary Magdalene might even increase grounds for the suspicion, put forward in recent times, that Jesus was married to Mary Magdalene (see *Holy Blood, Holy Grail* by Baigent *et al.*, published in 1983 and now fictionalized in Dan Brown's (2004) *Da Vinci Code*. In fact, in the Gospel of John it is *only* Mary Magdalene who is present at the tomb and sees Jesus and converses with him (John 20:13–17). Anyway, the first reaction of the other disciples was disbelief towards Mary Magdalene's claim:

> And they, when they had heard that he was alive, and had been seen of her, believed not. (Mark 16:11)

Jesus then appears to another "two of them," who were not believed either. Finally, he appears "unto the eleven as they sat at meat, and upbraided them with their unbelief and hardness of heart" (Mark 16:14). Mark then tells us that Jesus, having spoken to the disciples, was received into heaven:

> So then after the Lord had spoken unto them, he was received up into heaven, and sat on the right hand of God. (Mark 16:19)

Now that really does seem the waste of a good resurrection if ever there was one. It is only in the later written gospels that the post-resurrection time is made greater use of and further elaborated. In the last of the gospels to be written, that of John in the late 90s CE, again it is Mary Magdalene who first has the vision of Jesus, after which he appears to the other disciples apart from the famous "doubting Thomas." Although John tells us this was because Thomas was absent when Jesus appeared to the other disciples, another explanation is that Thomas was less suggestible or less stricken with grief. John also adds a further episode in which Jesus appears to Simon Peter and other disciples while they are fishing, though the dialogue is primarily with Simon Peter in which Jesus comforts him and even helps him to find the best side of the boat from which to fish. Such comforting hallucinations are typical of the types of hallucinations that the newly grieving participants reported in the Agneta Grimby study discussed above. The Gospel according to Luke, written in the late 80s CE, gives a different account in which Simon Peter rather than Mary Magdalene is the first to see Jesus, whereas in the Gospel according to Matthew, also thought to be written in the late 80s

CE, he again first appears to Mary Magdalene. The key point about the gospel accounts is that Jesus's appearances are very fleeting and take place eight days apart as John states, and sometimes he was not recognized by all of them. Reinterpreted, these accounts are more likely to mean that Jesus was not directly seen but was imagined by other than Mary Magdalene and Simon Peter, who seem from the four accounts to have been the two who most clearly had the grief-based hallucinations.

To return now to the more general issue of grief, one of the things that people do, especially following sudden, unexpected, and untimely deaths, is to search for *meaning* in the death as a way of coping with the subsequent grief. Religions not only offer social rituals around key events and transitions such as births, marriages, and deaths (see Chapter 4), but they also offer possible explanations and an understanding of death that can bring consolation to the bereaved individual. For example, a study by George Bonanno and colleagues (Bonanno *et al.*, 2004) followed up 1532 married older adults in Detroit in the USA. In the course of the study, 319 people lost their spouse, 86% of whom participated in at least one follow-up interview. Issues that the researchers examined included the attempt to find meaning in the death of the spouse and whether or not this had an impact on subsequent grief or depression. The study showed that almost one third searched for and attempted to find meaning in their spouse's death, and those who were resilient throughout the experience of the loss tended to show that they had found meaning in the loss. A further study by Fenix and colleagues (Fenix *et al.*, 2006) investigated 175 caregivers who were followed up following the death of their spouses from cancer. Those caregivers who scored higher on religiousness were *less* likely to be depressed than those who scored low on religiousness at a 13-month follow-up. In addition to religious beliefs providing meaning and solace to the bereaved individuals, part of the advantage was the social support obtained from religious groups over the time of the bereavement. We will examine in more detail in Chapter 6 the possible health and well-being benefits of religious belief and religious activity. The point to make here is that there are benefits from religion and religious belief at times of loss, and that these benefits can strengthen religious beliefs, whether or not they are true.

Our final example in this section on the effects of loss concerns so-called phantom-limb effects in people who have lost arms or legs. The French poet and novelist Blaise Cendrars (1887–1961) lost his right arm in the First World War in the Battle of the Somme in 1915. He taught himself to write with his left hand; however, he experienced phantom limb pain and phantom limb effects for the rest of his life. A large-scale study of military amputees in Germany (Kern *et al.*, 2009) showed that such phantom limb and pain effects were extremely common; thus, of the 537 amputees who participated in the survey, 74.5% reported phantom limb pain with sensations such as burning, cramp, prickling, electrification, and tingling experienced in the missing limb. Sensations other than pain were experienced by 73.4% of the sample and included movement, warmth, coldness, nakedness, clothedness, pressure and contortion. The important point for our argument is that loss of a limb leads to the experience that the limb still exists in approximately three-quarters of people who experience such loss. By extension, therefore, if a limb that no longer exists (and is likely to have been incinerated in the hospital furnace) still behaves as if it did exist, it is a short step to the sort of conclusion that claims something like the "soul" of the limb continues to exist. However, before believers in the supernatural get too excited by this bizarre phenomenon as a new form of evidence for the soul, there is an absurd consequence if one were to accept such a conclusion; namely, that there must be a special section in heaven full of amputated limbs that are sitting and waiting for their owners. Now that would be a theological conundrum that even the head of the Catholic "Congregation for the Doctrine of Faith" (more famous, as we noted in Chapter 1, under its previous name, The Inquisition) might struggle with.

In summary, we can see that death and other losses lead to the experience of phenomena such as illusions and hallucinations about the person or even part of one's own body that has been lost. At risk of a very bad pun, it can be seen that the more attached you are to what has been lost, the more likely you are to experience the person, or limb, as if they still existed. However, experiences such as illusions, hallucinations, and phantom limb effects will be interpreted by many people to mean that the lost person or limb continues to exist. What the effects actually demonstrate is that the representation, or memory, of body parts and significant others in the brain can create phantom phenomena after their loss that may mislead some into believing that the lost person or object actually still exists.

Of Parents and Gods

One of the questions that was raised in Chapter 1 was the possibility of the conception of god(s) as parent-like figures or ancestors, especially in Freud's analysis of god-as-father. While there may be some limited evidence in the monotheistic religions for aspects of Freud's proposal, the evidence suggests that it has little application among the polytheistic and deistic religions (see Argyle, 2000). Nevertheless, there is still an interesting question, both for developmental psychologists and for parents, which is whether children conceive of their parents as god-like creatures, and whether such conceptions thereby influence the child's conception of God. Ana-Maria Rizzutto (1979), in her book *The Birth of the Living God*, argued from a psychoanalytic object-relations perspective that our images of God derive from the early object relations that we form of our parents and other key figures; she also presents a number of clinical examples to illustrate the links between object relations and the conception of God, though as Kate Loewenthal (2000) points out, there have been little or no empirical studies that have specifically followed up these object relations proposals.

There are a number of more general and relevant empirical studies. Dickie and colleagues (1997) studied a total of 143 children aged 4 to 11 years from a variety of different ethnic backgrounds and religious affiliations. They found consistently that if mother was perceived as powerful and father as nurturing, then God was seen as powerful and nurturing. However, God was seen as more like father in younger children, but more like mother or like a mix of both parents in later childhood. Girls were found to conceive of God as closer to their parents' attributes than were boys. An earlier study by Johnson and Eastburg (1992) reported on 30 abused children and a comparison group of 30 non-abused children aged five to thirteen years. The self-concepts of abused children were found to be lower in comparison with non-abused children, and the abused children also reported lower concepts of their parents but not of God. The impact of abuse may therefore have been to make their parents seem less god-like, but that God became more like an ideal parent instead. A study by De Roos *et al.* (2004) of 363 Dutch preschoolers found that the stricter the child-rearing practices in the home, then the more punitive was the conception of God held by the children. These results add support to the idea that, for young children, gods and parents can be seen as very close to each other conceptually, especially with the good-enough parent who does not abuse the child. Some of the images in religion of gods as father-like or mother-like (or even both) are likely therefore to have originated with the child's conception of parents as god-like and, consequently, these attributes have been projected on to some conceptualizations of gods.

The equation of gods and parents in childhood leads to the interesting question of whether adolescents and young adults who lose their faith in God, so-called apostasy, are more likely to have come from certain types of problematic families, to perhaps have had difficulties in attachment to their parents, or even to have been more likely to have been abused by their parents (in the broadest sense of not just sexual or physical abuse, but including emotional abuse and neglect also). Before we address this question directly, we should note the appalling story told by Richard Dawkins in *The God Delusion* (2006) of the case of Sadiq Abdul Karim Malallah who on September 3, 1992, was beheaded in Al-Qatif in Saudi Arabia after he was convicted of apostasy and blasphemy. Sadiq had been held in prison from April 1988 and had been told by the judge at his trial that he had to convert from Shi'a to Wahhabi Islam, but he failed to do so and was eventually beheaded. Saudi Arabia is governed by an Islamic theocratic monarchy, who have imposed the strict Wahhabi Islamic code in which the government-run Religious Police are designated to prevent the public practice of all non-Wahhabi Islamic religions. Amnesty International reported that in 2009 at least 102 men and women had been executed in Saudi Arabia, many for blasphemy and apostasy.

To return to the issue of loss of belief or apostasy in adulthood, there are a couple of relevant studies that can be cited. Bahr and Albrecht (1989) interviewed 30 former Mormons about why they had abandoned their faith. Most of them described themselves as having been on the periphery of belief and so they had drifted away from the faith. However, a sub-group who had been fervent believers reported that the break-up of their families such as through divorce and separation had been key events in their loss of faith. Lawton and Bures (2001) examined a much larger sample using data from the US National Survey of Family and Households of whom 11 372 were either Catholic or Protestant. The data showed that parental divorce was most predictive of apostasy for the Catholic and conservative Protestant groups, but less so for moderate Protestant groups. What these data highlight is that how strongly we are likely to have religious beliefs and how likely we are to believe in God are strongly related to how we view our parents whilst we are children, together with the impact of family problems during development.

Good and Evil

The existence of evil in the world has provided religion and philosophy with some difficult and unresolved issues: if God is both omnipotent and benevolent, then why is there evil in the world? Why does an omnipotent benevolent God allow young children to die from disease? Or murder of one person by another? Or acts of genocide of one race against another? Or natural disasters that lead to the deaths of thousands of people? An apparently simple version of these questions is why do churches need lightning rods? If God exists, and he is being worshipped in the right church (mosque, synagogue, temple . . .), then why would he allow his own place of worship to be destroyed?

The existence of evil is used by many to argue against the existence of such a god, or even against gods altogether. Jack Smart and John Haldane (2003) in *Atheism and Theism* provide the arguments both ways and present a useful summary of "theodicy"—the attempt to resolve the omnipotent god in an evil universe problem. As Smart summarizes the argument:

1. If God exists there is no evil.
2. There is evil.
3. Therefore there is no God.

Philosophers and theologians have offered numerous possible solutions to this problem. As Smart notes, the "free will defence," in which God steps back and leaves us a choice, does not apply to the natural disasters, which represent a natural evil in the universe that is beyond the scope of human free will. One of the problems with the shift to the monotheistic omnipotent God is that it lost the more anthropomorphic capacities of the Greek and Roman gods, who, just like humans, could at times behave very badly and even do evil for which they had to atone. Because monotheism cannot deny the existence of evil, one of its solutions has been to split the universe into forces for good and forces for evil. The dualist tradition in Zoroastrianism (see Chapter 1) to split the world into such good and evil (the good Ahura Mazda versus the bad Angra Mainyu), became incorporated into the developing monotheistic world-view of the Old Testament. Of course, the early Abrahamic God of the Old Testament was anything but benign and loving, as Richard Dawkins and others have carefully catalogued. To give one example:

> The moral story of Noah is appalling. God took a dim view of humans, so he (with the exception of one family) drowned the lot of them including children and also, for good measure, the rest of the (presumably blameless) animals as well. (Dawkins, 2006, pp. 237–238)

Who needs Satan, when you have a god like that? However, the character of God changes dramatically from the older books to the newer books of the Old Testament to the New Testament to modern times. Such acts of genocide were subsequently ascribed to evil forces in the universe, personified by some as Satan, the Angra Mainyu of the Zoroastrians, with some influence from the Egyptians as well. The history of monotheism seems therefore to have increased the split between good and evil in the universe instead of integrating these forces within individuals. This split leads not only to the "existence of evil" problem for philosophers and theologians, but also, as we will argue throughout this book, to a range of psychological problems for each individual as well.

Most individuals have personal moral codes by which they can judge the good or evil nature of both their own and other people's actions. We say *most* individuals: we will return later to the issue of psychopathy, but for now we will focus on normal development. In the section *The Search for Meaning*, earlier in this chapter, we outlined four key stages of cognitive development based on Jean Piaget's approach. Lawrence Kohlberg (1969) proposed a system of moral development that is derived from Piaget's developmental system and that is worth outlining briefly here.

Level 1 Pre-Conventional
   1. Obedience and punishment orientation—Here the child is oriented to the avoidance of punishment and the need to obey authority and is therefore externally oriented.
   2. Self-interest orientation—The orientation is still external but it is guided by what is the benefit to the child, or what counts as a fair exchange.

Level 2 Conventional
   3. Interpersonal accord and conformity—Rules and values now become internalized, but rule adherence is to please and be approved of by others and be seen as the "good boy" or the "good girl."
   4. Authority and social-order maintaining orientation—To do one's duty and to maintain the social order and, therefore, a stage beyond which many adults do not progress.

Level 3 Post-Conventional
   5. Social contract orientation—Moral principles applied independently of social authority, with awareness that rules are relative to one's group, though some may have universal applicability.
   6. Universal ethical principles—Moral decisions are based on universal ethical principles.

As with Piaget's work, later revisions to Kohlberg's scheme have been proposed. In particular, the Post-Conventional stage seems to be found only in urban settings in developed countries, but the first four stages seem otherwise to reflect moral development.

The important point here for religion is that the moral approaches to good and evil by many religions operate at the Pre-Conventional and

Conventional stages. For example, in the Islamic religions even the name "Islam" conveys an expectation because it means "surrender," that is, to surrender to the will of Allah and to free oneself through moral struggle from the temptations of Satan. The strict Wahhabi Sunni Islam of Saudi Arabia referred to earlier, and the related Taliban Islamic group in Afghanistan and Pakistan, demonstrate moral imposition at the Pre-Conventional and Conventional levels. Wahhabism promotes the teachings of the eighteenth-century Saudi scholar, Ibn Abdul Wahhab, and involves a strict return to the Koran and Hadith (teachings of Muhammad). The restrictions on women in Saudi Arabia are particularly revealing. Women are segregated from men (purdah), such that they must stay in certain parts of their own home, and there are separate entrances for men and women into most buildings, shops, and offices. However, women must have a male guardian, normally the father or husband, who owns the woman; thus, the woman must be accompanied by her guardian in order to leave the home, and she must adhere to a strict dress code that includes a hijab and veil in order to cover the head and face. If honour (namus) is lost by the woman, her guardian has the right to punish her, including killing her. Women are not allowed into mosques, Saudi Arabia is the only country that prohibits women from driving, and it was one of the few countries that did not send a female delegation to the 2008 Olympics because women are banned from most sports.

One of the points to draw from definitions of good and evil within religions is that while there may be some universally agreed acts of evil such as murder, theft, and rape (though even here many religions condone even these actions under certain circumstances), religions also generate sets of actions considered bad or sinful that are completely arbitrary. We will consider the social control aspects of religion in more detail in Chapter 5, so for now we will just provide one example. Within Judaism, the rules governing kosher cooking definitely fall within the arbitrary category of religious morality. This was brought home to me on a trip to Beer-Sheva in Israel a few years ago. Near my hotel there was a very inviting looking pizza restaurant, so I went in and without thinking asked for my favourite pizza, pepperoni with extra mozzarella. The consternation caused in the restaurant was considerable because my pepperoni pizza with extra mozzarella broke every rule of kosher cooking imaginable, and not just because pepperoni is made from pork.

Finally in this section, mention must be made of two important concepts, those of "original sin" and of "psychopathy" because of their implications for morality and moral behavior. The concept of original sin (also known as "ancestral sin" in the Orthodox Christian faiths) arises in the Bible with the fall from grace when Adam and Eve ate the apple from the tree of knowledge, though the concept exists only in Christianity and not in the other biblical religions of Judaism and Islam. Clearly, knowledge is sin, at least in Christianity. The concept was developed most by St. Augustine of Hippo in the fourth century CE, who, based on his own depravity as a young man, linked original sin in particular to sexual libido and the suggestion that the sin of Adam and Eve was that of *carnal* knowledge. Augustine's proposal was enthusiastically taken up by the Protestant reformers such as John Knox, Martin Luther, and John Wesley. It also led to some theological conundrums such as whether or not unbaptized children could go to heaven; the Catholic Church invented "Limbo" as a place where such unbaptized children would go, lest it seem too harsh in its judgment to condemn these innocents to damnation in hell for eternity. Unfortunately, however, Pope Benedict XVI was reported in 2007 in the media as "The Pope Closes Limbo," which caused panic among those who had assumed that their unbaptized children were peacefully residing there. As a note of hope, we might also note that Father Gabriel Funes, the priest-astronomer in charge of the Vatican Space Observatory, has stated that there may be other planets where intelligent life-forms do not have original sin.

From the psychological point of view, the proposals for an original sin that can be removed by baptism could easily be dismissed as hocus-pocus that is designed to ensure that all Christian parents put their new-born infants through a money-raising ritual for the financial benefit of the Church. However, perhaps a more constructive question can be asked, namely whether or not there is an innate capacity for "sin" or "badness" within all humans. An interesting book, *The Psychopath: Emotion and the Brain,* by James Blair and his colleagues (Blair *et al.,* 2005) summarizes recent work on a category of people referred to as "psychopaths" in which there is evidence for the influence of genetic and developmental factors. As Blair and colleagues define it:

> Psychopathy represents a specific pathology where there is not only antisocial behavior but, more importantly, a particular form of emotional dysfunction . . .[that] puts the individual at risk for developing heightened levels of goal-directed, instrumental aggression. (p.17)

The emotional dysfunction in psychopathic individuals includes reduced anxiety levels, reduced responsiveness to threat, poor emotional learning, impairment of empathy, and impaired moral reasoning. Blair and colleagues estimate that psychopathic tendencies occur in about 1.23 to 3.46% in the community, with the incidence rate of psychopathy itself being about 0.75% in males in the community. Such individuals populate our prisons and special hospitals in high numbers, though they are also over-represented among those in leadership roles such as politicians and, clearly, given the recent world-wide economic crisis, among those who run our banks and other financial institutions. Psychopathy is by no means the same concept as that of original sin, which can be removed by baptism, but it does highlight the fact that some members of society do not share the personal moral and social values of others and can thereby come to represent all that has come to be labelled as evil.

Mystical or "Religious" Experience

In *The Varieties of Religious Experience* William James (1902) famously referred to a unique type of experience that people have and that he referred to as "quasi-sensible realities directly apprehended." There are many experiences that can be labelled as "religious" or as "proof of God", such as watching a beautiful sunset or admiring a beautiful landscape. However, William James's proposal goes well beyond experiences such as enchantment with nature, into a different quality of experience in which the experiencer is overcome with a conviction of the supernatural. If we look to famous religious figures writing about their experiences, their writings are replete with such examples. In the next chapter, we will return in detail to the visions described in the famous autobiography of the Spanish saint, Teresa of Avila, which is the second most read Spanish book (second only to Cervantes' *Don Quixote*). She also wrote extensively about the religious experiences that we are interested in here to the extent that William James described her as "the expert of experts in describing such conditions" (p. 408). Here are some examples of how she describes these experiences:

> There would come to me unexpectedly such a feeling of the presence of God as made it impossible for me to doubt that He was within me, or that I was totally engulfed in Him. (p. 71, 1957)

> When His Majesty wishes, he teaches us everything in a moment in the most amazing way. (p. 86, 1957)

St. Teresa referred to such experiences as her "mystical theology," and her autobiography is an extremely moving account of her suffering and of how her conviction that these experiences originated with God helped her cope with such suffering. St. Teresa's account is so moving and convincing that one almost feels it sacrilegious to consider any other possible account of what she went through. But this charismatic conviction, we know, is part of the impressive impact and power that such religious individuals have over the rest of us. For exactly that reason, therefore, we must stop and examine what the magnetism of such religious leaders is based on, especially because many other religious writers describe experiences that can be classified in the same way. Again, the ugly fact meets the beautiful theory.

In their book *The Psychology of Religious Knowing* (1988), psychologists Fraser Watts and Mark Williams summarize and attempt to provide an explanation for religious experience. However, their stance is that any psychological explanation is necessarily *reductionistic* and to be avoided, because such experiences should be taken as proof of a spiritual realm. The stance taken here is that because these experiences *are* psychological, a psychological explanation cannot, contrary to their view, in principle be reductionistic. Watts and Williams provide an informative overview of research on religious experience that is recommended as a very readable summary that also covers a range of psychological explanations including Freudian and Jungian approaches. In contrast to Freud, Jung was far more sympathetic towards religion and grew up in a religious family as the son of a Swiss pastor. Both Freud and Jung refer to the "oceanic feeling," or feeling of oneness with the universe, as a special experience that is taken by religious individuals to imply the existence of the supernatural, though Freud sees its origins in the infant's fusion with the mother rather than as evidence of the supernatural.

Freud's suggestion that the oceanic or mystical feeling might originate in the childhood fusion between the infant and the mother offers an interesting possible psychological account, but it ignores the fact that there is also a normal adult experience of fusion and oneness that is not normally given a spiritual interpretation. Indeed, some of the descriptions of oneness given by St. Teresa have led others towards similar conclusions (see, for example, David Lewis-Williams' (2010) *Conceiving God,* in which he explores a wide range of religious practices involving chanting, prayer, starvation, and hallucinogenic drugs, which are used to "inspire" such religious states). In St. Teresa's words (Avila, 1957):

> I wish that I could explain, with God's help, the difference between union and rapture, or elevation, or flight of the spirit or transport—for they are all one. I mean that these are different names for the same thing, which is also called ecstasy (p. 136).

And in her famous account of such an experience of union, beautifully portrayed in Bernini's statue, *The Ecstasy of Saint Theresa*, in the church of Santa Maria Della Vittoria in Rome:

> Beside me, on the left hand, appeared an angel in bodily form . . . He was not tall but short, and very beautiful; and his face was so aflame that he appeared to be one of the highest rank of angels, who seem to be all on fire . . . In his hands I saw a great golden spear, and at the iron tip there appeared to be a point of fire. This he plunged into my heart several times so that it penetrated to my entrails. When he pulled it out, I felt that he took them with it, and left me utterly consumed by the great love of God. The pain was so severe that it made me utter several moans. The sweetness caused by this intense pain is so extreme that one cannot possibly wish it to cease. (p. 210)

This is religious writing at its erotic best and must be one of the most beautiful descriptions of *sexual orgasm* ever written.

The serious suggestion that we wish to make here is therefore that the oceanic, mystical-union experiences are similar in type and effect to that of orgasm, and that orgasm-based ecstasy may have provided the basis for much of the religious "mystical experiences" of union described by St. Teresa and many other religious mystics. In a study of subjective descriptions of orgasm in over 1600 male and female respondents, Kenneth Mah and Yitzchak Binik (2002) found that both men and women described their orgasms in largely similar ways that reflected two key dimensions, one that focussed on physical sensory factors and a second that focussed on cognitive–affective factors. A key component of the cognitive–affective dimension focussed on emotional intimacy which included adjectives such as unifying, close, and loving. The experience of union in orgasm is, we suggest, one of the likely candidates to explain the experience of union in mystical states. Of course, sexual excitement is only one possible source of ecstatic experience, as we noted above, though it may be the major source for the experience of ecstasy with union. However, as Watts and Williams (1988) also point out:

> Early Israelite prophecy appears to have been associated with deliberately stimulated frenzy or ecstasy . . . and the book of Judges contains many identifications of religious inspiration with the excitement of battle. (p. 75)

In summary, there are a number of psychological "union" states in which the person may experience a sense of oneness with others and with the universe. Such states can include infant attachment states as originally suggested by Freud, but ecstatic states induced by a range of other factors can also lead to a feeling of union, in particular in the experience of sexual orgasm. These ecstatic union states are both powerful and immediate and may well provide the source of the "directly apprehended" supernatural realities that religious mystics such as St. Teresa write so movingly about.

Thou Shalt Not

Restrictions, "Thou shalt not," pervade all religions. The "shalt nots" range from not eating meat, to not using birth control, to not hanging your washing out on a Sunday (as we discovered on a vacation on the Scottish islands of Lewis and Harris, which are the centre of an extreme form of Scottish Free Presbyterianism). Many of the "shalt nots" make a considerable degree of sense, whereas others, at least from the outside, appear to be extremely arbitrary and even bizarre. As an example of some of the more rational and understandable "shalt nots", the most famous set of restrictions, the Ten Commandments, include some very sensible rules such as "Thou shalt not kill." To take an example of a much more arbitrary set of "shalt nots," let us again consider kosher cooking in Judaism, which was touched on in the earlier section on good and evil when the pepperoni pizza with extra mozzarella problem was raised. Basic rules of kosher cooking (kashrut) include no eating of pork or shellfish, ritual slaughter of animals including extraction of all blood from meat using salt, and separation of dairy and meat cooking requiring separate utensils and separate kitchen areas. The justification for these extensive rules and restrictions includes the fact that the pig is seen as a disgusting animal and that shellfish can be contaminated. Applying rules of disgust and possible contamination would of course lead to a rejection of virtually all meat and fish, which would be the conclusion of Buddhist and Hindu vegetarians. However, rules about the separation of dairy and meat, such that even separate kitchen utensils and kitchen areas need to be designated and that dairy and meat products must be eaten separately and at least one hour apart, place most of the world's finest French cuisine, in which meat and dairy-based sauces are exquisitely combined, completely out of bounds—not to mention burgers with cheese, and of course pepperoni pizza with extra mozzarella.

So what are the consequences of the range of "shalt nots" that religions hand out to their followers? You might well say, why not leave well alone: if Jewish people want to keep dairy and meat products separate, that is up to them and they are not doing anyone any harm. Granted, kosher cooking and other similar "shalt nots" are basically harmless, even if somewhat bizarre. The problem arises, however, with the "shalt nots" that can be harmful to the individual and to other people within the social sphere of that individual. A particularly sinister requirement in some religions is that of *celibacy* (voluntary abstinence from all sexual activity) for some of their practitioners, as we will briefly consider next but examine in more detail in Chapter 5 when we examine social structures and religion and discuss more generally the importance of sin and its avoidance by religious followers.

One of the origins of celibacy was noted in Chapter 1 when we examined the Ancient Egyptians and the contribution, often hidden or denied, that they made to the Abrahamic monotheistic religions, which included celibacy. However, the Egyptian priests of Amun were only expected to live in the temple for three months of the year. During that time they were expected to be ritually pure and so sexual intercourse was taboo. For the other nine months of the year, the priests of Amun were married members of the community who normally had other professions and were not required to be celibate (see Rosalie David's *The Ancient Egyptians*, 1998). In contrast to this more sensible tradition, Buddhism from its origins developed a completely celibate monastic tradition following Siddhartha Gautama, the Buddha, and his rejection of his wife and son in order to pursue an ascetic and celibate life. The tradition of celibacy within the Roman Catholic Church followed a long period of discussion and conflict over many centuries. Eastern and Egyptian influences led to a development of a monastic tradition from the earliest Church onwards, with St. Paul, who was celibate, seeing marriage as a frailty. Nevertheless, until the twelfth century, many of the clergy were married and it was only at the Second Lateran Council in 1139 that clerical marriages were finally declared unlawful (see Diarmaid MacCulloch's *A History of Christianity*, 2009). As we will explore in detail in Chapter 5, the motivation for imposing celibacy on the Catholic clergy seems to have been more to avoid hereditary rights over property inheritance, in which the families of clergy could have been in conflict with the Church, than to do with any sense of "ritual purity" that the Egyptian priests of Amun might have had.

One further comment that must be made about celibacy before we explore its possible personal consequences is that, as any schoolchild who has studied Darwin will tell you, if a species does not procreate, then surely it will become extinct. That is, if celibacy is held as the ideal for all, then surely any such religion must die out. In fact, the Christian sect, the United Society of Believers in Christ's Second Appearing, or "Shaking Quakers" as they were better known, provide an illustration of exactly this problem. They were founded by Mother Ann Lee in Manchester, England, in 1747, though Mother Lee and eight followers emigrated to New England in the USA in the search for more religious freedom in 1774. Over 500 Shaker communities were founded, and at its peak in the mid-nineteenth century it had over 6000 members. Unfortunately, however, this community believed in celibacy for *all* members of the community, not just for a religious elite. The Shakers were reliant on conversion and the adoption of orphans in order to maintain their numbers, but these methods have not been sufficient to counteract the consequences of celibacy; thus, there is now only one Shaker community left, in Sabbathday Lake, Maine, and with only three members (see their website at www.maineshakers.com). And looking at their photos on the website, it is clear that even if they finally decided to reject celibacy it would now be too late.

The tragic fate of the Shakers can leave one feeling pity for adherents of celibacy in such religious communities. However, as psychologists we must also ask: what are the personal consequences and risks for people such as Catholic priests, monks, and nuns who are forced into lives of celibacy? Again, we will return to this issue in more detail in Chapter 5 because of its social consequences, so will just mention briefly some facts and figures that reflect how the Catholic Church has been rocked by sex abuse scandals over recent years. A summary by Karen Terry (2008) on the situation in the United States summarized the findings of surveys carried out in Catholic dioceses and religious communities throughout the United States between 1950 and 2002. The findings showed that 4392 (4%) of US priests had allegations of abuse from a total of 10 667 victims who made allegations; that the Catholic Church by 2002 had already paid a total of $572.5 million for treatment and legal fees; and that victims had already received over $1.3 billion in compensation awards. What is worse is that these figures are a considerable underestimation of the problem because the Catholic Church hierarchy has worked hard to cover up allegations and publicity and avoid official reporting of the true figures. Moreover, these figures refer only to *child* abuse, so they do not include figures for adult heterosexual and homosexual relations, which are also common in priests. And how often priests commit the "sin" of masturbation may be something for which we will never get accurate figures. Of course, we are not proposing that celibacy is the only contributing factor to problems such as child sexual abuse; for example, Karen Terry's work shows that priests who were themselves abused in childhood are more likely to become abusers and to abuse more from an earlier time in their career than non-abused priests. The figures also show a steady increase in cases, especially in the 1970s and 1980s, with a dramatic increase in the 1990s. These increases not only reflect the likelihood of reporting abuse, but also something of the impact of the "sexual revolution" of the 1960s, which must have left many a priest in a heightened state of personal conflict about his own sexuality that may have been easier to contain in less permissive sexual times. Nevertheless, the conflicts between sexuality and celibacy for Catholicism are as old as the Church itself and one need only read Bocaccio's *The Decameron*, completed in 1353, to enjoy more entertaining stories of the sexual activities of priests and nuns. However, Bocaccio did not write about *child* sexual abuse nor about its horrific lifelong consequences for its victims.

Conclusion

In this chapter, we have examined some of the range of normal experiences, including such states as consciousness, dreaming, grief and loss, experiences of good and evil, and mystical experiences, in order to understand how everyday experience can be understood by so many people to indicate the presence of gods and the supernatural. We will return in subsequent chapters to consider the importance of ritual and prayer and the avoidance of sin. One of the themes behind this examination is that it seems unlikely that the religious experiences of a few charismatic leaders would be sufficient to convince so many people of the existence of the supernatural unless the many also had experiences that led to belief in such explanations. For example, we have argued that the experience of consciousness itself, with its consequent experience of uniqueness and being at the centre of a personal universe, already provides the foundation for beliefs in personal immortality and omnipotence. That said, the unique experiences of charismatic religious leaders such as St. Teresa of Avila are well beyond the range of everyday experience, though they have a ready and willing audience. The next chapter will therefore examine in detail the varieties of abnormal experience that are limited to only a minority of individuals, but which are also taken as evidence for the proof of the supernatural.

3

The Psychology of Religion—The Varieties of Abnormal Experience

Anyone who has had a true vision from God will detect a false one almost immediately.

St. Teresa of Avila

Introduction

In the last chapter the focus was on everyday experiences such as dreaming, consciousness, and issues of good and evil. This chapter will look at some of the more unusual or even "abnormal" experiences that people can have and that they and others use as evidence for the supernatural. As in the last chapter, we will try to outline what the experience is and provide some examples. We will then provide a psychological or biological explanation for what might cause such experiences. The first section, which is the most substantial, will focus on visions and hallucinations, because these seem to be of such importance in a variety of religions and religious practices. Later sections will look at phenomena such as false memories, fugue states, conversion, and miracles.

Visions and Hallucinations

In the last chapter we presented one of the most famous hallucinations from St. Teresa of Avila in which she is pierced with the red hot spear by a beautiful young angel. St. Teresa's autobiography (Avila, 1957) contains a number of

Adieu to God: Why Psychology Leads to Atheism, First Edition. Mick Power.
© 2012 Mick Power. Published 2012 by John Wiley & Sons, Ltd.

less well-known visions, some of which she found equally rapturous but others that were quite terrifying. She interpreted the rapturous visions to be from God, and the sinister visions to be from the devil. For example, compare the following two reports:

> Once when I was at Mass on St Paul's Day, there stood before me the most sacred Humanity, in all the beauty and majesty of His resurrection body, as it appears in paintings. (p. 196)

> Once when I was about to take Communion, I saw with the eyes of my soul, more clearly than ever I could with my bodily eyes, two most hideous devils. Their horns seemed to be about the poor priest's throat and . . . I knew for certain . . . that here was a man in mortal sin. (p. 291)

She also reports a unique and terrifying version of hell that must have been an inspiration to Edgar Allan Poe:

> One day when I was at prayer, I found myself, without knowing how, plunged into hell . . . The entrance seemed like a very long, narrow passage, or a very low, dark, and constricted furnace. The ground appeared to be covered with a filthy wet mud, which smelt abominably and contained many wicked reptiles. At the end was a cavity scooped out of the wall, like a cupboard, and I found myself closely confined in it. But the sight of all this was pleasant compared with my feelings. (p. 233)

From St. Teresa's own account of her life, she clearly suffered from a variety of different psychological disorders. As a young woman, she describes times when she seems to have been anorexic, and throughout her life she recounts long periods of depression and episodes of rapture and ecstasy. Her discussion of herself, her self-concept, displays extreme negativity:

> I beg anyone who reads this account to bear in mind . . . how wicked my life has been—so wicked, indeed that among all the Saints who have turned to God I can find none whose history affords me any comfort. (p. 21)

There are also extremes of positivity:

> I had experienced a continual tenderness in devotion, which is partially obtainable . . . by our own efforts; it is a gift not wholly of the senses, nor yet of the spirit, but entirely God-given. (p. 71)

This split in the self-concept, which we have labelled the ambivalent self (e.g. Power and Dalgleish, 2008), is characteristically found in depression, and is even more characteristic of manic depression or bipolar disorder as it is now known. St. Teresa's hallucinations have high affectivity and there is also a considerable grandiosity, not only of her specialness in relation to God, but also in her founding of a new branch of Discalced Carmelite nunneries in Spain with 17 new nunneries opened during her lifetime. Alternative accounts of St. Teresa's visions have included the possibility that, perhaps like St. Paul, she may have been epileptic (see Garcia-Albea, 2003), but this account does not take into consideration the extreme ambivalence in the self-concept and the well-documented episodes of depression and ecstasy that she experienced. Of course, to say that St. Teresa is likely to have suffered from anorexia and bipolar disorder and perhaps epilepsy is not in itself to dismiss the contribution that she made both to religion and to literature, but the point is that it is necessary to begin to understand the range of natural phenomena that can give rise to so-called supernatural experiences.

Some of the founders of the world's key religions did so on the basis of their visions. Zoroaster, the founder of Zoroastrianism, saw his first vision at age 30 as he was drawing water from a river. He saw a bright being, "Vohu Manah," on the river bank, who then led him into the presence of the supreme god, Ahura Mazda, and several other "radiant beings," from whom he received his great revelation. This vision was the first of many in which he either saw Ahura Mazda or heard Ahura Mazda talking to him, or, like St. Teresa, felt the presence of the god but without seeing or hearing him. Zoroaster also saw in a vision the great evil adversary of the good Ahura Mazda, that is, Angra Mainyu. Both are forever in conflict with each other and thereby represent Zoroaster's teaching that both good and evil exist in all of us so we must choose between one path or the other.

Another founder of a great religion, Muhammad, also experienced visions similar in nature to those of Zoroaster. At about age 40, Muhammad began the practice of taking retreats to a cave on Mount Hira near Mecca. On one of these retreats, and after a period of fasting and meditation, he had his first revelation and a vision of "one terrible in power" or The Angel Gabriel. In one of his most famous visions, which is said to have occurred just after the death of his wife, Khadija, Muhammad was transported on his night journey from the sacred shrine in Mecca to Jerusalem on a mythical beast, the Buraq. From Jerusalem Muhammad was transported to heaven where God is said to have instructed him in the need for the five daily prayers, the practice of which has since become part of the Muslim faith. Such "transportations" are common among ancient and modern shamans, in whom such experiences are often induced with a variety of hallucinogens such as the peyote cactus in Central America, fasting, and ritual rhythmic music and dancing, or even, in the case of the Jivaro tribe in South America, going a year without sex (see Robert Wright, *The Evolution of God*, 2009). Muhammad's use of meditation and fasting (the origins of the Muslim month of Ramadan in which fasting must occur between sunrise and sunset) is a continuation of a long shamanic tradition of which Muhammad would have been aware in the various religions, including the Christian Anchorites in Syria, which he had experienced before he received his own personal visions and revelations.

Religious visions are not of course a feature only of the past but continually re-occur throughout the modern history of religion. The American Joseph Smith, the founder of Mormonism in 1830, the headquarters of which are now in Salt Lake City, produced his equivalent to the Old Testament, the so-called Book of Mormon, in an alleged state of revelation. In this book, Smith tells the story of a Hebrew tribe who were led by the prophet Lehi from Jerusalem to America in about 600 BCE. The subsequent history then describes a split in the tribe and a war between the two groups. Smith claimed that their history was written on golden plates by the prophet Mormon, and that they spent 1400 years buried in the ground until the angel Moroni delivered the plates to Smith, who copied what was written on them into the book of Mormon and then returned the plates to the angel. As Christopher Hitchens details in his book *God Is Not Great* (2007), by the age of 21 Joseph Smith had already been convicted by a court of being "a disorderly person and an impostor," because he had defrauded his fellow citizens by organizing false gold-digging expeditions that were supposedly based on his "necromantic powers." Consistent with his interest in gold, 18 months after his conviction Smith then miraculously discovers the buried gold plates as directed by the angel Moroni. Because Smith could not write, he had to dictate the message on the gold plates first to his wife and subsequently to his neighbour, though they were never allowed to see the plates, which were hidden behind a blanket as Smith dictated from them in his kitchen. As Hitchens notes, Joseph Smith was clearly inspired by the methods and experiences of Muhammad and even announced, "I shall be to this generation a new Muhammad." It seems fairly likely, therefore, that Smith's revelations are more likely the work of a gifted psychopath than the result of hallucinatory-type experiences. Nevertheless, the Mormon Church is now one of the world's fastest growing religions, with the main sect, The Church of Jesus Christ of Latter-day Saints, estimated to have 12 million followers.

Our final set of examples of more recent religious visions reflects an apparent trend among lonely young shepherdesses in the various mountains around Europe to have visions and conversations with the Virgin Mary. Within a relatively short space of time, destinations such as Fatima and Lourdes have become major Catholic pilgrimage centres, with Lourdes in the French Pyrenees receiving over three million visitors a year as Catholicism's answer to Mecca. The right vision at the right time in the right place can really do wonders for the local economy. In the case of Lourdes, in 1858 a 14-year-old peasant girl, Bernadette Soubirous, had a vision of the Virgin Mary who announced, "I am the Immaculate Conception." This might of course seem to be a bizarre statement to have made until you realize that, just four years before, Pope Pius IX had issued a papal bull stating the dogma of the Immaculate Conception (that Mary was born free from original sin). The Virgin Mary also revealed a spring in the grotto, which has since been believed to have miraculous qualities such that an estimated 50 000 sick or disabled people bathe annually in the search for a miracle cure. Back in 1858, Bernadette's initial vision seems to have caused mass hysteria in the local village, in which other girls also claimed to have had visions and seen phantasmic lights, and who threw themselves from high rocks into the river. The Virgin Mary also taught some of the more cynical men of the village a lesson or two: a drunkard who defecated in the grotto was punished with a night of violent diarrhea, and disbelieving local officials who interrogated Bernadette were apparently visited by poltergeists. Diarmaid MacCulloch in *A History of Christianity* (2009) puts the Lourdes visions in the following context:

> The nineteenth century proved one of the most prolific periods for Mary's activity in the history of the Western Church . . . She seems to have made more appearances all over Europe and Latin America than in any century before or since: generally to women without money, education or power and in remote locations, and often in association with the political upheavals or economic crises which repeatedly hit a society in the middle of dramatic transformations. (p. 819)

The more recent case of the Virgin Mary's appearance to three children in Fatima in Portugal in 1917 follows a similar pattern. The visions were first seen by 10-year-old Lucia Santos, though she was accompanied by two younger cousins, Jacinta and Francisco. The Virgin Mary in the form of "Our Lady of the Rosary" appeared on the thirteenth day of three successive months, May, June, and July, and famously imparted three secrets to the children. The first secret included a vision of hell, and the second secret included the need to convert Communist Russia to Catholicism. The vision for the third secret included the Virgin Mary together with an angel with a flaming sword above her, very reminiscent of St. Teresa's famous vision discussed in the last chapter. However, the third secret was withheld by the Vatican and not released until 2000, though many claim that the full content of the third secret has still not been revealed. The vision for the third secret includes the death of the pope, which Pope John Paul II interpreted to mean his attempted assassination in St. Peter's Square on May 13, 1981, in which he said he was saved by Our Lady of Fatima on her feast day. Lucia Santos subsequently became a nun and continued to see visions of the Virgin Mary throughout her life until she died on February 13, 2005. Her two young cousins were much less fortunate and died aged 10 years in the influenza epidemic that occurred after the First World War.

The Marian visions continue into the twentieth and twenty-first centuries. Not to be outdone by their French and Portuguese Catholic rivals, many other Catholic countries, including Ireland, have had their fair share of Marian visions. In 1985 the good people of Ballinspittle in County Cork, Ireland, claimed that the statue of the Virgin Mary had moved—yes, moved, and as a consequence drew an estimated 100 000 visitors. The vision led to a spate of "moving statues" in 30 other locations throughout Ireland. The Virgin Mary also accounts for the majority of so-called "simulacra" in which her image is perceived in natural phenomena. One such occurrence was the "Clearwater Virgin" who appeared in Clearwater, Florida, on Christmas Day in 1996 in the glass façade of a finance building that subsequently drew over one million visitors. Back to Ireland: on July 9, 2009, BBC News (retrieved from news.bbc.co.uk on April 7, 2011, which also includes a short video) reported from the Holy Mary Parish Church in Rathkeale, County Limerick, that workmen who were felling trees found the image of the Virgin Mary in one of the tree stumps. People from all across Ireland travelled to see the tree stump, though the local parish priest, Father Willie Russell, was not convinced and said "I have seen the tree . . . it's only a tree." Perhaps Father Russell was mindful of the episode of the classic television comedy *Father Ted*, "Kicking Bishop Brennan Up the Arse," in which the local bishop is persuaded that an image of his face had appeared in the parish-house skirting board. As Bishop Brennan bends over to study the skirting board . . . well, the rest is television history as the sketch lived up to the title of the episode.

In her study of Marian Apparitions, Sara Horsfall (2000) reported that there have now been an estimated 21 000 sightings of Mary. In her study, she examined accounts of the visions and extracted a number of similarities between them that included the fact that they are more likely to occur to the young and poor, that the visionary typically enters a trance state during the vision, that more recent visions have become serial, occurring over days or weeks, and that, with the serial visions, the visionary may gain an overnight fame such that thousands of people may travel in the hope of witnessing the visions. There are various explanations offered for why there continues to be this increase in Marian visions. They include unconscious wish-fulfilment, sociocultural explanations, and an attempt to overcome the misogyny in Catholicism through assertion of a lost feminine principle. The truth may reflect some combination of all of these factors, but they must be understood in a social context in which large numbers of people rush to validate the visions against the perceived hostility of state and even sometimes the Church itself. We will return to the importance of shared pilgrimage and the social structures of religion in Chapters 4 and 5. However, to return to the theme of this section in which the aim has been to illustrate the various psychological states under which hallucinations might lead to a belief in visions, some people might argue, and they would have a point, that the process of applying modern psychiatric diagnostic criteria to famous religious leaders and visionaries from past historical and cultural times is a rather crass exercise that really does not explain very much. Our point is that we agree in part with such a criticism, but we still wish to note that there are a large number of phenomena that can lead to the experience of what have been interpreted as visions and the voices of gods. In modern parlance, these visions and voices are called visual and verbal hallucinations. As Richard Bentall summarizes in his book, *Madness Explained* (2003), the causes of such hallucinations can include grief (see Chapter 2), psychoactive substances, trance states, deprivation, the transition between sleep and wakefulness (hypnagogic hallucinations), and temporal lobe epilepsy, in addition to a range of psychiatric states with diagnostic labels such as bipolar disorders and schizophrenia. When all of these phenomena are added together, then a substantial number of people will experience visual, verbal, and other types of hallucinations at one time or another in their lifetime, with only a minority of these experiences being due to psychosis, especially if the phenomena of dreaming are included in this category (see Chapter 2). Whereas psychiatry and psychology argue that these phenomena are the result of natural causes, the Catholic Church and other religious groups are predisposed, because they believe in gods and angels, to attribute some of the phenomena to the work of supernatural forces. Take the example of the so-called miracle at Fatima. The 10-year-old Lucia Santos and her young cousins promised the world that they would witness a miracle at Fatima and the world turned up. On October 13, 1917, approximately 70 000 people arrived in Fatima to see the promised miracle. In a beautifully simple, childish fashion, Lucia asked the huge crowd to stare at the sun, which eventually appeared to many to start zig-zagging and changing colours, and the "Miracle of the Sun" was declared. If you stare at the sun or other bright light (even a flash from a camera will give these effects) for long enough, visual afterimages and phosphenes (e.g. from mechanical stimulation such as rubbing the eyes after seeing a bright light) appear like ghostly images and can cause apparent movement as the perceiver moves his or her head. The most likely explanation for Lucia Santos seeing the Virgin Mary in the mountains around Fatima or, as Lucia described her in the documents held in the Vatican, as a woman "brighter than the sun, shedding rays of light clearer and stronger than a crystal ball filled with the most sparkling water and pierced by the burning rays of the sun," is that the young, bored shepherdess found that staring at the sun made her very famous. What is more, she even persuaded 70 000 adults to stare at the sun and then convinced them that they had seen a miracle! The young shepherdess certainly found her flock of sheep and they were only too ready to follow her.

Meaning under Stress

A common belief about religion is that people turn to their god or gods under times of stress. Most people will experience times of worry or distress at one point or another during their lifetime such as the death of a loved one, periods of financial difficulty, and threats of unemployment. Currently there is also an increase in the number of natural disasters such as hurricanes, floods, droughts, and avalanches, which are linked to problems in global climate change. The combination of natural and man-made disasters such as war means that there is an increasing chance that some people will experience extremes of stress that are beyond everyday stressors such as birth, marriage, divorce, and retirement. These extreme stressors have begun to be studied in psychology, and it seems that, while they often impact dramatically on people's belief systems, they may lead to a turning away from religion as much as they might cause people to turn to it.

To give an example, many people who experience a severe traumatic event go on to develop post-traumatic stress disorder (PTSD). Research carried out by Janoff-Bulman and others (e.g. Janoff-Bulman and Frantz, 1997) has shown that the experience of a severe trauma can lead many people to experience "shattered assumptions" about, for example, their own personal invulnerability, to the extent that their subsequent feelings of extreme vulnerability and impermanence lead them to seek psychological help. That is, beliefs in invulnerability and permanence, the immortality illusion that we discussed in Chapter 2, can sometimes contribute to the experience of trauma such as a road traffic accident because the (typically) young male adult believes that it will not happen to him even if he drives recklessly. However, the experience after a serious accident can be a dramatic feeling of vulnerability and impermanence, the opposite of what was believed before the trauma. The point is that it is commonplace to hold such beliefs, in part because of the special nature of the experience of consciousness, but it is when life-threatening events occur that the questionability of such beliefs becomes apparent. Nevertheless, as we sit contemplating our own consciousness, it is easy to understand how beliefs about one's specialness and even permanence at the centre of an idiocentric universe can originate.

A theory developed in social psychology, the so-called terror management theory, is of relevance here. Developed by Solomon, Greenberg, and Pyszczynski (e.g. Solomon *et al.*,1991) and drawing on the earlier psychoanalytic work of Freud, Fromm and Rank, the theory argues that humans are unique in their knowledge of their own mortality, and, as a consequence, must find ways of defending themselves against that existential knowledge. The theory predicts that increases in mortality salience have important effects on our beliefs and actions because of the need to buffer the consequent anxiety. One of the functions of religion from the terror management theory approach is therefore to offer a sense of security against this existential death anxiety because of the promise of immortality. The theory gained particular prominence after the terrorist 9/11 attacks on the Twin Towers in New York. One of the predictions was that under such stress people seek out strong charismatic leaders, as evidenced by the subsequent outcomes of elections in the United States and the United Kingdom. Critics of the theory might, however, argue that the elections of Bush and Blair subsequent to 9/11 disprove this aspect of the theory. Nevertheless, the theory does support the god and stress proposal, in the sense that if the stress increases our awareness of our own mortality and the associated death anxiety, then religious beliefs can offer a strong buffer against that anxiety. For those people with weaker or ambivalent religious beliefs, however, the increase in death anxiety may undermine the belief and lead to belief change or apostasy as we considered in Chapter 2.

Consciousness (Out-of-Body and Near-Death Experiences, Fugue States and Glossolalia)

The normal experience of consciousness was considered in Chapter 2 with its associated range of altered consciousness states that most people typically experience. It was argued that the range of normal conscious experiences, indeed the existence of consciousness itself, draws the experiencer into quasi-religious interpretations that may include a sense of permanence and invulnerability. However, there is a further set of unusual consciousness-related phenomena that people sometimes feel convinced are evidence for the supernatural. In this section we will consider the phenomena of out-of-body and near-death experiences, fugue states, and glossolalia (speaking in tongues).

Out-of-Body-Experiences (OBEs)

Out-of-body experiences, and the related near-death experiences which will be considered in the next section, have long been considered as support for the supernatural in many different cultures and have been given a variety of names such as "astral projections" and "spirit walking." One of the first recordings of such an experience comes from St. Paul's Second Epistle to the Corinthians:

> I knew a man in Christ above fourteen years ago (whether in the body, I cannot tell; or whether out of the body, I cannot tell . . .) such an one caught up to the third heaven . . . How that he was caught up into paradise, and heard unspeakable words, which it is not lawful for a man to utter. (2 Corinthians 12:2–4)

The experience typically consists of a sensation of floating outside the body and in some cases seeing all or part of the body from a distance. For example, patients under anesthesia for medical procedures have reported a sense of floating at the height of the ceiling in the operating theatre whilst watching their bodies being operated on.

OBEs have become a subject for research in a number of cognitive neuroscience laboratories around the world. The Swedish neuroscientist Henrik Ehrsson reported a technique for the induction of OBEs, which consisted of the use of video cameras presenting a display as if seeing the self from behind, which, when accompanied by tactile stimulation, leads to a sense of dislocation in space similar to an OBE (Ehrsson, 2007). The Swiss neuroscientist Olaf Blanke has reported a case (Lenggenhager *et al.*, 2007) in which electrical stimulation of part of the temporal lobe, the temporal–parietal junction, led to the experience of OBEs in a woman suffering from epilepsy. Blanke and colleagues have also reported a technique similar to Henrik Ehrsson's, in which the use of a virtual reality technique that permitted discrepant visual and tactile input can lead to the experience of OBEs (Lenggenhager *et al.*, 2007).

The point about these neuroscientific studies of OBEs is that if such experiences can be created under certain conditions in which visual and somatosensory inputs are discrepant, or by electrical stimulation of one or more parts of the brain, then supernatural and "astral projection" types of explanation become superfluous.

Near-Death Experiences (NDEs)

There is some overlap in the experience of NDEs and OBEs because the NDE is often accompanied by an out-of-body experience. In a study of 183 cases of NDE, Bruce Greyson (1990) reported in the appropriately named *Journal of Near-Death Studies*, a number of common features that included the following:

- Time stopped and there was a sense of peace.
- There was bright illumination.
- The experience was out-of-body.
- "Spiritual" beings were experienced, including dead friends and relatives.
- There was a sense of joy on entering a mystical place.

Sometimes the experience was so powerful that the person felt a reluctance to return to join the living. These similarities have led Gregory Shushan, in his book, *Conceptions of the Afterlife in Early Civilizations* (2009), to argue that there is a considerable uniformity among largely unconnected ancient cultures regarding belief in life after death and that the core elements of these religious beliefs are largely similar to the core elements of NDEs. In his book he examines conceptions of the afterlife in Ancient Egypt, Mesopotamia, China (before the arrival of Buddhism), India (also before the arrival of Buddhism) and pre-Columbian Mesoamerica. Shushan compares the afterlife accounts in each of these five civilizations and concludes that the differences between the afterlife experiences in ancient texts and the NDE accounts are predominately on the symbolic, culture-specific level but that, "the NDE itself appears to be a collection of subjectively experienced universal phenomena." Shushan summarizes a number of key elements in the NDE that form the basis for afterlife conceptions in these early civilizations. These include:

- The out-of-body experience.
- Corpse encounters, for example with dead relatives (ancestors).
- The experience of passing through darkness or a tunnel.
- Passing into the presence of intense light.
- An experience of union (oneness) and enlightenment.
- The feeling of being in another realm or at the point of origin.

Shushan argues very persuasively that NDEs were clearly part of the experience of these ancient cultures and that they provided key evidence for the nature of the afterlife in an otherwise diverse set of religious beliefs and practices. He argues, for example, that, in contrast to conceptions of the afterlife, these same ancient cultures have extremely diverse accounts of creation or creation myths ("cosmogonies") because there is no shared experiential basis from which to develop a culture's creation myths.

There is considerable modern interest in psychology and neuroscience in NDEs, similar to the increased interest in OBEs because of their implications for the functioning of the brain. The development of cardiac resuscitation techniques has permitted researchers to study systematically the experiences of people who have been clinically close to death. The Dutch cardiologist Pim van Lommel and his colleagues studied a consecutive series of 344 cardiac patients who had been resuscitated after cardiac arrest (van Lommel *et al.*, 2001). They found that 62 patients (18%) reported NDEs. Those patients who did have an NDE were significantly more likely to die within 30 days of the experience compared with those who did not have an NDE. Of those patients who experienced an NDE and who survived, follow-up at

2 and 8 years showed, from an examination of life changes, that the NDE group were significantly more accepting, loving, and empathic towards others, that they were more spiritual and felt they had a deeper sense of purpose in life, and that they were more likely to believe in an afterlife and had less fear of death. These findings are dramatic in the sense that it is not just the near-experience of death itself that is important, because all of the patients in van Lommel's study were close to death, but, that, when combined with an NDE, one can gain an insight into the origins of religious beliefs in the afterlife as Gregory Shushan has elucidated.

Fugue States

A fugue state is a rare phenomenon in which the person suffers an amnesic episode and usually travels away from home and can assume a new identity. The state normally lasts a matter of hours or days, but in some cases has been documented to last years. There is normally an abrupt return of the previous self with amnesia for the time of the fugue state. The fugue state is normally precipitated by personal crisis or stress and not related to substance abuse or other medical condition because it is of psychological origin. The writer Agatha Christie is believed to have suffered such a fugue state when she disappeared from her home in Cornwall and then appeared in Harrogate in Yorkshire 12 days later but with no memory of the intervening period.

It is likely that the fugue state, in which there may even be the assumption of a new identity, has been a source of so-called mystical states, especially those in which the person has become "possessed" by another identity. Fugue states and trance states have been well documented in the anthropological literature in religious and shamanic practices. The anthropologist Michael Lambek, in *Human Spirits: A Cultural Account of Trance in Mayotte* (1981), describes trance behaviour among the inhabitants of Mayotte, a small island in the Indian Ocean off the coast of East Africa in the Comoro Archipelago. Lambek describes how the people of Mayotte (usually the women in the group) enter into what he calls trance states, during which they believe their bodies are inhabited by spirits. He then analyses the conventions for behaviour in trance and the process by which the individuals come to terms with the spirits in their midst. He proposes that trance can best be understood as a social activity within a defined system of cultural meaning rather than as a "psychological problem." However, his descriptions of "trance" include the absence of the person who becomes incommunicado and that a spirit has taken over as a new identity. The Mayotte spirits will then talk to the villagers and hold conversations with them, but the entranced person has no recollection of the spirit or the conversation afterwards.

One way in which those who participate in Haitian voodoo may enter a fugue state is to become possessed by the loa, one of the religion's spirits. It is believed that when the loa possesses someone, their body is being used by the spirits. These spirits can offer prophecies of future events and situations. Practitioners experience such possession to be an exhausting experience. The possessed person has no recollection of the possession and normally suffers amnesia for the time of the possession. It is said that only the spirit can choose whom it wants to possess and that those who become possessed are at a high spiritual level. The voodoo notion of the zombie, which has proven so popular amongst Hollywood film-makers, also presents many features of the fugue state. The zombie is considered to be a corpse that has been raised from the dead and that, at least in Haiti, was used to carry out some of the more boring and tiring agricultural work that the African slaves were originally brought to the Caribbean and Americas to carry out. It is also believed that there are those who feign possession because they want attention and status. A "chwal" (one who is being ridden by the spirit, derived from *cheval*, the French word for horse) will therefore undergo some form of trial or testing to make sure that the possession is indeed genuine. For example, someone who claims to be possessed by one of the spirits may be offered a liqueur made by steeping chili peppers in alcohol. If the possessed person consumes the liqueur without showing any evidence of pain or discomfort, the possession is considered to be genuine. The most important voodoo ceremony in Haitian history was the Bwa Kayiman ceremony of August 1791 that began the Haitian Revolution. In the ceremony a spirit loa possessed a priestess and received a pig sacrificed as an offering. All who were present at the ceremony pledged themselves to fight for the freedom of the slaves against French colonial rule, which was eventually achieved in 1804 with the establishment of the first black people's republic.

Another possible fugue example from the Christian tradition relates to one of the puzzling episodes in the life of Jesus in which, shortly after being baptized in the River Jordan by John the Baptist, Jesus mysteriously disappears into the desert for 40 days:

> And Jesus being full of the Holy Ghost returned from Jordan, and was led by the Spirit into the wilderness. Being forty days tempted of the devil. And in those days he did eat nothing: and when they were ended, he afterward hungered. (Luke 4:1–2)

In this state, Jesus seems to spend 40 days and 40 nights in conversation with the devil who tempts him with a variety of delights including bread for his hunger as well as power and glory, and even tempting him to throw himself off the temple in Jerusalem to see if the angels really would catch him before he died:

> And when the devil had ended all the temptation, he departed from him for a season. (Luke 4:13)

Again, a strange comment at the end of a strange episode in which the suggestion "[the devil] departed from him for a season" indicates that Jesus may have experienced other such similar episodes during his life. Of course, the accounts of the 40 days in the desert in the gospels such as Luke's do not provide definitive evidence that Jesus's experience was a fugue state, but the wandering alone in the desert after the intense emotional experience of his baptism suggests that a fugue state is one possible explanation.

Glossolalia

Glossolalia, which literally means "speaking in tongues," was first described in the New Testament:

> And when the day of Pentecost was fully come, they were all with one accord in one place. And suddenly there came a sound from heaven as of a rushing mighty wind, and it filled the house where they were sitting. And there appeared unto them cloven tongues like as of fire, and it sat upon each of them. And they were all filled with the Holy Ghost, and began to speak with other tongues, as the Spirit gave them utterance. (Acts 2:1–4)

Within the Christian calendar, Pentecost occurs 50 days after Easter and is also known as Whit or Whitsunday. It celebrates the episode from Acts in which the Holy Ghost descended upon the apostles. It has also become the focus of an American Christian revivalist movement that began in the 1900s. This was called the Pentecostal movement, and is part of a more general "Charismatic movement" within Christianity that is claimed to include a quarter of the world's two billion Christians. The Pentecostal and Charismatic movements make clear the importance of miracles, prophecy, and glossolalia for the modern church rather than simply being of historical interest. The movements now emphasize the practice of glossolalia in their ceremonies. The ceremonies, in which typically a believer may writhe on the ground whilst speaking in tongues, have become familiar sights through the media.

Pentecostal and Charismatic followers believe that glossolalia is, as in the extract from Acts quoted above, a gift from the Holy Spirit in which the person is given the gift to speak in a sacred or spiritual language. Linguists, however, who have now carefully examined recordings of glossolalia, have come to very different conclusions. In his now famous studies of the linguistics of glossolalia, William Samarin, in his book *Tongues of Men and Angels* (1972), showed that glossolalic speech consists of regular intonation, accent, rhythm, and pause patterns from the speaker's own language, that the spoken phonemes are also those from the speaker's own language and do not include phonemes from other languages, but that these regular phonemes are combined to give nonsense words and neologisms within the spoken utterance. Practitioners of glossolalia rebut such linguistic interpretations and claim that they are speaking other, often lost, languages (known as *xenoglossia*) and can sometimes be understood by other believers.

Glossolalia provides a classic example of a natural phenomenon that can be generated by anybody who is prepared to practice the repetition of quasi-nonsense syllables expressed with great emotion, but which is interpreted by religious believers to represent a sacred language in which the Holy Spirit speaks through the experiencer in a near-miraculous fashion. Unfortunately for the Pentecostal and Charismatic believers, these "miraculous" visitations are no more than well-practiced performances although they clearly create strong emotions in those who are present.

Loss and Absence of Consciousness

There are a number of medical conditions in which consciousness either does not develop in the first place (for example in anencephalic individuals), or it only develops in a limited but damaged form (as in autistic spectrum disorders). Similarly, there are a number of medical conditions in which, because of disease (such as Alzheimer's disease) or injury (e.g. traumatic brain injury leading to permanent coma), significant damage occurs to consciousness and to systems such as memory that underlie self-identity. For example, anencephaly results from a neural-tube defect that occurs when the head end of the neural tube fails to close early on in pregnancy, and that results in the absence of a major portion of the brain and skull.

Individuals with this disorder are born without a forebrain and are usually blind, deaf, unconscious, and unable to feel pain. Although some individuals with anencephaly may be born with a main brain stem, the lack of a functioning cerebrum permanently rules out the possibility of ever gaining consciousness, though reflex actions such as breathing and responses to touch and taste can occur.

The problem that these developmental and acquired disorders of consciousness raise is a straightforward one, yet theologically very difficult to deal with. The question is, if an individual never acquires consciousness or a sense of self-identity, or if someone damages consciousness and loses their self-identity, is there a separate soul that exists independent of our consciousness and that maintains self-identity even though damage or disease has led to its loss? From the psychological point of view, studies of damage to the functioning of the mind demonstrate that the mind is dependent on the brain for its existence; that if the brain develops in certain abnormal ways or becomes damaged in certain ways, then there is a loss of functioning of the mind, or the mind is also damaged. The mind does not exist separately from the brain, but it exists because of the brain. The theological problem is that the Descartes mind–brain split is a false one, therefore the soul must exist separately from the mind. How, though, can the soul have an identity and a self-consciousness if the individual never had these in the first place (such as in anencephaly) or if they have been lost through severe brain damage? The answer that we would support here is that the soul has been invented by self-conscious individuals in whom consciousness has led to an illusion of immortality, but, alas, their illusory eternal souls died when their brains died, just as for the rest of us.

The "Holy Fool"

A recent visit to the wonderfully eccentric but internally claustrophobic St. Basil's Cathedral in Moscow's Red Square highlighted for me the role that the so-called "Holy Fool" (or "Fool for Christ") has played in the history of religion. The story of St. Basil is worth the telling in that, for all of the pomp and hierarchy about which one might be cynical in organized religion (see Chapters 4 and 5), there has always been a place for the wonderfully eccentric, and eccentricity can even be revered. St. Basil (also known as Vasily the Blessed) is one of 36 *yurodivy* or Holy Fools that have been made saints within the Russian Orthodox Church. Basil (?1469–1552) was born to poor parents just outside Moscow and became an apprentice shoemaker. He showed early talent when a merchant asked him to make shoes that would never wear out, a promise that Basil was able to make because he had seen what the future held for the merchant who purchased the boots: the merchant died a few days after he bought the boots. At age 16 Basil then adopted his eccentric lifestyle, which included walking around barefoot and naked in both summer and winter, wearing heavy chains, and sleeping in the porches of churches. He is recorded as one of the few people who was able to challenge the then Tsar of Russia, Ivan the Terrible, and survive. On one occasion he criticized Ivan after a church ceremony for not paying attention, to which Ivan confessed his sin and said he had been dreaming about refurbishing one of his palaces. On another occasion Basil gave Ivan meat to eat during Lent when Ivan was supposed to be abstaining from meat. Basil gave Ivan the explanation that it did not matter if Ivan broke the fast because he had committed so many murders. At his death, Ivan was one of the pallbearers for Basil's coffin and he was buried on the site of an earlier church that was subsequently replaced at Ivan's behest by the cathedral that now bears St. Basil's name.

The role of the Holy Fool is identifiable in the Old Testament and also bears a relation to the court jesters who have an equally long history. Its significance in the Christian Church, however, did not begin until the fifth century in Syria with Simeon of Emesa, who now has the honour of being the patron saint of Holy Fools, the ultimate fool among fools. Diarmaid MacCulloch in *A History of Christianity* (2009) tells an equally fascinating tale. Simeon apparently first came to the notice of the good people of Emesa when he began dragging a dead dog around hanging from his belt, he started throwing nuts at women during church services, and he then caused a group of girls who were laughing at him to go cross-eyed, thereby clearly proving his divine inspiration. As MacCulloch suggests, the Holy Fool provides a "safety valve" against overly pious solemnity and prayerful silences, especially in the Orthodox tradition. It now has a modern American variant, which has been renamed "Crazy for God" in place of "Fool for Christ." This has become primarily associated with converts to Sun Myung Moon's Unification Church (now formally known as the family Federation for World Peace and Unification). Sun Myung Moon founded his church in Seoul, South Korea, after a vision in which Christ told him that he was the new Messiah who needed to continue his work. A number of so-called "Moonies" have written books about their experiences of being "Crazy for God" within the Unification Church. Many of these accounts have been highly critical of Sun Myung Moon's motives and have left worldwide suspicion hanging over the Church.

False Memories

One of the most heated debates in psychology in recent years has been the issue of whether or not traumatic memories can remain repressed for many years but then be "recovered" many years later, or whether in fact such memories are actually "false memories" that, either through suggestion from influential others or through the processes of memory reconstruction, feel real to the experiencer even though the events recalled never happened (see Graham Davies and Tim Dalgleish, *Recovered Memories: Seeking the Middle Ground,* 2001). The dispute between recovered versus false memory has been at its most public and painful over allegations of childhood sexual abuse; the American False Memory Syndrome Foundation was founded in 1992 by a married couple who, they claimed, were wrongly accused by their adult daughter of having abused her when she was a child. A survey of 4400 families who were members of the Foundation (McHugh *et al.,* 2004) found that there had been a peak in allegations in 1991–1992 in the United States with 579 such accusations, but that the numbers had declined significantly since. The accusations were almost all made by young white females, 86% of whom had been in psychotherapy, and the majority of accusations were against their biological fathers. The many subsequent US legal cases testify to the fact that there is no easy answer to whether or not a recovered memory is true or false, because there are clearly examples of both (Power, 2001).

One of the perhaps more intriguing aspects of the whole literature on false memory has to be the reports of *alien abduction*. If these increasing numbers of claims are to be believed, then it is estimated that several thousand Americans are *each day* taken on board fleets of spaceships hovering somewhere over the Midwest of the United States where lengthy medical examinations are carried out by groups of intergalactic physicians. The abducted individuals are then returned back to their humdrum lives and only manage to recall these abduction episodes using memory recovery techniques such as hypnosis. In their studies of these phenomena, Newman and Baumeister (1998) observed that about 80% of abductions occur in the US, with virtually none being reported in Asia and Africa. (It is possible to be facetious at this point and ask: why would apparently *intelligent* life-forms from other planets only be interested in middle-aged guys in camper vans in some unknown part of the US Midwest?) Newman and Baumeister have also noted an increasing trend towards reported sexual interference from the alien abductors. To give an example, Police Sergeant Herbert Schirmer claimed that he was abducted by aliens on December 3, 1967, while in Ashland, Nebraska. He was later examined under hypnosis by a psychologist on February 13, 1968. Under hypnosis he reported that he had seen a blurred white object that came out of what he had at first thought was a truck because of its blinking red lights. The white object communicated mentally with him and prevented him from drawing his gun. During hypnosis he reported that the aliens in the vehicle were quite friendly, that they had bases on Venus, and that they drew energy from power lines.

If we can assume that there is no such fleet of extraterrestrial, NASA, or Hollywood spacecraft, these reports of alien abduction are surely proof that individuals can recover "memories" of events that have never occurred. They are proof that suggestible individuals, when placed under the influence of credible experts such as therapists using hypnosis, are vulnerable to the recovery of false memories. The question of false memory therefore becomes not *whether* but *how* and *when*.

The other side of the argument about false memory, as we noted above, is whether or not a memory can be forgotten for a long period of time and then subsequently recovered. In contrast to the case of alien abduction (for which, at least as yet, I can offer no personal recollections), the following example is of a personal memory of an event that occurred when I was eight years old and which I did not recall until 38 years later. My family had recently moved to the city of Birmingham and my mother, my sister, and I had gone to visit some relatives some distance away by bus. As we returned that night, a very heavy fog descended, so that when we got off the bus we became completely disoriented. We were lost in an open park area and unable to find our way out. We were lost for some considerable time, wandering around in a cold and anxious state before we spotted some lights from a building and were then able to go and ask for directions.

The trigger or cue that led to this recollection was seeing a television program listed in a newspaper about a famous London fog of 1952 in which many thousands of individuals died. The newspaper summary of the program led to the complete recovery of the memory, together with a sense of certainty that I had not recollected this memory previously. In addition, the memory recovery was accompanied by a re-experiencing of the considerable anxiety with which the original experience had been associated.

The memory has now been corroborated by my mother who was present at the event, but obviously the additional recollection that this memory has never previously been remembered can only be trusted by virtue of my belief that this is the case. The fact is, and this could be put to an empirical test, most individuals probably have long-forgotten memories that, once cued, they would estimate not to have recalled for some considerable time. So why, therefore, is there such a debate about this issue? The question is whether or not *traumatic* events (that is, events that would be judged by most as difficult if not impossible to forget because of their nature) can in fact be forgotten. In addition, the question is whether special intrapsychic mechanisms such as "repression" need to be mooted to account for such forgetting or whether that forgetting can be accounted for by the characteristics of remembering and forgetting about which everyone would agree.

So what implications do these debates about false and true recovered memories have for religion and religious experience? One very famous ancient claim that is reminiscent of modern-day stories of alien abduction is that of Muhammad's "night journey," which is recorded in the seventeenth chapter of the Koran, the Sura Al-'Isra. Muhammad's night journey is still a major source of conflict between Muslims and Jews over the ownership of Jerusalem, but the Muslim claims based on what has every mark of a false memory of early alien abduction consequently appear to be extremely flimsy. Muhammad's night journey took place 12 years after he became a prophet, during the seventh century. Muhammad was in his home city of Mecca and praying at the Kaaba (the central shrine in Mecca to which all Muslims are meant to make pilgrimage or *hajj*), when the angel Gabriel appeared together with the mythical horse, the Buraq. Muhammad mounted the Buraq and flew with Gabriel to the "farthest mosque," which has been taken to mean the Temple Mount in Jerusalem. From the Temple Mount, the Buraq took Muhammad to heaven, where he met prophets such as Moses and then spoke to God (Allah). Initially, Muhammad was instructed to tell his followers that they must pray to God (Allah) 50 times a day, but he eventually managed, with the help of Moses, to negotiate this down to the current practice of five times a day. The Buraq then flew Muhammad back to Mecca.

Glory to (Allah) Who did take His servant for a Journey by night from the Sacred Mosque to the farthest Mosque, whose precincts We did bless,—in order that We might show him some of Our Signs: for He is the One Who heareth and seeth (all things). (Sura, Al-Isra 17:1)

Muhammad's ascent to heaven, in which he met biblical prophets, saw paradise and hell, and learned from Allah the teachings of the Koran, has become an article of faith in Islam with the addition of the following definitive proof: on the rock in Jerusalem that supports the Temple Mount there are grooves that show Muhammad's footprints. And that just about sums up the nature of religious belief and religious proof.

Conversion

William James was much taken with the issue of conversion. In *The Varieties of Religious Experience* (1902) he discusses different types of conversion and offers the following observation:

> Emotional occasions, especially violent ones, are extremely potent in precipitating mental rearrangements. The sudden and explosive ways in which love, jealousy, guilt, fear, remorse, or anger can seize upon one are known to everybody. Hope, happiness, security, resolve, emotions characteristic of conversion, can be equally explosive. And emotions that come in this explosive way seldom leave things as they found them. (p. 198)

As James notes, probably the most famous of all sudden conversions was that of St. Paul, formerly known as Saul of Tarsus who was born in a Mediterranean port of what today is Turkey. Paul was a Greek-speaking Jewish Pharisee who had hated the new Christians:

> As for Saul, he made havock of the church, entering into every house, and haling men and women committed them to prison. (Acts 8:3)

The famous incident on the road to Damascus happened just after Paul had witnessed the stoning to death in Jerusalem of Stephen, the first Christian martyr. Paul was travelling to Damascus in order to capture more Christians and bring them back to Jerusalem when:

> As he journeyed, he came near Damascus: and suddenly there shined round about him a light from heaven: And he fell to the earth, and heard a voice saying unto him, Saul, Saul, why persecutest thou me?... And Saul arose from the earth; and when his eyes were opened he saw no man... And he was three days without sight, and neither did eat nor drink. (Acts 9:3–9)

The fact that Paul fell to the earth and saw a bright light has led some to speculate that he had experienced an epileptic seizure. However, even if this were true, it still does not explain the more important fact that Paul was suddenly converted from being a persecutor of Christians to becoming a Christian himself, and, moreover, became the leading proselytizer in bringing Christianity to Gentiles so that it was no longer merely a Jewish sect.

Sudden conversions such as that of St. Paul are just one of the types of conversion that have been identified. In her insightful discussion of conversion, Kate Loewenthal in *The Psychology of Religion* (2000) summarizes a number of studies that show that sudden conversions are a rarer form of conversion, because most are gradual and occur over long periods of time in which individuals struggle at both an intellectual and an emotional level with the religious belief system that might be best for them. Furthermore, conversions need not only consist of individual personal struggle, but can also result from group pressure, as we will explore in more detail in Chapters 4 and 5. For example, of the recent new religious movements, the Unification Church (Moonies) has been studied in most detail. Members of the Church identify young and perhaps lonely individuals and then invite them back for a meal to their communities where they would be "love-bombed" by the whole group and then gradually isolated from previous family and friends in order to become more dependent on the religious group. Such procedures highlight the fact that some people are more vulnerable to "conversion" than others. Factors such as early problems in attachment relationships, stress and unhappiness in the pre-conversion period, and degree of intrinsic religiosity of the person are also important (see Loewenthal, 2000).

Miracles

Last but not least, what better way to end this chapter than with a miracle? If only.

David Hume (1748) famously wrote about miracles, on the topic of which he noted:

> A miracle is a violation of the laws of nature ... The plain consequence is ... that no testimony is sufficient to establish a miracle, unless the testimony be of such a kind, that its falsehood would be more miraculous, than the fact, which it endeavours to establish. (p. 35)

One of the examples of a putative "miracle" that Hume quotes was that of the Emperor Vespasian, who, at the start of his reign in the first century CE, is reputed to have cured a blind man by spitting in his eye and cured a lame man by touching him. However, the context of the supposed "miracle" was that it was at the start of Vespasian's reign, that he was a "common" man who had risen through the ranks of the military, and that a well-stage-managed miracle or two was used to establish his authority and quasi-divinity in order to overcome the uncertainty about him in the eyes of the populace.

In his essay, Hume deals only implicitly with the miracles that are used as proof of the divinity of Jesus in the New Testament, in that he prefers to focus on the Pentateuch, the first five books of the Old Testament, in order to dismiss the claimed miracles therein concerning creation, the fall, the flood, and so on. Hume notes that these are stories written centuries later than the claimed events and for which there is no direct testimony. At first sight, therefore, the miracles of the New Testament appear more challenging, so the argument goes, because the miracles were the direct testimony of the writers of the gospels, Matthew, Mark, Luke, and John. In fact, we know that the gospels and other documents of the New Testament were not written contemporaneously with the life of Jesus. The documents were written in "common dialect" Greek, such that later Christian Fathers, trained in classical Greek, found them ugly and unattractive. The four gospels (their name deriving from the Old English "godspell" and meaning "good message") were selected from a large number of "godspells" by the Church in the fourth century at the Council of Nicaea and other Councils. Although the four gospels are attributed to the apostles Matthew, Mark, Luke, and John, little or nothing is actually known about who the authors were. The three so-called "synoptic" gospels of Matthew, Mark, and Luke give a more coherent and consistent account of Jesus. The gospel of Mark is thought to be the earliest, written in about 70 CE, with those of Matthew and Luke written in the late 80s CE and likely to have drawn in part on the earlier Mark but another source also. The gospel of John is thought to have been written in the late 90s CE and is very different from the three synoptic gospels. It has the most well-known opening of any of the books of the bible "In the beginning was the Word, and the Word was with God, and the Word was God" (1:1) and has had the greatest impact on Christianity of the four gospels. It is possible that John was written in Egypt, because fragments have been found there, and it also presents more hostility towards the Jews than is found in the other gospels. The subject of the authorship and accuracy of the gospels has been and will continue to be a major theme of scholarship, but the key point that we wish to highlight here is that the gospels do not provide a contemporaneous eyewitness account of the supposed miracles that Jesus performed. Indeed, the synoptic gospels do not even present Jesus as the divine "Son of God;" it is only with the gospel of John that this presentation of Jesus begins to appear, and many of these statements may even have been additions made in later centuries as the theological shift towards the "Son of God" movement gained prominence until officially endorsed again at the Council of Nicaea.

Even if a modern-thinking Christian were to accept these doubts about the authenticity of the miracles reported in the New Testament, he or she might still point to the recorded recent past and the present day and the miracles that the Church has testified. What about the "Miracle of Fatima" that was witnessed by a crowd of 70 000 people in 1917? As we discussed above, however, this "miracle" seems to have consisted of a 10-year-old child persuading the crowd of 70 000 to stare at the sun for longer than they should have done and then interpreting the visual after-effects as miraculous visions. Even if the modern-day Christian concedes that Fatima need not have been miraculous, he or she could point to all the miraculous cures that have been documented for the pilgrimage site of Lourdes in the Pyrenees. Well, let us run some figures for the alleged miracles that are said to have occurred at Lourdes. The official Lourdes website is very informative about the miracles at Lourdes (www.lourdes-france.org). At the time of accessing the website (April 21, 2011), there were 67 recorded miraculous cures, beginning with the first in 1862. Because of the regular declarations of "cures" made by visitors to Lourdes, in 1905 Pope Pius X set up the Medical Bureau to investigate claims, and an additional International Medical Committee of 20 members was established in the 1940s. The Committee needs a two-thirds majority vote before a declaration can be made that "the cure is inexplicable according to present scientific knowledge." The Lourdes website helpfully gives details of the 67 cures; thus, one cure was recognized in the 1990s for Jean-Pierre Bely of La Couronne, France, who was cured of multiple sclerosis; one cure was declared for the 1980s for Cirolli Delizia from Paterno, Italy, who was cured of "Ewing's sarcoma of the right knee." The rate of one "miraculous cure" per decade does actually sound very low by unexpected medical cure standards given that Lourdes has approximately five million visitors per year, that is, a rate of one miracle per 50 million visitors each decade. Take, for example, Ewing's sarcoma, named in 1921 by the Cornell University Professor of Pathology, James Ewing. The sarcoma is a type of cancer that affects bone or soft tissue, typically in the leg, pelvis, or arm. Its peak occurrence is in children in the age range 10–20 years with about 250 new cases diagnosed in the United States every year. The prognosis is increasingly good, with figures suggesting a 66% 5-year survival rate. The Lourdes website states that in 2005 the Medical Bureau investigated 40 declared cures, of which five are being followed up. It hardly seems necessary to comment on the influence that psychological factors have been shown to play in recovery from all somatic disorders, even when physical medicine has apparently failed. The regular visits to pilgrimage sites in all religions, the miraculous cures that living religious gurus claim to make, or the power that the relics of a saint have in curing the incurable, raise general issues of religion, belief, and health that will be examined in Chapter 6 when we consider the links between religion and health.

A final comment on miracles: one common use of the term is when someone experiences something very unusual, for example, "It's a miracle that I won the National Lottery" or a survivor from a disaster declares, "It's a miracle that I survived the plane crash." However, the problem with the winning-the-lottery miracle is that the lottery is designed for someone to win a large amount of money, so it is simply an issue of *probability* that has nothing to do with the miraculous. A very different issue arises with the survival of one person in an aircraft disaster in which hundreds of people die; such a "miracle" potentially leads to a very perverse view of miracles if a disaster is to be viewed in this way because in this situation the miracle requires the death of many other people in order to miraculously save one person. Even the psychopathic god of the Old Testament might be hard pushed to label that degree of human loss as a "miracle," though, on second thoughts, the miracle of the Passover with the deaths of the first-born of humans and animals comes pretty close.

Conclusion

In this chapter we have reviewed an extremely diverse range of phenomena that relate in one way or another to the varieties of abnormal psychological experience that have often provided evidence in favour of religious phenomena. We considered in detail the hallucinations or visions that a number of important spiritual leaders have presented as voices or visions from their gods and angels. We examined a variety of disorders of consciousness and of unusual conscious states such as fugue states, false memories, out-of-body experiences, and near-death experiences. The argument is that, although these phenomena are not commonplace in that the majority of people are unlikely to experience them, nevertheless, all of these phenomena are psychological rather than supernatural in origin and we need only understand them at a psychological level for which there is no need for supernatural explanations. Other phenomena such as conversions and miracles have also been discussed because these too are rare but understandable phenomena for which we have psychological explanations. In summary, therefore, it is argued that, as with the range of normal experience considered in Chapter 2, the varieties of abnormal experience do not require any form of supernatural explanation even though those who have had such experiences have sometimes firmly believed in and been able to convince others of their supernatural origin. On that point we therefore now move to a consideration of the social structures and processes that have worked to make religions such an enduring part of the human experience.

4

Social Structures and Religion

Lighthouses are more useful than churches.

Benjamin Franklin

Introduction

In Chapters 2 and 3 we examined some of the range of normal and abnormal psychological experiences that can be used as evidence for the supernatural and religious belief systems that are derived from such phenomena. However, the initial focus on the individual psychological level of explanation is not meant to lessen the importance of the fact that religions are social systems that also need to be understood in terms of their social structures and social processes. Whereas William James was notoriously opposed to organized religion and favoured private experience as the route to spirituality, on the contrary we believe that the great majority of religious believers hold their beliefs because of their social development, and maintain their beliefs in the complex social systems that reflect the diversity of extant religions.

In contrast to the individual psychological focus of William James, the great sociologist Emile Durkheim (1912) in his analysis of religion saw that religions reflect the social structures of the group or crowd but in an idealized form. Later sociologists have developed Durkheim's argument and argued that there are many significant types of social structure that range from the dyad, to the family, to the group, and to the society, all of which must be understood in relation to the social structures and processes that provide the rock on which religion is built. In this chapter we will begin

Adieu to God: Why Psychology Leads to Atheism, First Edition. Mick Power.
© 2012 Mick Power. Published 2012 by John Wiley & Sons, Ltd.

with an examination of how some of these different types of social system are reflected in or help us to understand the dynamics of religious systems.

How to Be a Social Success—A Case Example

Pope Benedict is no fan of Halloween, according to the press: "Halloween is 'dangerous' says the Pope as he slams 'anti-Christian' festival." So ran the headline in the *Daily Mail* on October 30, 2009, and in many other national newspapers. In fact, contrary to the claims of the *Daily Mail*, it does not appear to have been Pope Benedict XVI himself who made the comments, but the writer of an article in the Vatican newspaper *L'Osservatore Romano*. Nevertheless, Pope Benedict must experience some discomfort when good Catholics all over the Western world appear to re-enact the ancient pagan ceremony of Samhain, celebrated by the Celts on the eve of November 1, the start of winter, and designed to frighten away the ghosts and ghouls who were believed to become more powerful during the harsh winter months. The Pope probably does not read Harry Potter either. In fact on July 13, 2005, *The Times* ran an article in which it stated, "Pope Benedict XVI has condemned the Harry Potter books as 'subtle seductions,' capable of corrupting young Christians, in two letters which have now been published online."

The Vatican's problems with the ghosts of religions past highlight a number of issues about modern religions. We will examine a key aspect of these issues here because of their psychological implications. The first issue is that of "syncretism" as it has been called, which is the incorporation into a new religion of some of the beliefs and practices of earlier religions, which enables the new religion to be more successful in its conversion of practitioners. The second issue that we will highlight is why wizards have always had a better press than witches. That is, most of the world's major religions are misogynistic, an issue that will also be discussed in Chapter 5 when we look at the issue of power and control in religions.

First of all, let us consider the issue of syncretism within the Catholic Church and how it has incorporated the practices of other belief systems. In Chapter 1 we saw that many of the basic theological beliefs, including those of monotheism, paradise, and semi-divine men (the pharaohs) who were born from the union between a god and an earthly woman, originated in the ancient belief systems of the Egyptians which in turn influenced the Jewish belief system into which Jesus was born. As the Christian Church spread through western and northern Europe, however, it incorporated many of the Celtic and Germanic pagan religious belief systems into its practices. For example, the festivals and celebrations that we now think of as Christian ones, including Christmas, Easter, and Halloween, were simply borrowed from the Celtic and Germanic tribes as part of the means of their conversion. In the case of Christmas, as Diarmaid MacCulloch (2009) notes:

> We must conclude that beside the likelihood that Christmas did not happen at Christmas, it did not happen in Bethlehem. (p. 79)

December 25 seems to have been chosen as the date for Christmas, Christ's birth, by the Christian Church some time in the fourth century. The date is significant because it coincides with the winter solstice and with the Roman holiday *Sol Invictus*, in which several sun gods were worshipped together, and it follows the Roman *Saturnalia*, which ran from December 17 to 23, which was a time of merry-making, gift-giving, and visiting friends and family. As Christianity spread north through Europe, Christmas also came to incorporate Germanic and Scandinavian winter-solstice celebrations, including the "12 days of Yul" such that in some areas Christmas is still known as "Yule-tide" and includes the adornment of the house with plants such as holly and ivy from these pre-Christian celebrations.

The arbitrariness of the date of Christmas has not gone unnoticed among some of the later Christian reformers. The Protestant Reformation saw attempts to ban Christmas. Following the English Civil War, Cromwell banned Christmas in 1647, but it led to rioting in England so Charles II restored Christmas to the English calendar on the restoration of the English monarchy. Nevertheless, some of the Scottish Protestant Churches still take a dark view of Christmas. If you log on to the website for the Scottish Free Presbyterian Church (www.fpchurch.org.uk), there is an article entitled "Why Christians Should Not Celebrate Christmas," which includes the warning:

> The all too common depiction of the Son of God in the form of a plastic doll is therefore nothing short of blasphemous.

By the way, do not make the mistake of trying to log on to the website on a Sunday, as I innocently did without thinking, because the site is closed on Sundays and simply states, "Remember the Sabbath Day to Keep It Holy", with the relevant quote from Exodus in support.

The timing of the Christian celebration of Easter shows even more "syncretism" than the timing of Christmas. At least Christmas is predictable and falls on the same date every year (although in Eastern Orthodox Churches, which still use the older Julian calendar, it falls on January 7), but the calculations for Easter have to be carried out in a Druid-like moon ceremony at midnight in the back garden of the Vatican. Yes, that is a slight exaggeration, but the truth for the dating of Easter is equally bizarre, yet two billion Christians seem happy that the supposed death and resurrection of Jesus are marked on a different date every year at a time that is calculated according to the position of the moon. Why didn't Cromwell target Easter as well as Christmas, one wonders? The actual calculation for the date of Easter is extremely complex and it turns out to be one of those questions that you probably wished you had never asked. The starting point is the ancient Sumerian/Babylonian lunar calendar, which was based on 12 lunar months each beginning at the first sight of the new crescent moon and with the year beginning at the spring equinox at about March 21 in modern terminology. However, the lunar cycle and the solar cycle bear no relation to each other, so, in order to keep the lunar cycle aligned with the seasons, a thirteenth month needs to be added every few years, according to a 19-tropical-year cycle known as the Metonic cycle after the astronomer Meton of Athens who was one of the early identifiers of this cycle. During the Hebrew Babylonian exile in the sixth century BCE, the Jews adopted the Sumerian/Babylonian luni-solar calendar, and this Hebrew calendar is still used for the determination of Jewish religious dates. One of these key dates is that of the Passover, one of the most gruesome feasts in any religion, which celebrates the angel of death killing all the first-born children and animals of the people of Egypt, apart from those Jews who had marked their doors with the blood of a ritually sacrificed lamb. This is celebrated following the full moon on the fourteenth day of the lunar month of Nisan, the start of spring and the vernal equinox. The importance of Passover for Christians is that the crucifixion of Jesus is meant to have occurred just after the celebration of Passover which meant that many in the early Church celebrated Easter at the same time as Passover. Many non-Jewish Christians (Gentiles), however, opposed the linking of Easter to a Jewish feast and preferred that the resurrection be celebrated on a Sunday rather than a moveable day of the week, which is what happens with the calculations for Passover. At the Council of Nicaea in 325 CE, therefore, Easter was recommended to be the first Sunday after the full moon after the vernal equinox, in which the vernal equinox is set as March 21. However, even this apparently simple equation is not quite accurate in that the vernal equinox does not always occur on March 21, and the so-called Paschal full moon (the fourteenth day of the month of Nisan in the Hebrew religious calendar) does not always coincide with the actual full moon! In practice, these calculations mean that Easter Sunday can occur anywhere between March 22 and April 25. The early and late dates occur very rarely, such that the next time Easter Sunday will be on March 22 will not be until 2285 CE.

The point about these digressions into the dates for Christmas and Easter is that one of the classic ways in which a new religion succeeds and becomes the majority religion is through a process of syncretism, in which some of the existing beliefs and practices of the older religion become incorporated into the new one. For example, just after the vernal equinox, pagan Anglo-Saxons celebrated the arrival of spring with a festival for the fertility goddess Eostre (as the Venerable Bede recorded in the eighth century). They found the name of their goddess (the origin of the name "Easter"), together with fertility practices symbolized by rabbits and eggs, part of the new religion on the block, Christianity.

The sacred springs, caves, temples and mountains that were significant in the old religion also became part of the new religion. To give just one example, from archaeological evidence we know that Glastonbury Tor in Somerset, England, had been occupied and used as a place of worship from pre-Christian times. It is still considered the location of the mythical Avalon of Arthurian legend. St Michael's church was built there in medieval times, though all that remains now is the rebuilt tower of the church because the earlier building was destroyed in an earthquake. The master symbol of Mexico, the famous Virgin of Guadalupe, also presents a fascinating example of syncretism, as spelled out in the classic paper by the anthropologist Eric Wolf (1958). In brief, shortly after the Spanish invasion of Mexico, a Christianized Indian, Juan Diego, claimed to have had visions of the Virgin Mary on Tepeyac Hill, just to the north of Mexico City, who gave him instructions to tell the archbishop to build a church on the hill. Eventually, the Church of Our Lady of Guadalupe was built there, and it has now become Mexico's major pilgrimage centre receiving hundreds of thousands of visitors every year. However, what Juan Diego failed to tell the archbishop was that Tepeyac Hill was already a pilgrimage centre for the Aztec fertility goddess Tonantzin, known as Our Lady Mother, who was associated with the moon. Later church commentators in Mexico were known to complain that the Christianized Indians used apparent worship of the Virgin Mary as a cover for worship of the Aztec goddess Tonantzin and even referred to the Virgin Mary with the same name as the Aztec goddess (see Wolf, 1958).

The point is that the incorporation of earlier sacred sites occurs regularly in the spread of new religions, which makes the acceptance of those new religions easier for potential new converts. However, the problem with syncretism for religion is that although the process helps in the conversion of new believers because they do not have to reject all their previous beliefs and practices, at the same time practitioners can carry too many of the old beliefs into the new religion to the discomfort of the leaders of that new religion. Hence, Pope Benedict XVI's apparent discomfort with people dressing up as ghosts and ghouls at Halloween on October 31. There are of course many more extreme examples where syncretism can backfire on the new religion. A good example comes from Macumba, the African-Brazilian religion of which the best-known sect is Candomblé, based in Salvador de Bahia to the north of Brazil. During a stay in Salvador at a beachside hotel, when I was kept awake by an all-night Candomblé ceremony (a mixture of baptism and all-night African drumming), the syncretism was very apparent. Candomblé is one of the religions of slavery that was part of the African diaspora. It draws primarily on the Yoruba people of Nigeria and surrounds, where there is worship of the *orishas* or religious deities. Macumba was viewed by the slave-owners as paganism and witchcraft, such that the slave population was put under pressure to adopt Christianity. In many parts of Latin America, orishas are now equated with Catholic saints, which allows worship of the original Macumba deity under the guise of the Catholic saint.

Candomblé was originally confined to the slave population, and was subsequently banned by the Catholic Church. Over the centuries Candomblé has incorporated an increasing number of elements from Christianity. Crucifixes are sometimes displayed in Candomblé terreiros (temples), and Candomblé houses in Brazil often display statues of the Catholic saints. In addition, Candomblé followers often participate in Catholic celebrations for the particular saint that corresponds to their Candomblé deity. Even after the end of slavery, the claim that ritual dances of Candomblé were in honour of Catholic saints was often used by practitioners and authorities alike as an excuse to avoid confrontation. The slave context has led Candomblé to be one of the ultimate syncretic religions, even if the Catholic Church has come to reject it. The anthropologist Mattijs van de Port has written recently of "Candomblé in pink, green, and black" (van de Port, 2005), meaning that Candomblé appeals not only to the blacks (the black

Africans brought to Brazil by the slave trade), but also now to the pink (gays, who are treated badly within Catholicism) and to the green (the environmental movement which is growing in Brazil). There is even an Islamic sect within Candomblé because some of the slaves from West Africa had already been exposed to Muslim ideas, plus there has been some incorporation of local Native American gods. Hence, not only does the new religion take hold through the incorporation of some of the old beliefs, but, in cases such as Candomblé, the old religion actually survives through the superficial adoption of some of the beliefs and practices of the new religion. Still, the Candomblé practice of the ritual sacrifice of animals such as chickens in public was always hard to disguise as anything other than of African origin rather than Catholicism.

The Dyad and Religion

Normal social structures contain dyadic relationships of many forms, for example, mother and father, husband and wife, brother and sister, parent and child. As we noted earlier, Emile Durkheim (1912) argued that the supernatural structures typically reflected idealized forms of our own social structures. Durkheim's ideas have been developed by sociologists such as Guy Swanson in his *The Birth of the Gods* (1960), in which a more sophisticated analysis of social structures than Durkheim's group or crowd was put forward. Swanson proposed that the key social structures that are reflected in the supernatural are those in which the legal force of "sovereignty" operate, because these structures are the groups that often direct our behavior without our realization:

> A group has sovereignty to the extent that it has original and independent jurisdiction over some sphere of life—that its power to make decisions in this sphere is not delegated from outside but originates within it. (p. 243)

There is of course no inherent reason why the eternal gods should also have similar social structures to mere humans given that they are the eternal gods. The fact that the relationships between the gods often seem to mirror those of humans provides at least some evidence that the gods were invented by humans rather than humans being invented by gods. Of course, some might argue that there are examples of unique relationships between the gods, such as the Trinitarian view of God within Christianity, but even in the Trinity of Father, Son, and Holy Ghost, there is a key dyadic relationship of father–son, which highlights our initial point that human dyadic relationships are imposed on to the religious view of the gods.

The mother–father theme has to be the most prominent theme throughout world religions, given that there is no religion that is without some form of maternal theme among its gods. The mother-goddess theme is often different from the earth mother, because the latter may simply be the origin of the earth and the cosmos. In contrast, the mother goddess is typically young and very sexually active, and often dominates her male consort or even regularly replaces him with new consorts, thereby reflecting seasonal fertility cycles. In some versions, the mother goddess emphasizes the nurturing role of the mother, and in her depictions is therefore large-breasted (such as the famous statuette, the *Venus of Willendorf,* carved about 22 000 BCE) or many-breasted (such as the statue of Artemis of Ephesus carved about 550 BCE in the Temple in Ephesus that was one of the Seven Wonders of the Ancient World). For the Ancient Egyptians, Isis became a major mother goddess, whose consort was her brother Osiris and their son was Horus (see Chapter 1 for a summary of the Osiris death-and-resurrection myth). Isis was often depicted in statues and murals as a mother nursing her child Horus in a manner familiar in later Christian iconography of the Virgin and child. In fact, some historians believe that because the cult of Isis spread beyond Egypt and became very popular in both Greek and Roman civilizations following Alexander the Great's conquest of Egypt, the Christian church suppressed the cult from the fourth century CE onwards, but that the development of the mother-and-child worship and imagery within Christianity represented a syncretism based on the cult of Isis.

God-as-father has become a more predominant theme in modern religions as the monotheistic religions in particular have seen the rise of the masculine and subjugation of the feminine (see also the section in Chapter 5 on misogyny) so mother goddesses have been downgraded into lesser roles. The obvious proposal to explain these apparent changes in the roles and relationships of the gods to each other is that it has nothing to do with the gods themselves, but the changes have everything to do with the dynamics of the power relationships between human males and females, old and young, and between the male religious elite and their followers. In Chapter 1, which outlined the development of religions, we saw that the development of agriculture at the beginning of the Neolithic period (about 10 000 years ago) saw the development also of mother goddesses such as Isis in Egypt, Asherah and Anat in Syria, Inanna in Sumer, and Demeter in Greece. These mother goddesses represented the fertility of the earth, such that agriculture was equated with sexuality in which the male seed was planted into mother earth. The goddesses are heroic in their annual battles with the gods of death who bring winter and destruction, which can only be overcome by the mother goddess whereas the other male gods are seen as impotent in this battle.

The coming of urbanization with the early cities from about 4000 BCE eventually saw the rise of monotheism as urban life became liberated from the annual agricultural fertility cycles of the Neolithic period. Monotheism arose initially within Egypt, then subsequently in Jewish society with the development of a patriarchal system in which male gods came to predominate (see, for example, Gerda Lerner's *The Creation of Patriarchy,* 1986). It would of course be possible to write whole books about the change from polytheistic matriarchal to monotheistic patriarchal religions and societies, and in the next chapter we will return to the issue of power and misogyny within the monotheistic religions. However, the acknowledgement of the importance of the mother goddesses within Neolithic agricultural societies raises the possibility that factors other than urbanization may also have played a part in the shift towards the patriarchal misogynistic monotheistic religions. Staying with the issue of fertility, and the fact that the male consorts played secondary roles to the mother goddesses, there is perhaps another dynamic at work with men's envy of female creativity and fertility playing a role. Psychoanalysts such as Freud mistakenly saw envy the wrong way round: that women suffered from penis envy (Freud, 1914). However, a more potent type of envy that has latterly come to be recognized is men's envy of women's capacity for childbirth. The neo-Freudian psychoanalyst Karen Horney (1885–1952) rightly dismissed Freud's focus on female envy of the penis, but proposed instead that men are motivated by womb envy. Horney argued that, because of men's envy of women, they are driven to dominate them and to be creative and to compensate for their inadequacy. We can, however, only speculate as to whether or not such a process might have operated in the shift from the small Neolithic agricultural communities into the larger urbanized cities, where the scale of social organization demanded a different type of social structure, which, as Durkheim and Swanson would argue, was then reflected in the idealized structure projected on to the supernatural, and from which patriarchal monotheism emerged.

How is the monotheistic God-the-Father actually viewed by those who believe in him? Does the psychological evidence provide any support for

Freud's father-figure hypothesis? Vergote and Tamayo (1980) summarized a number of studies that they carried out in Belgium. Young Catholic children saw God as very much like a parent, with properties of both mother and father and depending on which was the more dominant parent. Dickie and colleagues (Dickie *et al.*, 1997) explored the relationship between Bowlby's attachment theory and children's belief in God. They also found that the children's perceptions of God were drawn from characteristics of both parents, not just the father, though girls tended to see God more in relation to their parental disciplinary style. Dickie and colleagues found support for an attachment view of God rather than God being the substitute father of Freudian theory. Findings such as these show that the older polytheistic religions provided a more balanced view of the masculine and feminine principles in the view of gods. This balance can still be seen in polytheistic religions such as Hinduism in which male and female gods and goddesses are normally paired, but the monotheistic god has come to be seen as the ultimate alpha male in accordance with the dominant alpha males of church, synagogue, mosque, and state.

Family Structure and Religion

Guy Swanson's (1960) extension of Emile Durkheim's structural analysis of religions locates the family as a key social structure that is apparent cross-culturally and that has sovereign power. The family therefore should be an evident structure within the supernatural. We must, however, be mindful of Clifford Geertz's (1966) warning against a simplistic structuralism since religion does not merely describe the social order but also shapes it. We also reiterate the point that there is no reason why the eternal gods should in any way reflect human family relationships other than that these are idealized structures of our earthly forms.

All of the polytheistic religions present family relationships between the gods, and even the monotheistic religions have family relationships within them. The Egyptian Isis–Osiris–Horus myth that we have discussed previously presents a classic and repeating theme within Neolithic agricultural communities in that the mother goddess, Isis, must overcome the evil forces (Seth) that destroy her husband, Osiris, so that each springtime the land can be refertilized and give birth to the next season's crops (their child, Horus). The Greek god Zeus was born from his father, Cronus, the king of the Titans, and his mother, Rhea. Cronus discovered that one of his children was set to dethrone him, so he swallowed his children as they were born. However, Rhea hid Zeus in a cave on Crete, where he eventually grew to manhood and dethroned Cronus. Zeus then ruled the heavens and married his sister, Hera, who became queen of the gods of Olympus. Hera was also driven to distraction by the constant philandering of Zeus and the many children that he sired both by other goddesses (for example, Apollo and Artemis with the goddess Leto) and by mortal humans (among them Helen of Troy with Leda of Sparta, whom he approached disguised as a swan). Zeus clearly deserves to be the god of modern-day football players who seem to model themselves on him.

Another example that was mentioned earlier is provided by Eric Wolf's (1958) analysis of the Virgin of Guadalupe, the patron saint of Mexico. In addition to the syncretism between the Aztec goddess Tonantzin and the Virgin Mary, Wolf's analysis links the significance of the Virgin of Guadulupe to two types of family structures within Mexican society. The first family structure was that of the indigenous Indian population in which there was a basic equality between the male and the female with all tasks shared equally. These families suffered defeat by the Spanish, but her appearance to the Christianized Indian, Juan Diego, in 1531 offered some triumph to the old religion and the old ways, and the Virgin Mother provides nurturance and protection for her defeated children. Wolf then argues that the second type of family, which he calls the Mexican family, was a product of the invasion and reflected issues of male dominance over women and children within the family. Eventually, the Mexican nation sought independence from Spain, in which the new Mexican families threw off the dominance of a distant father figure in Spain and Mexico itself became dominant. For these families, the Virgin of Guadalupe signified survival and hope after the defeat of the crucified Christ. As Wolf (1958) notes:

> The Guadalupe is important to Mexicans not only because she is a supernatural mother, but also because she embodies their major political and religious aspirations. (p. 163)

To continue with the Christian theme, the concept of the Trinity of God can seem both puzzling and absurd to outsiders (see, for example, Richard Dawkins' account in *The God Delusion*, 2006). The Trinitarian view is at best implicit, if represented at all, in the New Testament, but grew in subsequent centuries with the notable work of the Carthaginian Tertullian (160–220 CE), who first proposed the notion of the "Trinity" and of "Three

Persons, One Substance." Tertullian's proposals and the notion of the Trinity were a source of great conflict in the early Church until 325 CE when the Council of Nicaea declared in favour of the Trinitarian view, which elevated Jesus to divine status along with the Father and the Holy Spirit. Although the Trinitarian view obviously gives masculine roles to the Father and the Son, there has always been some ambiguity over the Holy Spirit and exactly what it was meant to represent. The Nicene Creed, however, failed to delineate what the Holy Spirit was. That task was left to Athanasius (293–373 CE), Bishop of Alexandria, who argued for the divinity of the Holy Spirit. You may now wonder, though, how or why this "family" seems to have only three male members and what happened to the female. In fact, although the Holy Spirit is generally taken to be a male spirit, in some of the early traditions, some languages (e.g. Syrian) used the feminine form to refer to the Holy Spirit. Even in modern times some Messianic groups, such as the Branch Davidians and some members of other Protestant denominations such as the Southern Baptist Convention view the Trinity as being comparable to a family, with the implied role of mother for the Holy Spirit.

Although the Catholic Church is unlikely ever to declare that the Holy Spirit is anything other than masculine, the absence of a female goddess within its ranks has left a substantial gap. One of the steps it has taken to fill the gap is through the elevation of the Virgin Mary, who is worshipped widely within Christianity despite her obviously human origin. However, the Church has in recent times promoted her significance with two declarations, that of her Immaculate Conception, and that of her Assumption. We saw in Chapter 3, when we discussed the visions of the Virgin Mary witnessed by St. Bernadette at Lourdes, that the Virgin Mary announced herself by saying, "I am the Immaculate Conception," meaning that she was the only human to be born without the stain of original sin. The debate about the Immaculate Conception had engaged the Church for hundreds of years until Pope Pius IX declared it to be so *ex cathedra* (meaning from the "chair" or office of the Pope) in 1854, just a few years before the declaration in Lourdes. A further elevation of Mary came when Pope Pius XII in 1950 further declared with the privilege of papal infallibility that Mary was taken bodily into heaven, the so-called Assumption of Mary, though he left it ambiguous as to whether she was still alive at her Assumption or if she had died before it. Anyway, the key point about the elevation of Mary within Church doctrine accompanied by widespread worship of her reflects the fact that the Christian version of monotheism, especially in its Trinitarian version, is excessively masculine. By the conveyance of the family schema with the "Father" and "Son" concepts, Christian monotheism evokes the need for a feminine mother principle within its deities. As the "Mother of God" Mary completes the Christian family circle.

To return to more earthly families, one of the questions that must be asked, given the sovereignty or power of the family, is how much influence the family has on the religious beliefs of the children in the family. Earlier research by Cavalli-Sforza *et al.* (1982) showed that, as would be expected, children hold similar beliefs to their parents such that there is a correlation of between 0.5 to 0.6 for activities such as church attendance and prayer. This research also showed that there are higher correlations for religious beliefs and practices than for other comparable activities such as politics and support of sports teams. The parental influence is strongest when there is religious activity in the home, for example praying and Bible-reading together (Erickson, 1992). A study of over 3000 nationally representative adult children (aged 16 and over) in Australia showed that parental influence from both mother and father was the strongest predictor of religious activity in contrast to other socio-demographic factors which generally did not predict religious activity (Hayes and Pittelkow, 1993). Stokes and Regnerus (2009) found, from the American National Longitudinal Study of Adolescent Health, that teenage children report more discordant family relationships if their parents are more religious than they are and they do not share their parents' religious beliefs. However, there is significantly *less* discord if the teenagers are more religious than their parents. Research by Saroglou and Fiasse (2003) suggests that birth order may have an effect on religiousness such that in a study of three-sibling families they found that middle-born children were most rebellious and least religious, whereas the last-born were more religious.

One of the questions that has arisen in European trends in religiosity has been the apparent decline in religious belief since the early twentieth century. One interpretation that has been made of the decline in Church attendance has been "believing without belonging;" namely, that although Europeans attend church less often, nevertheless, they still retain their religious beliefs. However, Voas and Crockett (2005) report analyses of the British Household Panel Survey and the British Social Attitudes surveys to show that in the United Kingdom there has been a decline in both belief and attendance at about the same rates. Their further analyses show that these effects are not due to specific cohorts, nor due to specific experiences (e.g. the Second World War), but are generational; thus, their results show that the absence of religion in a family is almost always passed on to the children, but only about half of the children in religious families share their parents' religiosity. In further analyses of the UK data, Crockett and Voas (2006) found that although immigrant nonwhite ethnic-minority groups are more religious than the indigenous population, the generational rate of decline in religiosity is nevertheless similar to that in the indigenous population. Nor do people become more religious as they get older. As Richard Dawkins comments in *The God Delusion* (2006), the contrasting fortunes of religion in the United Kingdom and the United States are at first sight a paradox given that the USA was founded as a secular non-Christian nation, in contrast to the United Kingdom which has an established church headed by a constitutional monarch. Richard Dawkins is at a loss to explain the increase in religiosity in the USA, but Michael Shermer in *How We Believe* (2003) tackles the issue head on. Shermer summarizes data to show that, in the past 150 years, the percentage of the US population having church membership has increased from 25% to 65%, and that about 90–95% of Americans believe in God in one form or another. The increase in religiosity seems particularly evident among American evangelical Protestant groups. Lindsay (2008) suggests that the US–UK differences may in part be due to minority groups (e.g. African-Americans and Southerners) in the United States feeling more marginalized and excluded in comparison to their UK counterparts, so these marginalized groups in particular have turned to the Protestant evangelical movements that charismatic church leaders such as Martin Luther King have provided in the recent past. We will return to this issue in Chapter 5.

In summary, in this section on the family we have argued, as sociologists from Durkheim onwards have proposed, that the structure of the family influences the idealized structure of the relationship between supernatural beings even in monotheistic religions. Equally, the family is a very significant source of influence for the transmission of religiosity from one generation to the next. The contrasting trends in the United States and the United Kingdom, however, illustrate that the family is only one component among the range of social factors that influence religiosity and that other factors such as the recent history of exclusion and marginalization of African-Americans in the United States are also powerful factors that influence changes in patterns of religiosity.

Mega-Churches

The church and its congregation have always provided an important social structure within society and therefore, by its nature, are an important point of social influence and social participation for its members. In places such as England, the area of a parish may also be that used by local civil government for administrative purposes. The parish priest is the religious leader for that parish and therefore plays an important role in sustaining and influencing the local congregation. In this section, however, we have chosen to focus on the Korean mega-churches, which highlight many important issues about the development of so-called "New Religious Movements" over the recent period in order to help us understand why, in some parts of the world, religion is on the increase whereas elsewhere it is on the decrease.

The history of Korea has been nothing if not turbulent over the past hundred years or more. Japanese expansionism saw Korea come under Japanese rule in 1910 until the end of the Second World War in 1945. Korea was then divided into two states, a Communist North and a non-Communist South, but North Korea invaded South Korea in 1950. Intervention by the United Nations eventually saved the two-state system. This turbulent history created a rich bed in which New Religious Movements began to flourish. From the mid-nineteenth century onwards, Korea had been a target for Catholic and Protestant missionaries, who were particularly influential in the post-war period. By 1995 an estimated 25% of the population were now Christian, but many were of quasi-Christian New Religious Movement forms that have developed out of the American Protestant evangelical movements.

A mega-church is defined as a church with more than 2000 members in the congregation, though it typically refers to Protestant rather than Catholic congregations. Although many of the mega-churches are based in North America, five out of ten of the world's largest congregations are in South Korea, the world's single largest congregation being that of David Yonggi Cho's Yoido Full Gospel Church in Seoul, which had an estimated 830 000 members in 2007. The Yoido Full Gospel Church is part of the Assemblies of God movement. David Cho's life is classic of modern Korea. He was born in 1936 and was a Buddhist but converted to Christianity at age 19. At that time, he was dying of tuberculosis and was visited by a young Christian missionary, then converted to Christianity and recovered. His first service began with just a few members in 1958. The Yoido Church includes an auditorium that initially seated 10 000 but has now been expanded to 25 000 seats and holds seven services every Sunday (see the Church's website at www.fgtv.com). Because of the rapid growth of the Church, there are now smaller satellite churches to which the services and sermons are relayed simultaneously.

The main practices of movements such as the Assemblies of God (or technically The World Assemblies of God Fellowship), of which the Yoido Church is a member, focus on fundamentalist beliefs closely based on the Bible, inspirational preaching, highly emotional services, faith healing, and exorcism. The Assemblies of God are the world's largest Pentecostal group and therefore emphasize the experience of the apostles at Pentecost and include baptism in the Holy Spirit and glossolalia or speaking in tongues (see Chapter 3). The Pentecostal revivalist movement began in the early twentieth century in the US, first in Topeka and then in Los Angeles. It has quickly spread world-wide and now has an estimated 60 million followers. As part of an American Protestant movement, it makes strong use of all modern marketing methods including television evangelism via channels such as the God Channel (now known as God TV: see www.god.tv). It encourages a "big is beautiful" view in which it directly competes with modern large gatherings such as pop festivals and sports events by offering religious ceremonies on a similarly large scale. The fact that David Cho's Yoido Church entered the *Guinness Book of Records* for the largest church gathering illustrates the view that biggest is best that clearly motivates the Protestant mega-church movement.

Theocracies: "For God and Country"

The separation of church and state is normal for Western-style democracies, even where such countries have a strong majority religion. However, *theocracies* (literally "rule by god", but in practice political rule by a religious elite) are not just an historical anomaly of the Ancient Egyptians or the Israelites under the leadership of Moses, but are part of modern society in countries such as Iran, the Vatican State, and, until recently, Tibet. We discussed the fourteenth Dalai Lama of the Yellow Hat order of Tibetan Buddhists briefly in Chapter 1. Tenzin Gyatso was enthroned in 1940 at the age of five years as head of the order and, until he fled to Dharamsala in India in 1959, was the leader of a feudal theocracy in Tibet. Tibetan Buddhism is divided into four distinct traditions: Gelugpa, Sakya, Kagyu, and Nyingma. The Dalai Lama's efforts to unite them under his leadership has occurred over many years, though he recently seems to have tired of these attempts. The first phase started after he arrived in Dharamsala when he tried to get the different traditions to agree to come together as a single form of Buddhism, a pro-posal that was rejected by lamas of these traditions (the Gelugpa tradition maintained a neutral position at the time). The female head of the Black Hats, the twelfth Samding Dorje Phagmo (the only prominent female lama in Tibet) was quoted in 2008 as saying that "The sins of the Dalai Lama and his followers seriously violate the basic teachings and precepts of Buddhism and seriously damage traditional Tibetan Buddhism's normal order and good reputation," adding that "Old Tibet was dark and cruel, the serfs lived worse than horses and cattle."

Nor has the fourteenth Dalai Lama and head of the Yellow Hats proven very popular with another branch of Tibetan Buddhists. During a teaching tour of the United Kingdom in May 2008, members of the Western Shugden Society demonstrated against the banning of a prayer to Dorje Shugden. Similar protests occurred in Sydney when the Dalai Lama arrived in Australia in June 2008. The Dalai Lama says he had not banned the practice, but strongly discourages it as he feels it promotes a spirit as being more important than Buddha, and that it may encourage cult-like practices and sectarianism within Tibetan Buddhism. The Shugden worshipers in India protest that they are denied admission to hospitals, stores, and other social services provided by the local Tibetan community. The Western Shugden Society have now published a book, *A Great Deception: The Ruling Lama's Policies* (2010), which provides a very different view from the Nobel-prize winning media star of the West. To quote:

> With a role for every occasion—holy man, politician, international states-man, simple monk, pop icon, Buddhist Pope, socialist, movie star, autocrat, democrat, Marxist, humanitarian, environmentalist, Nobel Peace prize win-ner, nationalist, Buddha of Compassion, communist, God-King—the Dalai Lama weaves a complex web of religion and politics that entraps his audiences wherever he goes. Nobody has seen anything like it. People are easily swayed by the historical mystique of Tibet and its 'God-King', and feel captivated and convinced by his charm. (p. 229)

However, to quote from the book cover itself:

> A courageous and compelling account of Tibetan history and the activities of the current Dalai Lama that stand in stark contrast to popular percep-tions of a "holy" politician. With an extensive compilation of news stories, documents, personal accounts, and chronologies, a tangle of religion and politics is revealed that plays out in Tibetan exile communities and across the international stage, embodied in the person of the 14th Dalai Lama. The aims of this book are religious to end an illegal ban on a mainstream Buddhist

practice that the Dalai Lama has personally rejected and maligned. However, to get to the heart of this human rights issue and to gain the support of those who can affect its resolution, the book endeavors to follow knotted threads of political ambitions, deception, greed, and betrayal to unravel the popular mythology that surrounds the iconic Dalai Lama of Tibet.

The fourteenth Dalai Lama has mediagenic appeal in the West. No one there, however, would wish to have a feudal theocracy imposed on them, whoever were to lead it: the current increase in Islamic theocracies in countries such as Iran and Saudi Arabia, and the power wielded by the Taliban in Afghanistan, have left almost all Western commentators united in their distaste for these theocratic states. Unlike other religious leaders, Muhammad was also a civil leader and, after his emigration or *Hijra* to Medina from Mecca in 622, ruled that area before eventually conquering Mecca itself. The combination of prophet, warrior, and leader makes Muhammad's legacy for modern Islamic states more understandable, but it leaves Islam as currently the most aggressive of the Abrahamic religions in terms of its motivations to convert and bring "salvation" to non-believers. These aims suggest that Islam's supporters regard it as a *Pax Romana* for modern times. (During the "Roman Peace" the Roman Empire expanded to northern, southern, and eastern Europe and across North Africa.) Sam Harris in *The End of Faith* (2004) quotes from the *Hadith* (the collection of sayings attributed to Muhammad). Here is an example:

> Paradise is in the shadow of swords . . . Jihad is your duty under any ruler, be he godly or wicked. (p. 112)

Jihad can refer to both the internal religious struggle that an individual may experience, and also to external struggle and the declaration of holy war against the enemies of Islam. Sam Harris explores the issue that Muslims are "convinced of the superiority of their culture, and obsessed with the inferiority of their power" (p. 130). Perhaps, Harris argues, we should be grateful for Islamic "insularity and backwardness," otherwise:

> If Muslim orthodoxy were as economically and technologically viable as Western liberalism, we would probably be doomed to witness the Islamification of the earth (p. 133).

The theocracy, like other autocratic political systems, is the most conservative form of social structure. Modern democracies, for all their flaws, have evolved as mature political systems that protect against the religious and secular excesses of totalitarian regimes. Democracies do not declare war against each other, as Kant claimed in his essay, *Perpetual Peace* (1795), because he thought that a majority of the people would never vote to go to war unless in self defense.

Social Rituals

The importance of social rituals in religious practice cannot be underestimated. The anthropologist Clifford Geertz (1973) thought that part of the function of the religious ritual was actually to gain religious conviction: "In these plastic dramas men attain their faith as they portray it" (p. 114). Roy Rappaport, in *Ritual and Religion in the Making of Humanity* (1999), emphasizes that ritual is the basic form of social connection or social contract through which commitment and trust are established and maintained. That is, the act of engaging in religious and other social rituals serves to reaffirm a social commitment. However, there are certain conditions of the speech act "performative" aspects of rituals that ensure that the ritual performance does not backfire. For example, many religious rituals have strict rules about who, when, and where the ritual performance can be carried out; thus, religious rituals can normally only be performed by specially authorized individuals, at certain times, and often only in special places, or under certain circumstances. Rituals typically consist of formalized speech and can include song, formalized body movements that can include dance, and formalized material symbols that can work without language. Unlike ordinary discourse, however, the repetitive and predictable nature of spoken ritual provides a fixed structure to the social world that is not normally present in everyday interaction. Maurice Bloch (1989) also argued that ritual normally instantiates power and establishes a power relationship between the "holder of the office" (the priest or leader) and the inferiors who are part of the ritual performance but who are of a lesser rank than the power-holder.

One of the social rituals that we will examine here is that of prayer. St. Teresa of Avila, whom we met earlier, described prayer as "an intimate friendship, a frequent conversation held alone with the Beloved." Prayer can, however, be carried out both as a private and as a public activity, but the private enactment of prayer is still a social ritual because of its origin in social practices and the ritualistic nature of the perceived exchange with

God. Kate Loewenthal (2000) summarizes a number of approaches to the categorization of types of prayer and includes the following:

- *Petitionary prayer*—the asking for help for oneself.
- *Intercessory prayer*—similar to petitionary prayer but the request is for someone or something else.
- *Thanksgiving*—giving thanks for benefits received.
- *Adoration*—the expression of wonderment and giving praise, considered the most noble form of prayer, which can include prostration, kneeling, and other forms of physical submission.
- *Confession*—honesty and seeking forgiveness from God.

There are of course other possible ways to categorize prayer, but they fall roughly under these headings. The petitionary/intercessory categories can be usefully combined because there is a request for something. Petitionary prayer is also considered by many to be the most characteristic form of prayer and it is the category most typical of the prayers of children. An example can be seen in the Hindu Rigveda: "In payment of our praise, give to the head of the family, who is imploring you, glory and riches."

Most religions have prayer liturgies, that is, set forms of prayers that are recited at particular times or on particular occasions, and these prayer liturgies may be the primary mode of expression for the religion. Some religions have objects that facilitate prayer. The Tibetan prayer wheel consists of an embossed metal cylinder with an inscribed sacred mantra, such that each rotation of the prayer wheel is seen as equivalent to one utterance of the sacred mantra. The rosary, a string of beads on a knotted cord, was originally used by the early Christians, but similar strings of beads are used in Hinduism and Buddhism, and in Islam (the "subha"). The worshipper normally proceeds around the beads with each bead leading to the recitation of a prayer (typically a Hail Mary with the Christian rosary) or a particular formula ("Glory to Allah" is typical with the subha).

A recent survey of religious practices in the United Kingdom with a representative sample of 1000 people aged 16 and above showed that 42% of UK residents reported the use of prayer, with 1 in 6 praying daily, and 1 in 4 praying once a week (see www.bbc.co.uk, news item, November 11, 2007). There were generational differences in the use of prayer, only 25% of 16- to 24-year-olds praying, increasing to 51% of 55- to 74-year-olds, which further increased to 61% for those aged 75 and over. These figures reflect the observation noted above that there is a generation-by-generation decline in religious belief and practice in the United Kingdom. In contrast, equivalent figures from the USA for the use of prayer show very different rates. Joseph Baker (2008) provides figures from the Baylor Religion Survey carried out in 2005 on a representative sample of 1721 US adults. In the survey, 81.2% of men and 91.2% of women reported that they used prayer at least occasionally. Although there was a slight increase with age in the use of prayer, even the young adults, categorized as 18- to 29-year-olds in the study, reported using prayer in 85.2% of the cases surveyed. Despite the very high rates of prayer reported, statistical analyses showed that marginalized groups (e.g. African-Americans, those of low income) reported greater use of prayer, and, perhaps not surprisingly, they tended to use more petitionary prayer. Overall, however, the figures demonstrate the dramatic differences in religiosity between the United States and the United Kingdom, especially in the younger generations where the differences are the most apparent.

We will consider the health aspects of prayer in more detail in Chapter 6, but will provide a taste of research on the subject here. Harvard Medical School gave a news release (web.med.harvard.edu, March 31, 2006) in which they summarized the results from a six-centre study, funded in part by the Templeton Foundation, of 1802 heart bypass surgery patients, some of whom received intercessory prayer. The study had three conditions: Group 1 were told that they might receive prayer and actually did; Group 2 were told that they might receive prayer but actually did not; and Group 3 were told that they would receive prayer and actually did. The results showed that there was no overall difference in complications of the procedure for those who did receive prayer compared with those who did not; however, the highest rate of complications (59%) occurred in Group 3 who knew that they were receiving prayer compared with Group 1 (52%) who received prayer but were uncertain of it. In sum, this study showed that there was no benefit from intercessory prayer, but that patients actually had more complications when they knew they were definitely receiving intercessory prayer. We will reconsider both this study and a number of other related studies in Chapter 6 when we consider possible health and coping benefits of prayer.

Religious Wars

In the Middle Ages the Crusades were classic examples of religious wars that, many would say, have been re-enacted in the George Bush and

Tony Blair invasions of Iraq and Afghanistan. The Crusades were religious wars between Christianity and Islam over the jurisdiction of Jerusalem and the Holy Land. They were launched under papal initiative, the First Crusade being by Pope Urban II in 1095. Over the following 200 years various campaigns were launched with differing degrees of success, but attempts to liberate the Holy Land from the Muslim expansion ultimately failed. Occasionally, the Crusaders even turned against their own at the whim of the papacy if it was felt that the pope's authority was threatened. The Fourth Crusade diverted to Constantinople and sacked the city even though they were fellow Christians. A similar fate befell the Albigensians when a crusade was launched against them by the inappropriately named Pope Innocent III because of their opposition to him and their apparently heretical Christian views.

The theme of Christian against Christian makes good reading for understanding many of the wars in the past two millennia. The "Wars of Religion" involved most European powers over a period of nearly 130 years (approximately 1524 to 1648). Conflicts that can be placed in this category took place in France, Germany, Austria, Bohemia, The Netherlands, England, Scotland, Ireland, Switzerland, and Denmark. The cause of the wars was the Protestant Reformation beginning with Luther in Wittenberg in 1519. Protestantism spread rapidly throughout Germany, which was then part of the Holy Roman Empire. The first conflicts took place in 1524 with the German Peasants' War in which there were an estimated 100 000 deaths.

It is clear that although religions teach love, they also teach war. There is no major religion that has not fought war with another religion, or within its own religion as splits have occurred. To the naïve outsider, these holy wars or jihads or whatever, in which each side believes that God is only on their side, seem completely contradictory to the supposedly high moral principles and the claim that morality would fall apart if we all became atheists. Current and recent religion-based conflicts include Sudan (Islamic–Christian), Northern Ireland (Christian–Christian), Pakistan–India (Islam–Hindu), Afghanistan (Islam–Islam, with Christian interference), Iraq (Islam–Islam, with Christian interference), the Balkans (Islam–Christian), and Sri-Lanka (anti-Buddhist). Of course, we are not claiming that wars are fought *only* on religious grounds. Even the two Marxist-atheist states of the USSR and China in 1968 and 1969 fought battles along the disputed 2738-mile border between the two countries, and many at the time were worried that the conflict would lead to a nuclear world war because the Soviets came close to a nuclear strike against the Chinese nuclear test site at Lop Nur. The point is that while all religions take the high moral ground, at the same time they seem to consider that the initiation of war and the forced imposition of religious belief on conquered peoples is perfectly acceptable. The world's major axis of conflict is no longer the cold war of Capitalism versus Communism: it is now the holy war of Christianity versus Islam. In their histories, both Christian and Muslims have been guilty of unspeakable atrocities and of war-based expansion into peaceful territories. Add to this mix the continuing conflict in the Middle East between Islam and the third Abrahamic religion, Judaism, and you have to wish that Abraham and his bloody religions had never been born. If one were to estimate how many deaths occurred as a result of conflicts within the Bible-based religions, it would be an unbelievable number and one that the war-mongering God of the Old Testament would have been proud.

Conclusion

In this chapter we have ranged across some of the social structures and social processes of religion. Not only do we make the gods in our own likeness, but we also make their relationships, their families, and their hierarchies in our own likeness too. Our everyday dyads of husband and wife, mother and child, father and child, brother and sister are projected on to the gods with an anthropocentric narrowness that is both laughable and absurd. Even some of the more superficially bizarre social structures, such as the Trinitarian view within some Christian denominations, fits on to a family triad given that, within the Father, Son, and Holy Spirit, some Christian religious groups view the Holy Spirit as feminine. For those denominations that see the Trinity as all masculine, the gradual promotion of Mary, the Mother of God, from a human to a divine form has occurred in order to give the divine family some gender balance.

Sociology and anthropology continue to study the larger-scale social structures that we considered in relation to the development of mega-churches in the United States and South Korea. Big seems to be beautiful for the Protestant evangelical denominations. Beyond that there are the theocracies. Many sociologists and other commentators believe that the United States is heading towards becoming a theocracy in that the preferred separation of church and state is becoming increasingly blurred. At the same time the United States shows increasing levels of religiosity, as witnessed in indices such as church attendance, use of prayer, belief in intelligent design, and so on, in contrast to western European countries such as the United Kingdom, which has been witnessing a steady decline across recent generations in the same indices of religiosity. Religious organizations do, however, have important social functions and add to social capital, an issue that we will consider in more detail in Chapters 6 and 7. First, though, we will examine the importance of power in religious social structures.

5

Religion, Power, and Control

*Why should we take advice on sex from the Pope? If he knows anything
about it, he shouldn't.*

George Bernard Shaw

Introduction

Jane Stork was born in Western Australia and brought up in a Catholic
home. She married and had children and seemed to be living a standard,
respectable life until she experienced some difficulties when she reached her
thirties. She sought help for her personal issues at a local meditation centre,
and then became enthralled by the Indian guru Bhagwan Shree Rajneesh,
also known as "Osho." She persuaded her husband also to become a fol-
lower of the Bhagwan, then in 1978 she and her family moved to Pune in
India where the Bhagwan had set up an ashram and to whom she gave up
everything. The Bhagwan, who became known in India as the "sex guru,"
decided that India was not enough, so he moved to Oregon in 1981 where
he bought a 65 000-acre ranch and established the town of Rajneeshpuram
for himself and 7000 followers who joined him there. The local town of An-
telope in Oregon, population 50, seemed initially tolerant but then became
alarmed as the orange-robed "sannyasims" (disciples of the Bhagwan) tried
to take over and control the town. Jane Stork, now known as "Ma Shanti
Bhadra," having abandoned her husband and children, joined the Bhagwan
in Oregon where she worked closely with the Bhagwan's personal secretary,
Ma Sheela. At this time, the Bhagwan became notorious in the United States
for his collection of cars (including 93 Rolls-Royces), diamond watches and

Adieu to God: Why Psychology Leads to Atheism, First Edition. Mick Power.

bracelets bought for him by his followers, such that Americans gave him the name the "Rolls-Royce guru." Unfortunately, increasing conflict with the American authorities led to a range of criminal activities, including Jane Stork personally being involved in the attempted murder of a doctor and a US attorney who was investigating the Bhagwan, and the first bioterrorism attack on US soil, when they tried to spread salmonella poisoning among the good people of Oregon. The Rolls-Royce guru was arrested in 1985 and then deported from the United States, eventually settling back in Pune, where his ashram is still a popular visitor destination. Jane Stork, however, was not so lucky: she spent nearly three years in an American jail. She has published an account in 2009 of her life with the Bhagwan called *Breaking the Spell: My Life as a Rajneshee and the Long Journey Back to Freedom* in which she describes her story in harrowing detail, which included discovering that her children were sexually abused while in the ashram. Nor is Jane Stork alone in her experiences with the Bhagwan: similar accounts have been written by Hugh Milne, an ex-bodyguard of the Bhagwan, in his book, *Bhagwan: The God That Failed* (1986), and Satya Bharti Franklin in her book, *Promise of Paradise: A Woman's Intimate Story of the Perils of Life with Rajneesh* (1991). On a lighter note, we might highlight the view of Jane Stork's fellow Australian Clive James, who renamed the Rolls-Royce guru "Bagwash" and likened the experience of listening to him to sitting in a laundrette and watching "your underwear revolve soggily for hours while exuding grey suds. The Bagwash talks the way that he looks . . . [he is a] rebarbative dingbat who manipulates the manipulatable."

Stories such as Jane Stork's raise the issue of power and control within religions both old and new. In Chapter 4 we examined the range of social structures that reflect human society, and looked at how these structures impact on religious social structures and, in turn, are projected on to the imagined social structures. In this chapter we want to focus specifically on power and control in religion. Of course, from the influential work of Max Weber onwards, sociologists and anthropologists have for many years singled out the issues of power and control that we will draw on throughout this chapter. However, we will begin with and examine in detail an issue that stands out more than any other in the extraordinary history of religion, and that is the subordination of women and the domination of the world's religions by men. Patriarchy and misogyny in the world's religions have only recently come into focus and come to be questioned. Ultimately, these issues may well lead to the collapse of many a house of cards on which religious patriarchal hierarchies have been built.

Misogyny

Mount Athos has to be one of the most extraordinary places on the planet. Located on the Halkidiki peninsula in northern Greece but only accessible by sea, it is an autonomous region of 130 square miles known as the Autonomous Monastic State of the Holy Mountain. It is home to 20 Eastern Orthodox monasteries, with a population of over 2000 that consists of monks and workers who help in the monasteries (see their website at www.inathos.gr). It is a spectacularly beautiful place and absolutely unique in one feature. Despite the population of over 2000, there are no women, girls, or female animals allowed on Mount Athos, not even as visitors. Females have to stay at a minimum distance of 200 yards offshore from Mount Athos, as did Queen Elizabeth II when her husband Prince Philip visited the peninsula. The male monks believe that the presence of women (and presumably girls, cows, ewes, sows, and the like) would interfere with their contemplation and the achievement of spiritual enlightenment. Even more bizarrely, though, Mount Athos is known by the monks as the "Garden of the Virgin Mary" because the story is that the Virgin Mary was shipwrecked there with John the Evangelist and that she loved the place so much that she asked God to give it to her as a present (see www.inathos.gr). Therefore, in religious terms Mount Athos is owned by a female, but men have decided that no other female is allowed to go there.

The existence of Mount Athos stands as a pinnacle of misogyny that is present not only in Christianity but in all other major religions. Misogyny is complex in its societal origins and is clearly pre-Christian in origin. We are not laying the blame for misogyny solely at the door of St. Paul and St. Augustine, though they must bear a large share of responsibility for the misogynistic teachings in Christianity. Gerda Lerner, in her monumental work, *The Creation of Patriarchy* (1986), identifies the more general issue of the subordination of women to men in the shift from small hunter-gatherer communities to the larger groups and urbanization of the early civilizations in Mesopotamia, Egypt, and China. Lerner observes that, in early warfare at this time, the defeated males were slaughtered but women and children were taken into captivity, such that early slavery and ownership was of women by men. Women became the property of men, which became the norm even for the women who were part of the ruling class. We also observed in Chapter 1 how the Neolithic farming groups invariably worshipped fertile mother goddesses because they linked female fertility with their dependence on the fertility of the earth and the seasonal cycles. However, urbanization in the early civilizations saw the subordination of the female goddesses to one or more primary male gods, reflecting the emerging social structure of these early civilizations. The key point is that misogyny, subordination, and sexuality seem to have become linked through the ownership of female slave-concubines.

In the example of Mount Athos, the location of sinful sexuality is clearly placed in the female of all species: yet another example of blaming the victim. It is the equivalent to the asymmetrical sexual relationship that occurs in prostitution: the female prostitute is labelled as the sinner rather than the man who visits the prostitute for sex. As Gerda Lerner (1986) argues, this is the advantage of the power relationship in a patriarchy. Male spiritual and political leaders can present themselves as being led astray by the subordinate temptresses who will do anything in order to survive.

The location of the "sin of sex" in women who are viewed as constantly trying to lead astray these otherwise innocent spiritual men would lead one to predict that most sex crimes should be committed by women. But what does the evidence on crime show us? Just to set the context, recent figures from the US Federal Bureau of Investigation (see www.fbi.gov/stats-services/crimestats) show that of 15 760 murders committed in the United States in 2009, in only 7.6% of cases was the murderer female. If we look specifically at murder in marital partners, 141 husbands were murdered by wives, but 609 wives were murdered by husbands (a ratio of 4.3 to 1 for male to female murderers), and, similarly, 138 boyfriends were murdered by girlfriends, but 472 girlfriends were murdered by boyfriends (a ratio of 3.4 to 1 male to female murderers). Crimes of violence in intimate partners were 82 360 incidents for male victims, but 564 430 incidents for female victims (a ratio of 6.9 to 1 for male to female perpetrators of violence), and in the case of sexual assault and rape there were 55 110 female victims but no male victims. If we ask specifically about the crime of incest, a variety of factors mean that these figures are notoriously unreliable and likely to be considerable underestimations of the true figures. Nevertheless, a national study in Canada was published by Statistics Canada in 2001 called *Family Violence in Canada: A Statistical Profile* (see http://www.statcan.gc.ca/pub/85-224-x/85-224-x2010000-eng.htm). Figures for children aged 0 to 15 years show that 69% of the victims of sexual abuse were girls and 31% were boys. The perpetrators of sexual abuse were in 3% of cases the biological mother, 2% a stepmother, 8% the biological father, and 8% a stepfather. In 44% of cases the perpetrator was an older male sibling, uncle, grandfather, or other relative. Overall, what these figures for murder, violence, sexual assault, and incest show dramatically is that men are many times more likely to be the perpetrators of such crimes, whereas women are many times more likely to be the victims of these crimes. Hence, any patriarchal religion that attempts to locate sexual sin in women has got it completely the wrong way round. The majority of crimes, especially those of a sexual nature, are carried out by men, not by women.

Fear of Witches (Wiccaphobia)

The projection of sexual sin by men on to women is just one of a number of such projections that seem to have been institutionalized in the misogynistic beliefs of many of the world's religions. The next issue that we will touch on briefly here in the context of the social structure and power relations within religion will focus on the example of the persecution of witches by the Christian church during the Middle Ages. There are of course many other examples of misogyny throughout the world's religions that we will consider as we discuss different aspects of the social structure of religions, but the institutionalized misogyny that is part of the Christian church clearly reached its peak in the Middle Ages. The publication of the *Malleus Maleficarum, The Hammer of the Witches,* in 1487 by two Dominican monks, Heinrich Kramer and Jacob Sprenger, provided a handbook for the detection, interrogation, and torture of witches. The Dominican order had been appointed as the inquisitors by Pope Gregory IX in the thirteenth century, a task at which they excelled to the extent that they were known at that time as the "Domini canes", a Latin phrase that translates as the "Hounds of the Lord." Estimates of women who were put to death as a result of accusations of witchcraft in the sixteenth and seventeenth centuries range from 50 000 to 200 000. Infamous witch trials such as those in Salem, Massachusetts, are remembered to this day. Even what is today the pleasant seaside town of North Berwick near Edinburgh in 1590 witnessed witch trials with over 100 people accused of witchcraft, and all because King James VI had experienced bad storms at sea while travelling back from Denmark, storms that were blamed on witchcraft in North Berwick. The trials there were the first major witchcraft trials in Scotland, and although some men were included in the accusations by far the majority of the accused were women. One such woman was Agnes Sampson who was brought to the palace of King James at

Holyrood House in Edinburgh where she was held in a witch's bridle with a rope around her neck, and prevented from sleeping:

> This aforeaside *Agnis Sampson* which was the elder Witch, was taken and brought to Haliciud house before the Kings Maiestie and sundry other of the nobility of Scotland, where she was straitly examined, but all the perswasions which the Kings maiestie vsed to her with ye rest of his counsell, might not prouoke or induce her to confesse any thing, but stood stiffely in the deniall of all that was laide to her charge: whervpon they caused her to be conueied awaye to prison, there to receiue such torture as hath been lately prouided for witches in that country: and forasmuch as by due examination of witchcraft and witches in Scotland, it hath latelye beene found that the Deuill dooth generallye marke them with a priuie marke, by reason the Witches haue confessed themselues, that the Diuell dooth lick them with his tung in some priuy part of their bodie, before hee dooth receiue them to be his seruants, which marke commonly is giuen them vnder the haire in some part of their bodye, wherby it may not easily be found out or seene, although they be searched: and generally so long as the marke is not seene to those which search them, so long the parties that hath the marke will neuer confesse any thing. Therfore by special commaundement this *Agnis Sampson* had all her haire shauen of, in each parte of her bodie, and her head thrawen with a rope according to the custome of that Countrye, beeing a paine most greeuous, which she continued almost an hower, during which time she would not confesse any thing vntill the Diuels marke was found vpon her priuities, then she immediatlye confessed whatsoeuer was demaunded of her, and iustifying those persons aforesaid to be notorious witches. (From www.sacred-texts.com)

Following successful torture, Agnes Sampson subsequently confessed to 53 crimes of witchcraft, despite having worked as a respected healer and midwife in her community. On January 16, 1590, she was hanged, garotted, and then burnt to ashes.

The Exceptions that Prove the Rule

For the sake of argument, let us assume that men are not inherently more spiritual than women, and that they are not closer to their gods. Let us assume instead that men and women are equal in spirituality, but that the factors that we have discussed such as urbanization in the early civilizations, the development of patriarchal systems of control, and the move towards monotheistic religions have created the illusion that men are more spiritual and women are more sinful. If such supposed differences are illusions man-ufactured by patriarchy, then under certain conditions we would expect women rather than men to be the spiritual leaders, similar to how, in the Neolithic communities, female fertility goddesses seem to have been dom-inant because of the preoccupation with seasonal cycles and the fertility of the earth. One example of a matrilineal religion of recent origin is Macumba, the African-Brazilian religion that has a number of sects throughout Brazil. The religion has its roots in the enslavement of African peoples who were shipped to South America to work on the plantations. Part of the interest for anthropologists and sociologists of Macumba is that through enslavement any patriarchal power of the enslaved men was undermined by enslave-ment, so that spiritual power within the slave communities became female. However, in order to survive within a dominant culture of European origin, Macumba is a highly syncretic religion (see Chapter 4) that draws not only on African religions, but also on Catholicism and on Brazilian Spiritualism. The Macumba sect that has been studied most is that of Candomblé, which is predominant in Bahia state and its capital Salvador de Bahia, a beautiful coastal city with an old Portuguese centre that is reminiscent of Lisbon. An-other sect is that of Umbanda, which is more predominant in Rio de Janeiro and São Paulo. Umbanda also includes Hindu and Buddhist influences and has become attractive to the white middle classes. We will, however, focus on Candomblé because it is seen as the most African of the Macumba sects with strong links to the African Yoruba culture.

The priesthood of Candomblé is organized according to families, al-though the family members need not be blood relatives in the usual mean-ing. Each family owns and has the management of a temple, which can be a house, plantation, or yard (*terreiro*). In most temples, especially the larger ones, the head of the family is always a woman, the *mãe-de-santo*, or *ialorixá*, mother-of-saint in Candomblé, with her deputy being the *pais-de-santo*, or *babalorixá*, father-of-saint. During the earlier times of slavery, in contrast to the original African tradition, women became the diviners and healers. Upon the death of an *ialorixá*, her successor was often chosen from among her *filhas-de-santo* and by means of divination using consecrated cowrie shells. However, the succession can be disputed or fail, so can lead to the splitting or closure of the temple. In some *terreiros*, leadership has been inherited by the late *ialorixá*'s female blood relative, typically a daughter. Most Candomblé houses are small, independently owned and managed by the female high priests. A few of the older and larger houses have a more formal hierarchy, though there is no central administration.

As we noted in Chapter 4 with reference to the anthropologist Mattijs van de Port's (2005) study, "Candomblé in pink, green, and black," part of the general attraction of the Macumba sects such as Candomblé is in their appeal not only to marginalized minority groups such as those descended from former black African slaves, but also to other minority groups such as homosexuals (the "pinks"), and to environmentalists (the "greens"). The significant role that women play within this matrilineal religion is clearly part of the growing appeal of Macumba throughout Brazil and in other areas of South and Central America.

Charismatic Leaders

The sociologist Max Weber (1922/1947) famously defined three types of authority, namely traditional, rational-legal, and charismatic. He analysed both political and religious domination by charismatic leaders and defined charisma as:

> A certain quality of an individual personality, by virtue of which he is set apart from ordinary men and treated as endowed with supernatural, superhuman, or at least specifically exceptional powers or qualities. These are such as are not accessible to the ordinary person, but are regarded as of divine origin or as exemplary, and on the basis of them the individual concerned is treated as a leader. (p. 10)

Weber emphasized that charismatic authority is not a quality that is solely inherent in the individual but is one that is expressed in the relationship between leaders and their followers. Thus, the religious leader or guru (from Sanskrit, meaning "heavy" in the sense of commanding respect) may have charismatic authority over his followers so long as they believe that he has been touched by God, or even in some cases that he is God, but if for some reason that belief is damaged, then followers can desert the leader, who no longer has charismatic authority. Weber also pointed out that many religions and political systems that have been started by charismatic leaders eventually suffer routinization, in that their initial challenges to existing authority and society become integrated into that society.

The great religious leaders of the past may no longer be alive in order to be studied by sociologists and psychologists, but, fortunately for sociology and psychology, every generation throws up new sets of gurus who can be studied. Anthony Storr, in *Feet of Clay: A Study of Gurus* (1996), has provided a very readable summary of a number of recent gurus who have gained notoriety, including Jim Jones, David Koresh, Georgei Gurdjieff, and, our favourite, the Bhagwan Shree Rajneesh. From an examination of their biographical details, Anthony Storr has extracted a number of features that these gurus seem to share:

> Many gurus appear to have been rather isolated as children, and to have remained so. They seldom have close friends. They are more interested in what goes on in their own minds than in personal relationships . . . In other words, they tend to be introverted and narcissistic . . . Gurus tend to be intolerant of any kind of criticism, believing that anything less than total agreement is equivalent to hostility . . . Conviction of a special revelation must imply that the guru is a superior person who is not as other men are. (p. xiii)

Most notable among Storr's observations is the comment on the narcissistic characteristic, which in the case of some gurus would take them into the *Diagnostic and Statistical Manual Version IV* (American Psychiatric Association, 1994) category of Narcissistic Personality Disorder which requires at least five of the following symptoms:

- Has a grandiose sense of self-importance (e.g. exaggerates achievements and talents, expects to be recognized as superior without commensurate achievements).
- Is preoccupied with fantasies of unlimited success, power, brilliance, beauty, or ideal love.
- Believes that he or she is "special" and unique and can only be understood by, or should associate with, other special or high-status people (or institutions).
- Rarely acknowledges mistakes and/or imperfections.
- Requires excessive admiration.
- Has a sense of entitlement, i.e. unreasonable expectations of especially favorable treatment or automatic compliance with his or her expectations.
- Is interpersonally exploitative, i.e. takes advantage of others to achieve his or her own ends.
- Lacks empathy: is unwilling or unable to recognize or identify with the feelings and needs of others.
- Is often envious of others or believes that others are envious of him or her.
- Shows arrogant, haughty behaviors or attitudes.

In a comparison of the Bhagwan with Gurdjieff, Storr writes:

> Rajneesh, like Gurdjieff, was personally extremely impressive. Many of those
> who visited him for the first time felt that their most intimate feelings were
> instantly understood; that they were accepted and unequivocally welcomed
> rather than judged. He seemed to radiate energy and to awaken hidden
> possibilities in those who came into contact with him...Hugh Milne, a
> Scottish osteopath who became his bodyguard, wrote of his first meeting: 'I
> had the overwhelming sensation that I had come home. He was my spiritual
> father, a man who understood everything, someone who would be able to
> convey sense and meaning into my life.' (p. 47)

The Bhagwan clearly fits with Max Weber's description of the charismatic leader in that he was believed to possess an extraordinary supernatural power or grace, and subsequently through the adoption of the name
"Bhagwan" seemed to think that he was God, but he also rejected any other
authority or institution and so appeared revolutionary to his followers while
ultimately imposing a new and at times paranoid dictatorship within his
own community.

The Bhagwan's excesses with his 93 Rolls-Royces and domination of
his followers seem relatively benign in comparison with two of the other
modern gurus whom Anthony Storr discusses, Jim Jones and David Koresh.
In brief, Jim Jones was born in Indiana in 1931 and, in support of Storr's
proposal, was isolated and always alone as a child. He joined the Pentecostal
Church while still young, then set up the People's Temple in Indianapolis in
1956. At a time of considerable racial tension in the US, he adopted a black
child and opposed racial discrimination, which brought many African-
Americans into his congregation. In 1965 he moved the Temple to Redwood,
California, then to San Francisco, then ultimately they established Jonestown
in the jungles of Guyana in South America, where they moved in 1977. The
majority of followers who moved with him to Guyana were black females.
As Storr writes:

> Jones perfectly illustrates the difficulty in defining the boundaries between
> conviction, delusion, confidence trickery, and psychosis...Jones was a con-
> fidence trickster. He had no scruples about faking cures of illness...or in
> inventing attacks from imagined enemies. (p. 11)

By 1974 Jones had declared himself to be God. On November 18, 1978,
over 900 people died in Jonestown, in a mass suicide through cyanide

poisoning (though it is clear that some were murdered), including Jones who shot himself in the head. The dead included 260 children. The power of life and death over others was also a feature of David Koresh's brief reign as head of the Branch Davidian Seventh Day Adventist sect. Koresh was extremely narcissistic and paranoid and had complete sexual domination over his followers, whether man, woman or child. After a shootout with the FBI at their appropriately named Ranch Apocalypse in Waco, Texas, on April 19, 1993, 86 followers, including 22 children, were burned to death by Koresh, who also died with a gunshot to the head.

The charismatic leader can therefore be a mixed blessing. Gurus from the distant past, such as Zoroaster, Buddha and Jesus, who have had much myth built around them, from this vantage point do seem like genuine great teachers or "gurus." However, many of the recent examples, whether in religion, such as Jim Jones or David Koresh, or in politics, for example Mao Zedong, Joseph Stalin, and Adolf Hitler, have been severely disturbed individuals who, nevertheless, have used their charisma to bring about the destruction of many of their followers and others. All of them deal with an individual's need to find meaning and purpose and to cope with existential issues that can often feel overwhelming. However, each of these religious and political leaders was highly narcissistic and highly exploitative, often of the people who had helped them the most. We must hearken back to sociology's reminder that there are no leaders without followers, so, as Sheldon Kopp (1986) warns in the title of his wonderful book, *If You Meet The Buddha On The Road, Kill Him.*

How to Start a New Religion

From the last section it seems clear that having a charismatic leader is one factor in the start of a new religion, though, in the case of leaders such as Jim Jones, David Koresh, and Joseph Smith, they started new sects within Christianity rather than new religions *per se*. The so-called cargo cults that developed in the South Pacific islands over the past 150 years provide further clues about how religions can develop. The indigenous islanders were confronted initially by huge boats and subsequently by aeroplanes filled with white people who had mysterious objects such as radios with which they seemed to perform religious rites. Islanders believed that the "cargo" delivered to these white colonialists was of supernatural origin, so if they too built jetties and aeroplane landing strips the mysterious cargo would be delivered to them.

As we saw in Chapter 1, religion and religious beliefs often step in to offer supernatural explanations for natural and other phenomena that are otherwise difficult to understand. The Third Law of the science-fiction writer Arthur C. Clarke states, "Any sufficiently advanced technology is indistinguishable from magic." This provides a foundation with which to understand the preoccupations of recently developed religions. From the time of Copernicus and Galileo onwards, the Catholic Church has seen its power in the West challenged and increasingly diminished by science and by scientific advances such that it has been fighting a rearguard action for several hundred years. One would therefore expect that many of the New Religious Movements (NRMs) would try to encompass scientific-like beliefs into their belief systems because, as Arthur C. Clarke notes, many of the advances in science and technology do seem like magic to most people and run counter to everyday experience. Two such NRMs that we will consider that attempt exactly this integration are Scientology and Jediism.

The Church of Scientology was started in the 1950s by the science fiction writer L. Ron Hubbard (1911–1986), who at the time was better known for pulp science fiction such as *Masters of Sleep, Man-Killers of the Air, Beyond All Weapons,* and *Battlefield Earth: A Saga of the Year 3000.* In 1950, however, he published *Dianetics: The Modern Science of Mental Health,* in which he described a new type of psychotherapy, which involved using an "E-meter" to access destructive "engrams" in the person's unconscious. The E-meter is basically a galvanic skin response (GSR) machine that picks up small fluctuations in the conduction capacity of the skin in response to changes in its sweat gland activity, a response that is also used in so-called lie-detectors. In Dianetics, an "auditor" asks pertinent questions of the person while watching their GSR fluctuations in order to guide them towards more emotional material for that person. What began as a highly criticized pop therapy eventually metamorphosed into the Church of Scientology in 1953, with the addition of a new cosmology that included the proposal that humans were originally intergalactic divine beings called "Thetans." Part of the current practices of Scientology include gradual initiation into "Operating Thetan" (OT) levels that range from OT I to OT XV, with new secret knowledge about the intergalactic Thetan past being revealed at each new OT level. Cynics point out that the financial and personal cost of proceeding through these levels is considerable and that it adds substantially to the wealth of the Church. Hollywood celebrities such as John Travolta and Tom Cruise have helped to promote Scientology worldwide through their celebrity status. Many now believe that Tom Cruise is second in command, which presumably puts him at Operating Thetan level XV, and that he has become a Thetan divine. The narcissistic grandiosity to which L. Ron Hubbard's bad science fiction appeals hardly needs comment. Although Anthony Storr did not include Hubbard in his study of gurus, he could well have done, because, in addition to the clear narcissism and grandiosity, Hubbard was against authority (other than his own); and he was dominating and demeaning towards his followers, a confidence trickster, and sexually exploitative of teenage girls. As with the Bhagwan, there has been a steady stream of former followers who have become disillusioned with the guru and his teachings and who have provided highly critical accounts of Hubbard and the Church of Scientology; see for example Bonnie Woods (2009), *Deceived: One Woman's Stand Against the Church of Scientology*, and Marc Headley (2010) *Blown for Good: Behind the Iron Curtain of Scientology*.

Another even more bizarre NRM science-fiction religion is that of Jediism. Jediism developed from the very successful Hollywood Star Wars films written and directed by George Lucas. Lucas was raised in a strongly Methodist family, but in his Star Wars films has stated that he has combined religious themes from both Christianity and Buddhism, especially in his depiction of the forces of good and evil. However, in contrast to L. Ron Hubbard, Lucas did not set out to start a new religion, merely to use the universal appeal of religious themes in his movies. Nevertheless, what seems to have started as a movie-goer's joke is now becoming a new religion; today Jediism or the Jedi Realist movement is followed by thousands of people world-wide and has already been given official religious status in Canada. For readers wishing to take this further, Matthew Todd Vossler (2009) has published the *Jedi Manual Basic—Introduction to Jedi Knighthood*, which introduces the requirements for becoming a Jedi Knight. Daniel Wallace (2010) has published *The Jedi Path: A Manual for Students of the Force* (Vault Edition), for which it is worth quoting the advertising blurb:

> Fully illustrated, with removable features and a Mechanical Vault. With the push of a button, the doors of the vault open in a wash of light and *Star Wars* sound effects. The inner platform rises, revealing this exclusive edition of *The Jedi Path*. This ancient training manual, crafted by early Jedi Masters, has educated and enlightened generations of Jedi. It explains the history and hierarchy of the Jedi Order, and what Jedi must know to take their place as defenders of the peace in the galaxy—from mastery of the Force to the nuances of lightsaber combat. Passed down from Master to Padawan, the pages of this venerable text have been annotated by those who have held it, studied it, and

lived its secrets. From Yoda and Luke Skywalker to Count Dooku and Darth Sidious, they have shaped the content of the book by leaving mementos tucked within the pages, tearing out pages, and adding their personal experiences as tangible reminders of the lessons they've learned. Through wars and rebellion, only a single copy of this manual has survived. It is now passed on to you. The ancient Masters who wrote the text: Fae Coven, Grand Master and head of the Jedi Council; Crix Sunburris, Jedi Ace starfighter pilot; Restelly Quist, Jedi Chief Librarian; Skarch Vaunk, Jedi Battlemaster and lightsaber expert; Bowspritz, Jedi Biologist and expert on the Living Force; Sabla-Mandibu, Jedi Seer and Holocron expert; Morrit Ch'gally, Jedi Recruiter; Gal-Stod Slagistrough, Jedi leader of the Agricultural Corps.

Who can deny that it makes for great films, fun computer games, and a science-fiction story that should be enjoyed but then left at the movie theater? Instead, an out-and-out science-fiction story has given rise to a religion, which highlights how easily people turn myth and fiction into reality, and how the constant search for meaning to deal with our existential questions leads us into psychological traps and illusions, the Prozac of the soul.

Prophecy

There is nothing like a good prophecy to put the fear of God into people, literally. To be able to predict the future with confidence and certainty, and then to get it right, can have a very powerful effect. But beware the famous Oracle at Delphi effect. In 547 BC, Croesus of Lydia is reported to have asked the Oracle if he should make war against the Persians, to which the Oracle answered that if he made war against the Persians he would destroy a mighty empire. Croesus interpreted the prediction to mean that the mighty Persian Empire would be destroyed, but in the event it was his own that met this fate. Any critical reading of the daily horoscopes that appear in tabloid newspapers will have the same message; namely, that the oracular predictions are notoriously ambiguous and open to multiple interpretations that increase their chances of appearing to be correct.

One of the favourite, and therefore most terrifying if believed, predictions that many religions have made is that of the "end of days." So-called Millennialism in Christianity is derived from prophecies in the Book of Revelation of St. John the Divine, which forms the last apocalyptic book of the New Testament, with the Book of Daniel in the Old Testament also providing fertile ground for millenarians. Although Revelation is attributed to John the Apostle, many modern biblical scholars doubt that John was the source of Revelation: "I am Alpha and Omega, the beginning and the end, the first and the last" (22:13). Revelation expresses the belief that Christ will establish a 1000-year reign before the Last Judgment. This has led to numerous eschatological predictions ever since, depending on the numerous different calculations of either 1000 years or 6000 years (a combination of the six days of work in Genesis, with the idea from Psalms that "1000 years is a day in the sight of the Lord" (90:4)). The revolutionary aspects of Millennialism became predominant with the Protestant Reformation and its attempts to overthrow the evil empire of Rome, that is, Roman Catholicism. English and Scottish Puritanism led to the English Civil Wars and the overthrow of the monarchy by millennial groups such as the Levelers, Diggers, Ranters, and Quakers. Some of these millennial groups such as the Pilgrim Fathers emigrated to America and have provided the basis of many American Protestant groups ever since, for example the Mormons, the Seventh Day Adventists, and the Jehovah's Witnesses.

The millennial Adventist movement was started in the United States by William Miller (1782–1849), who predicted Christ's second coming somewhere between March 21, 1843, and March 21, 1844. This prophecy clearly failed, so Miller set a second date of precisely October 22, 1844. This date subsequently came to be known as the "Great Disappointment," but it failed to prevent further prophecies from the Adventists. Some of the followers of Miller persisted in the belief of the second coming, but believed that the coming would be aided if they switched the Sabbath back to the seventh day, Saturday, thereby becoming known as the Seventh-Day Adventists. These failed prophecies have not deterred would-be followers, with Seventh-Day Adventism now having an estimated 12 million followers worldwide.

Another Protestant Christian group that continues to expand despite its failed prophecies is that of the Jehovah's Witnesses. It was founded in Pittsburgh in 1872 by Charles Taze Russell (1852–1916), initially under the name of the International Bible Studies Association. Russell was heavily influenced by the Adventists and their eschatological predictions. Russell himself claimed from 1877 onwards that Christ had made an invisible return in 1874, and that the end of the non-believers would happen in 1914 when Christ would establish the promised 1000-year kingdom. The First World War is therefore considered a successful prediction by his followers, even if the promised kingdom and reappearance of Christ failed to occur. Russell's successor, Joseph Franklin Rutherford (1869–1942), changed the name of the association to Jehovah's Witnesses, arguing that God's true name is the anglicized version of the Tetragrammaton (the four letters YHWH in Hebrew and Aramaic that are used in the Bible to refer to God and which are translated as Yahweh or Jehovah). Among their claimed scripturally based beliefs are the rejection of medical interventions such as blood transfusion, their refusal to do military service or to salute any national flag, and their doorstep policy which by now probably means that most people in the world have had a visit from a Jehovah's Witness several times because of the belief that there is one convert for every 24 000 calls that they make. Michael Shermer in *How We Believe: Science, Skepticism, and the Search for God* (2003) offers much insightful discussion of how believers retain their beliefs despite failed prophecy, noting that:

> The Jehovah's Witnesses must hold the record for the most failed dates of doom, including 1874, 1878, 1881, 1910, 1914, 1918, 1920, 1925, and others all the way up to 1975. (p. 203)

Before we consider how belief systems can be maintained despite failed prophecy, we will briefly consider one further tragic group. The Heaven's Gate religious movement was founded by Marshall Applewhite (1931–1997) who, following a heart attack and a near-death experience in the 1970s, founded the Heaven's Gate movement with his nurse, Bonnie Nettles (1928–1985). Applewhite believed that he and Nettles were extraterrestrial beings from another world that represented "the evolutionary level above human" and that they had been planted on the garden of Earth to help other humans to mature to this higher evolutionary level. In order to achieve this higher level, followers had to relinquish their animal selves including their sexuality, such that many of the men in the movement, including Applewhite, castrated themselves. In March 1997, the appearance of the Hale-Bopp comet in the sky was claimed by Applewhite to be the arrival of the spaceship to collect them, following which the apocalyptic end of the Earth would occur. On March 26, 1997, police found the bodies of Applewhite and 38 followers on a ranch near San Diego. All of them had committed suicide and all were wearing armbands saying "Heaven's Gate Away Team."

One way of protecting yourself from failed prophecy is to die by suicide or to be murdered (as with many of Jim Jones's followers) before the prophesied date occurs. However, social psychologists since the classic study of

Leon Festinger have examined the impact of failed prophecy on belief and belief change. In Festinger's study, reported in the book *When Prophecy Fails* (Festinger *et al.*, 1956), a housewife from Michigan, given the name Marian Keech for the purpose of the book, received messages through automatic writing from the planet Clarion that the world would end on December 21, 1954, and so she started a doomsday cult. Keech had been involved in L. Ron Hubbard's forerunner of Scientology, the Dianetics movement, and had collected a group of like-minded followers who believed her prophecy that a great flood would overwhelm the Earth before dawn on the appointed day. Keech's group, who happened to have been infiltrated by a social psychologist, sat and waited for midnight on December 20 when an alien visitor was supposed to arrive in Keech's apartment and take the group to an awaiting spacecraft. They even removed all metal objects from their persons because metal apparently interferes with the transportation system. The group became very distressed as midnight passed and they awaited the apocalypse. At 4.45 a.m. Keech received another automatic writing message from the planet Clarion informing the group that because they had "spread so much light" and prayed so hard, God had called off the apocalypse. The following day the group contacted all the media to explain how they have saved the world. Festinger and colleagues were particularly interested in how the group would handle the disconfirmed prophecy, having invested so much in it. In Festinger's terms, there was high cognitive dissonance between the belief and the non-event that had to be resolved in some way. Options included rejecting the original belief and therefore leaving the group (which some members did), whereas for other members the disconfirmation actually strengthened their belief because they were able to incorporate the new belief into their model that the apocalypse would have occurred but for their efforts. Festinger emphasized, however, that such strengthening of belief in the face of disconfirmatory evidence would require the strong social support that a group such as the doomsday cult could provide for each other. Further analyses of how beliefs can be maintained in the face of contradictory evidence such as occurs with failed prophecies can be found in Phil Johnson-Laird's (2008) book, *How We Reason*.

As a tail-note about the human need for prediction of the future, during the recent football World Cup in summer 2010, an octopus named Paul, based at the sea-life centre in Oberhausen, Germany, became world famous for his correct prediction of the outcome of all of Germany's world cup matches, then went on to predict correctly that Spain would win the final. In probability terms, Paul the "Psychic Football Pundit" had a 1 in 256 chance (calculated from 2^8, given a 1 in 2 chance for each individual prediction) of getting all eight matches correct, assuming there were no drawn matches. However, the fact that there were hundreds of zoo animals all over the world also being used as "psychics" (with Paul's closest psychic rival, Mani the Parakeet of Singapore, failing at the last because it predicted incorrectly that The Netherlands would win the final) meant, again in probability terms, that it was surprising that only one animal managed to "predict" eight matches correctly. Paul subsequently retired and died, but one can be sure that at the next football World Cup his psychic successors will be in place because of our bias towards seeing mere correlations and probabilities as if they were causes.

Sin and Celibacy

In Chapter 2 we examined briefly how the definitions of good and evil within religions normally include laws, commandments, or prohibitions on certain actions that would be generally agreed to be evil, such as perhaps some universally agreed acts of evil, for example murder, theft, and rape, while noting that many religions condone these actions under particular circumstances. However, religions also produce laws and prohibitions against actions considered bad or sinful that are completely arbitrary and religion-specific. To other people these arbitrary rules often become defining characteristics of the religion because of the unique but arbitrary nature of the rules. The example within Judaism of the rules governing kosher cooking definitely fall within the arbitrary category of religious morality. For example, in Chapter 2 we considered the kosher pizza problem; namely, that you just cannot get a decent pepperoni pizza with extra mozzarella when you are visiting Israel. In this section we will consider how religious control is exerted over the issues of profanity, blasphemy, and sexuality, plus what both the benefits and costs to religions are for the exertion of such control.

Blasphemy

A comment will first be made in this section about the use of swearing to express emotions. The words and phrases used for swearing have a clear propositional structure in addition to their immediate emotional expression and impact. In fact, swear words provide an interesting example of the evocation of emotion by propositional material that has been frequently repeated automatically. Any language or culture can create such "taboo" words. In Western cultures during the Middle Ages, when the Christian Church was more politically powerful, swearing involved blaspheming against God (as in "blimey" from "God blind me!" or "zounds" from "God's wounds!"). Today certain body functions and parts are more generally used as swear words (Allan and Burridge, 2006). Although the expression used is often only a single word, typically there is an implicit propositional structure with an implied subject and object, which is why we include them under the rubric of "propositional". Swearing is typically used to express intensity or suddenness of emotion or to evoke an emotional reaction in someone else, but the meta-emotional skill is in knowing the "rules of usage," for example, how its use indicates status or intimacy in a relationship (Allan and Burridge, 2006). The over-use of swearing can be seen as excessively aggressive and inappropriate, but it can also be indicative of other problems, as in coprophilia in Tourette's syndrome, or a loss of the capacity to inhibit swearing in some neurodegenerative conditions (Jay, 2000).

Swearing may be tolerated even if considered sinful by many religions, but other forms of blasphemy can lead to far greater punishment. In Islam, verbal criticism against Allah, the Koran, the Hadith, or Muhammad can lead to charges of blasphemy. The writer Salman Rushdie is the most famous recent case: following the publication of his novel, *The Satanic Verses* (1988), he was charged by the Iranian Ayatollah Khomeini with having insulted the Prophet Muhammad. The resultant *fatwa* (which simply means an opinion stated by a senior Islamic figure) led to many attempts to kill or injure Rushdie and those associated with the book's publication. For example, on August 3, 1989, a book bomb being primed by Mustafa Mahmoud Mazeh in a hotel in London exploded prematurely, destroying the hotel and killing Mazeh. A Lebanese group stated that Mazeh died preparing an attack "on the apostate Rushdie." In fact, the *fatwa* is still in place and technically cannot be removed because the Ayatollah died in 1989 without having revoked it. Rushdie has reported that he receives a "Valentine's card" from Iran on February 14 every year reminding him of the *fatwa* so that he knows that Iran has not forgotten the vow to kill him.

Islamic problems with the visual image are even more severe than they are with verbal blasphemy. Although there is no clear ban on figurative art in the Koran, the development of Sharia law eventually led to the exclusion of figurative art from Islamic art forms, which present instead complex geometric patterns. Before the statement of this Sharia ban, there were many artistic depictions of Muhammad in a similar tradition to that of Christian iconography. In the first edition of his *Islam: A Very Short Introduction*, the author Malise Ruthven included an illustration of Muhammad and the Angel Gabriel published in a book in 1307 and held in Edinburgh University Library. However, for the second edition published three years later in 2000, Ruthven decided to replace the illustration with a text box that explained that he had received complaints from Muslim readers that the image was blasphemous. The case in 2005 of the Danish cartoonist Kurt Westergaard who had his life threatened for drawing a cartoon of Muhammad gained a similar notoriety as that surrounding Salman Rushdie for Islamic intolerance of what it considers to be visual blasphemy.

Given that we started this chapter with a section on misogyny, it is also worth noting Islam's problems with depictions of the human body, especially the female body. In the secular West, one becomes very used to semi-naked presentations of both the male and the female body in the media, walking along the high street, on the beach, or wherever. In considerable contrast, Islamic Sharia law has a very restrictive dress code for women in comparison with men; thus, men have a more relaxed dress code in which the body must be covered from the knee to the navel. However, under Sharia law, women are required to cover all of their bodies except their hands and face. The Muslim headscarf or hijab is commonly worn, though in more extreme places such as Taliban Afghanistan, the burqa is worn; this covers all of the woman's body and includes a net over the woman's eyes. The rationale given for these rules is that men and women are not to be viewed as sexual objects. However, the Taliban punishment for women not wearing a burqa was typically a public beating with a cable; the sexual sadism of the punishment seemed to go unnoticed. Given Islamic problems with figurative art and the female body, the following story that affected the Indonesian editor of *Playboy* magazine comes as little surprise. Prosecutors were searching for the former editor-in-chief of *Playboy Indonesia* after he failed to show up to begin his two-year jail sentence for publishing pictures of scantily clothed women. They wanted to present Erwin Arnada with a warrant for his arrest. Arnada faced loud protests from the time the toned-down version of the American magazine hit news stands in 2006. Within weeks, members of the hard-line Islamic Defenders Front stormed the magazine's offices in south Jakarta. They also started legal proceedings against him, but judges at the South Jakarta District Court acquitted the editor in 2007, saying that pictures that appeared in the magazine could not be categorized as obscene. The hard-liners appealed to the Supreme Court, which later that year overruled the acquittal and found Arnada guilty of violating the predominantly Muslim nation's indecency laws.

Celibacy

In Chapter 1 we saw that the idea of celibacy (defined as voluntary abstention from marriage and sexual relations, which includes refraining from masturbation and sexual fantasy) among religious elites originated with the early pre-Christian religions. The Ancient Egyptian temple priests and priestesses practiced celibacy in order to be ritually pure, but only during the periods of the festivals for the temple gods: they do not seem to have practiced celibacy at other times. However, subsequent development of the Isis cult required celibacy from its priesthood. The Roman Vestal Virgins were priestesses who had to remain virgins during their 30-year service to the goddess Vesta. The punishment for failure to maintain chastity was to be buried alive. In Eastern religions, Buddhism has a tradition of celibacy because its founder, the Gautama Buddha, renounced his wife and son to become celibate as part of his attempt to become enlightened. Nevertheless, there has been much variation within Buddhism surrounding the practice of celibacy among its monks and nuns, including, in Tantric Buddhism such as Vajrayana the use of ritual sexual practices in order to re-enact and achieve special states of union. The appearance of celibacy in Christianity followed centuries of debate and re-interpretation of the disputed belief that Jesus was celibate, and from the misogynistic writings of St. Paul who does indeed seem to have been celibate:

> He that is unmarried careth for the things that belong to the Lord, how he may please the Lord: But he that is married careth for the things that are of the world, how he may please his wife. (1 Corinthians 7:32–33)

Furthermore:

> For I would that all men were even as I myself . . . I say therefore to the unmarried and widows, It is good for them if they abide even as I. But if they cannot contain, let them marry: for it is better to marry than to burn. (1 Corinthians 7:7–9).

It was not until the Second Lateran Council in 1139, over a thousand years after the founding of Christianity, that celibacy became a requirement for the clergy. As Diarmaid MacCulloch comments in *A History of Christianity* (2009), one cynical interpretation of the move to celibacy was that secularization of land ownership at this time put the Christian Church at risk of land inheritance rules, which meant that Church lands could now be passed to the legal heirs if the clergy were allowed to marry and have children. The deciding factor for Christian celibacy seems therefore to have been rather more worldly than spiritual, which may explain why celibacy is not required for the religious clergy in the other two great monotheisms, Judaism and Islam. Indeed Muhammad actively spoke out against celibacy and had at least 11—possibly 13—wives of his own. The Scottish surname *MacTaggart* and its variations literally means "son-of-the-priest", and its prevalence shows how the clergy continued to father children despite the introduction of celibacy in the twelfth century.

The current practice of clerical celibacy in Christianity is now primarily restricted to Roman Catholicism because the churches of the Protestant Reformation (such as the Lutheran and Anglican) abandoned celibacy as a requirement for their clergy. In contrast, the Catholic Magisterium has become even more conservative in matters of sexuality in the time since. Pope Pius XI in 1930 condemned all forms of contraception, and Pope Paul VI reinforced this view in *Humanae Vitae* (1968), which continued the ban on all forms of artificial contraception. In relation to celibacy, modern pressures to relax celibacy requirements for Catholic clergy have fallen on deaf ears. There is no doubt that the failure of the Catholic Church to modernize its views on celibacy in particular and on sexuality more generally has contributed to the global sexual-abuse scandals that have rocked the Catholic Church to its foundations. Next we will therefore examine the role of both celibacy and general views on sexuality within Catholicism and their contribution to sexual abuse perpetrated by Catholic clergy, because these problems reflect issues of power and control at all levels within the Catholic hierarchy.

In recent decades the Catholic Church has been overwhelmed by repeated scandals of sexual abuse. Karen Terry (2008) summarized US data from the John Jay College study showing that, between 1950 and 2002, 4392 priests had allegations of sexual abuse against them from 10 667 victims (plus a further 3000 victims who had not made allegations) and that the Catholic Church in the United States had paid out more than $1.3 billion dollars in legal, treatment, and compensation fees as a consequence. One case in particular drew public attention to the problem in the United States. This concerned John Geoghan, a Boston priest accused of abusing over

130 children over three decades, who was sentenced and sent to prison where he was murdered by another inmate. A report published in 2009 of an investigation of the Dublin Archdiocese in Ireland found that in the period between 1975 and 2004 there were 46 priests accused of abusing over 320 children, with one priest alone admitting to the abuse of over 100 children. However, the additional scandal for the Catholic Church has not just been the existence of large numbers of abusers among its clergy, but the fact that the patriarchal church hierarchy had known all along about the extent of the abuse and simply chose to close ranks about it because it would have been damaging to the Church to be more open. Many of the serial abusers in the United States, Ireland, Germany, Belgium, and other countries were simply moved from one diocese to another as bishops and archbishops tried to cover up to prevent potential scandals.

We have raised these issues about sexual abuse by clergy in this section on celibacy, but we do not mean to imply that celibacy is the *only* cause or contribution to the occurrence of abuse. Indeed, we concur with Myra Hidalgo (2007) in her book *Sexual Abuse and the Culture of Catholicism* in which she presents a more sophisticated analysis of sexual abuse perpetrated by priests and nuns. Hidalgo argues persuasively that a key factor is the general Catholic view that sex is shameful into which children are socialized from an early age. This shame-based view means that many children view their sexuality in a traumatic fashion. It can lead them to be more vulnerable to being abused themselves, though abuse is one among many traumatic sex-related experiences. What sort of person, Hidalgo asks, would then be attracted to a life of supposed celibacy? When a decision to join the clergy is typically made in mid- to late teenage years, such individuals would be likely to be very confused about their own sexuality while at the same time unable to manage sexual impulses appropriately. Data from the John Jay College (2004) study showed that although the age of the priests at the time of abuse ranged from 18 to 90 years, most priests (40%) abused between the ages of 30 and 39, and the majority of victims (81%) were boys of whom 40% were aged 11–14 years. Hidalgo argues, however, that although the majority of victims of priests are boys around pubescence, many such priests actually report themselves to be heterosexual rather than homosexual, and that therefore the pattern indicates in many cases problems in sexual development and sexual identity. Immature individuals come to believe that their shame-based reactions to their developing sexuality can best be managed through taking vows of celibacy, which for many is an approach that is clearly not effective. Indeed, how do the religious police prevent masturbation and sexual fantasy which in theory a life of celibacy also demands? As Hidalgo argues, removing the requirement for celibacy will not make the problem of sex abuse by religious clergy go away on its own. Nevertheless, it is clear from many of the Protestant Christian religions that Christianity neither requires celibacy among its religious elite nor does it need to treat sexuality as something shameful and sinful.

Secret Societies and Secret Knowledge

Every boy loves a secret society, but some boys never grow up. Living for the past 15 years in the world capital of Freemasonry, Edinburgh, the workings of this secret society within society have been brought home to me on a regular basis. When I first arrived at Edinburgh University to take up the Chair in Clinical Psychology, my then head of department recommended her family law firm to carry out the conveyancing for my house purchase. I innocently went along to meet one of the senior partners of the firm, who, because I came family recommended, assumed that I must also be a Freemason. When I explained that I was not a member, he stated that almost every lawyer in Edinburgh was a Freemason and that at least half of the medics too, and that if I wanted to make my life a lot easier I should join them. Well, as you might have guessed by now, I have a problem with thinking that there really is a Supreme Being, The Great Architect of the Universe or whoever, even if a Great Scientist of the Universe such as Isaac Newton (after whom the Cambridge University Masonic Lodge is named) was a Freemason. In fact, I would go so far as to say, only consider moving to Edinburgh if you are prepared to join the Freemasons. Some locals joke that, if you do have to move to Edinburgh and do not want to be a Freemason, the only people you should trust are Catholics. Why? Because Pope Leo XIII banned Catholics from becoming Freemasons, a position that Cardinal Ratzinger endorsed before he became Pope Benedict XVI. You know there is a problem with the Freemasons if Pope Benedict is worried about their secrecy, when (if the author Dan Brown is to be believed) the Vatican archives on which the Pope sits contain secrets enough to blow the Church apart.

But let me step back for a moment from personal reminiscence and catharsis to explore the power of secrecy and secret knowledge that Freemasonry and other religious groups build into their societies. To continue with our examination of Freemasonry, there are many fanciful claims about its origins, none more fanciful than those presented in a book by two Freemasons, Christopher Knight and Robert Lomas, entitled *The Hiram Key* (1997). There they claim that Hiram Abif was the builder of the Temple of Solomon and one of the first Freemasons, who took many of the initiation ceremonies of the Egyptian Pharaohs and incorporated them into the Masonic rituals that are still practiced today. (As noted in Chapter 1, however, of all the ancient architects it is surely Imhotep, vizier to Pharoah Djoser and builder of the first step pyramid at Saqqara, from whom the great Masonic traditions should be derived.) Furthermore, Knight and Lomas claim that these rituals were passed down through historical figures such as Jesus, who, they claim, was a Freemason, and through organizations such as the Knights Templar. In contrast, what the historical records show is that the world's oldest Masonic Lodge is that of St. Mary's Chapel, in Hill Street in Edinburgh (where else?), whose records date back to July 31, 1599, and which is also known as Lodge of Edinburgh No. 1. The so-called Grand Lodges did not appear until the eighteenth century, the first being the Grand Lodge of England in 1717; others included the Grand Lodge of the USA in 1730, and that of Scotland in 1736. As in any good secret society, there are special gestures, handshakes, and passwords that are used to indicate membership, though the passwords differ between the different Lodges and can be changed from time to time as a protection. Freemasonry is patriarchal, with women allowed to be associate members but not allowed to become full members, nor can they participate in the rituals held in the Inner Sanctum. Members pass through the Rites for three degrees: 1, Entered Apprentice; 2, Fellow Craft; and 3, the "third degree" of Master Mason. In the Scottish Rite that is practiced in some Lodges, the Master Mason can pass through further degrees to the thirty-third degree (see the Scottish website at www.grandlodgescotland.com). At each degree, new secrets, codes, and rituals are revealed to the initiate. The Church of Scientology, which we considered earlier, has adopted a similar model of initiation, secret knowledge being passed to initiates as they pass through levels up to Thetan level XV.

Secret societies such as the Freemasons present themselves in a number of contradictory ways that serve to fuel many of the conspiracy theories that spring up around them, though the fact that they claim *not* to be a secret society only serves to add to the sense of conspiracy. The problem is that at least some of the conspiracies have been at least partly true. The Grande Orient de France, the French Grand Lodge founded in 1733, is considered by many to have played a major role in the French Revolution that began in 1789; the Jacobin Clubs that were influential during the early years of the revolution seem to have been re-badged Masonic Lodges; and the French motto, "Liberty, Equality, Fraternity," emerged from the various rallying cries used by the Masonic Jacobin Clubs in revolutionary France. One notable member of the French Grand Lodge was Benjamin Franklin during his time as the first American Ambassador to France, based in Paris, who helped export the American Declaration of Independence in 1776 to France. Moreover, in addition to Benjamin Franklin, perhaps a total of 19 of the 56 signatories of the American Declaration including Thomas Jefferson are thought to have been Freemasons. The problem for Freemasonry is that Masonic conspiracy theories will continue to survive because of the nature of the power wielded by this secret boys' club.

Conclusion

In this chapter we have highlighted some of the issues of power and control that have become institutionalized within religious systems. Although the early Neolithic religious practices seem to have focused on the issue of fertility and the role of mother goddesses, the shift to urban settlements in the early civilizations and their domination by male leaders was accompanied by the promotion of the male gods such that eventually the patriarchal monotheisms emerged in the Jewish, Christian, and then Islamic traditions. These patriarchal monotheistic religions have promoted a single male god and a male religious elite, while subordinating the role of women and other minority groups. However, there have been many backlashes from such oppression. They include religious movements that have emerged as the religions of the oppressed, such as the Evangelical movement in the US, the conversion of low-caste Hindus to Buddhism and Christianity (almost all Christian converts in India are from the low caste), and the development of New Religious Movements that can offer something other than traditional patriarchy. We also noted that there are consequences of excessive and inappropriate religious control, with the example of the global sexual-abuse scandals that have hit the Catholic Church in recent decades. It has been argued that these are a consequence of the celibacy imposed on a religious elite that is then in a position of power over women and children in their care. A celibate Catholic patriarchy will always be at increased risk of abusing those that it is meant to care for. The sooner that Catholicism learns from other monotheisms including Protestantism, Judaism, and Islam that celibacy is not the path to godhead but the path to abuse, and that sexuality is not inherently sinful and is not only for the purpose of procreation, then the sooner that millions of lives worldwide will be safer and healthier. However, as George Bernard Shaw noted, and as we quoted at the beginning of this chapter, "Why should we take advice on sex from the Pope? If he knows anything about it, he shouldn't."

6

Religion and Health

Religion provides the solace for the turmoil that it creates.

Byron Danelius

Introduction

Religion is good for your health, or so many people would have us believe. In a fascinating book, *Aging With Grace,* David Snowdon (2001) presented a summary of the findings of a longitudinal study of old age in a group of American nuns (see also the study's website at www.nunstudy.org). The study began in 1986 with a group of 678 members of the School Sisters of Notre Dame, who are a group of nuns primarily involved in teaching. At the beginning of the study they ranged in age from 75 to 102 years. Among its findings was that autobiographies written when they started in the religious order at average age 22 years predicted morbidity and mortality approximately 60 years later. Positive emotional content and ideational complexity in these early autobiographical sketches are significantly predictive of better outcome in later life. Lower levels of smoking and alcohol use than in matched age and gender comparison groups are also associated with overall increased longevity, with the exception that the nuns have higher rates of breast cancer and genital organ cancers because of nulliparity (absence of children). Higher educational qualifications such as having a bachelor's degree or better was also found to be associated with greater longevity (average 89.4 years) in comparison with those with the lowest educational

Adieu to God: Why Psychology Leads to Atheism, First Edition. Mick Power.
© 2012 Mick Power. Published 2012 by John Wiley & Sons, Ltd.

attainment (average 82.0 years). The nun study is fascinating on two counts: first, the nuns on average live longer than women in the general population; and, secondly, within the group it is possible to examine why some of the nuns live even longer than others.

Before we conclude that all that is needed for a long and healthy life is to be like Julie Andrews at the beginning of the *Sound of Music* with the addition of a university degree, we must consider whether there are certain elements of the nun's lifestyle, other than their religious beliefs, that contribute to their longevity or whether the religious beliefs themselves are the major cause of the longevity. For example, we must ask whether factors such as lower levels of smoking and alcohol consumption, a positive outlook on life, and good social support would be sufficient in themselves to account for the enhancement to longevity that the nuns experienced. In this chapter, therefore, we will attempt to disentangle the evidence on whether or not religion *per se* is good for your health. Before the evidence is reviewed, however, the cautionary note must be added that, even if we conclude that religion *is* good for one's health, this is not evidence for the existence of god(s); all that it would be evidence for is that the *belief system* is good for your health, but it would not be evidence that the belief system is therefore true. Otherwise, one ought to find that only belief in the true god is good for your health, because surely belief in *false* gods should be bad for your health and should even be punished by the true god? (Indeed, the First Commandment from the Old Testament, Thou shalt have no other gods before me, suggests such a punishment.) While it is conceivable that the true god could punish those who believed in false gods by inflicting short brutish lives on them, it is extremely doubtful that the actual evidence would ever go so far as to support one god over another. Certainly, the research to date has not set out with that intention.

The Evidence

So what does the general evidence on the relationship between religion and health look like? Fenix *et al.* (2006) reported a study in which they followed up 175 primary caregivers of cancer patients who subsequently died in a hospice in Connecticut. The caregivers were followed up for over a year after the deaths of their loved ones and the research found that those with high religiousness were significantly less likely to suffer from major depression in comparison with caregivers with low religiousness. Religiousness was therefore strongly protective for bereaved caregivers in the difficult period following the death of a family member.

Green and Elliott (2010) analysed data from the 2006 General Social Survey (GSS), a nationally representative survey of US adults that is carried out regularly and is run from the University of Chicago. Earlier studies had established that church attendance seemed to be beneficial for both physical and mental health (e.g. Idler and Kasl, 1992), but Green and Elliott were interested to know whether or not other confounding factors such as employment, financial status, and family support might account for these apparent benefits from church attendance. In multiple regression analyses that partialled out the effects of these variables, a positive effect of religiosity on both self-reported health and happiness was still found, which indicated that these particular variables did not explain away the health benefits from religiosity. Interestingly, the authors reported that, among the religious groups, those with more liberal views tended to report better health whereas by comparison those among more fundamentalist groups reported more happiness.

A summary of studies on mortality by Hummer *et al.* (2004) concluded that while there is good evidence that church attendance is linked to greater longevity, there is still a variety of other factors and mechanisms that need to be explored in order to understand the links better. Koenig (2009) reviews the positive effects of religious belief on mental health while noting that for some vulnerable individuals in some religions there may also be increased risk. For example, in a reanalysis of the US Epidemiologic Catchment Area (ECA) survey, Levav *et al.* (1997) reported that Jewish men had significantly higher rates of depression in comparison with men from all other religious and non-religious groups, such that the 2:1 ratio for adult female to male rates of depression that is normally found is not present in the Jewish population, where the ratio is 1:1. Kate Loewenthal (2008) has summarized research that suggests that the higher rates of depression in Jewish men may be linked to factors such as low use of alcohol in the Jewish community.

In an attempt to disentangle religion from other confounding factors, Baetz and Toews (2009) examined a range of social, psychological, and biological factors that must be taken into account. As these authors point out, the social domain has probably been best explored in order to understand the possible mediation of the religion–health links. In the social domain, religions often proscribe the use of alcohol and drugs, proscriptions which can therefore impact on health behaviors in a positive way. Equally, church attendance can provide an important source of social support and group membership. On the psychological level, the Allport and Ross (1967) distinction between intrinsic and extrinsic religious orientation has received wide consideration in research. Those people with intrinsic orientation obtain meaning and purpose from their religious beliefs, whereas those with an extrinsic orientation are considered simply to use religion for reasons such as sociability and security. There is evidence that intrinsic orientation is protective against depression, whereas extrinsic may increase depression risk (e.g. Smith *et al.*, 2003). The work of Pargament (1997) has extended the earlier Allport and Ross work with findings that are largely consistent with the view that religion can be both positive and negative in its impact on health depending on the approach to religion that the person has. Baetz and Toews' third group of factors are biological, which includes an area of study that has been labelled *neurotheology*. One of the questions for religious belief is whether, in times of stress following significant life events and other adversity, religious belief can help to buffer the effects through, for example, enhanced immunological system functioning and better regulation of stress-related hormones such as cortisol. For example, Carrico *et al.* (2006) found in HIV-positive men and women that religiosity was related to lower urinary cortisol levels, findings that supported the possible stress-buffering role of religious belief.

This brief overview of the impact of religious belief on physical and mental health supports the general proposal that religious belief can have positive benefits for health and happiness. However, it is still early days in terms of understanding the social, psychological and biological mechanisms through which belief can exert beneficial effects. There are also problems with understanding what "religiosity" actually is and how it should be defined. Earlier research which simply looked at church attendance has shown positive benefits for physical health, mental health, and longevity, but church attendance can occur for many different internal or external reasons, not all of which appear to be beneficial. Recent research has taken a more complex approach to the understanding of religiosity, but again this work shows that there can be both positive and negative impacts of religious belief that depend on the type of religiosity and the type of outcome being measured. In the remainder of this chapter we will therefore try to disentangle further some of these positive and negative effects, beginning in the next section with studies of prayer.

The Power of Prayer

There are several different types of prayer, as we noted previously, which are typically used for different reasons and in different situations. In their impressive *Handbook of Religion and Health* (2001), Harold Koenig, Michael McCullough and David Larson have summarized a range of studies that have shown the positive effects of prayer on well-being and on coping with a number of health-related disorders. However, such beneficial effects might always be attributable to a placebo effect, namely, that if you believe strongly enough that prayer is going to help you, then the chances are that there will be some beneficial effects. A number of empirical studies of prayer have therefore directly addressed the placebo issue, so we will focus on such studies in this section.

There have now been a number of studies that have tested empirically whether or not intercessory or petitionary prayer (prayer that requests an intervention) is effective in health states. The best tests of these are, as we suggested, not where the person prays for their own recovery (we will return to this issue of religion and coping in the next section), but rather where others pray for the persons who are unwell unbeknownst to those people. One of the better designed of the earlier studies of the effect of prayer was by Byrd (1988), based at the San Francisco General Hospital. The study included 393 coronary patients, half of whom were randomly allocated to the prayer group plus usual treatment, and half of whom only received the usual treatment. In the prayer group condition, the patients were prayed for by over 2000 Christians outside the hospital who were given first names plus medical condition of the people they were to pray for. The patients themselves did not know that they were being prayed for, nor did the doctors who did the follow-up assessments know which patients were being prayed for (a double-blind design). Over a 10-month prayer period, the results showed that on one or two measures such as the need for antibiotics, the prayed-for group performed better than the control group, though, importantly, there were no significant differences between the two groups in relation to mortality. Nevertheless, the results were considered sensational by many who took the results as evidence for divine intervention as a result of intercessory prayer.

Promising initial results always need replication in independent centres because of the inevitable flaws and biases that can enter even the apparently best-designed studies in medicine and psychology. One well-designed replication of Byrd's study was by Krucoff *et al.* (2005) and published in

The Lancet. The group, based at Duke University, investigated the effects
of intercessory prayer in 748 cardiac patients in nine different hospitals in
the United States. Again, the design was double-blind so that neither the
patients nor the staff knew who was in the prayed-for group. The results
from the study showed no health benefits in the prayed-for group during
the time of the three-year clinical trial.

To date, the most impressive and extensive study of prayer and cardiac
patients is the so-called STEP study (Study of the Therapeutic Effects of
Intercessory Prayer). The study was led by Howard Benson of Harvard
Medical School (Benson *et al.*, 2006) and funded by the Templeton Foundation, the scientific religious organization that is so hated by Richard Dawkins
(see his comments in *The God Delusion*, 2006). The study included leading
centres in Boston, Rochester, Memphis, Tampa, and Washington DC, together with a total of 1802 bypass surgery patients. The patients in the study
were randomly assigned to three groups:

- Group 1 were told that they might or might not receive intercessory
  prayer and actually did.
- Group 2 were told that they might or might not receive intercessory
  prayer but did not.
- Group 3 were told that they would receive intercessory prayer and actually did.

The study design thereby allowed the investigators to disentangle the
effects of expectations about prayer from the effects of prayer itself. The
prayers were carried out by three Christian groups, two Catholic and
one Protestant, who were provided with patients' first names and last initial.
The prayers commenced on the evening before surgery and then continued
for the next 14 days. The results published by Benson and his colleagues
showed that major complications and mortality at 30 days were similar
across the three groups. Additional results showed that complications occurred in 59% of the patients who were certain of receiving prayer compared
with 52% of those who were uncertain but who actually received it; thus,
the patients who knew that they were receiving intercessory prayer had a
worse outcome than the other two groups.

Cardiac patients have not been the only group studied for the possible
benefits of intercessory prayer. Cha *et al.* (2001) published a study in the
Journal of Reproductive Medicine in which the effect of intercessory prayer

on pregnancy rates in women undergoing in vitro fertilization (IVF) was examined. The study investigated 219 women aged 26 to 46 years, half of whom were randomly assigned to the prayed-for group and half of whom were assigned to the control no-prayer condition. The results reported in the paper found a pregnancy rate of 50% in the prayed-for group, which was significantly higher than the rate of only 26% in the not-prayed-for group. When the findings first appeared in 2001, they were widely reported in the US media, including ABC News, as the "Columbia Miracle Study." However, the study has not proven to be quite what it seemed at the time. In 2004 the paper's supposed lead author, Dr Rogerio Lobo of Columbia University, withdrew his name from the paper following an investigation by Columbia University and the US Department of Health, because of a number of anomalies that included the fact that the patients did not know that they were participating in a study and that Dr Lobo himself did not even know that the study was being carried out until almost a year after the study had finished. To make matters worse, the paper's second author, Daniel Wirth, a California lawyer who has published papers on parapsychology and who had supposedly arranged the prayer groups, was subsequently convicted and imprisoned for fraud of $1.2 million that involved the use for financial gain of names of people who had died (see *New York Times*, December 4, 2004). Following these scandals, the *Journal of Reproductive Medicine* initially withdrew the paper from the journal, but then reinstated it following a review so that it is now listed as Cha and Wirth (2001). Despite the nature of the serious question marks that hang over the study, it is still referred to as the "Columbia Miracle Study" and its results are still cited and used as evidence for the power of prayer when all they show is that religion attracts its fair share of crooks and quacks who exploit its power for financial and other gain.

Religion and Stress

Throughout this book we have touched on the role of religion as a coping mechanism in times of stress. A number of studies have investigated whether or not religious belief can help people at times of stress such as during illness to themselves and to loved ones, in times of financial hardship, and after natural disasters such as earthquakes, floods and tsunamis (e.g. Baker, 2008). Johnson and Spilka (1991) studied women with breast cancer in the United

States and found that 85% reported that religion helped them cope with the stress. However, when they looked at the effect of Allport's *intrinsic–extrinsic* classification, which was mentioned earlier, the researchers found that the benefits of religion were primarily for those with an *intrinsic* orientation.

Researchers such as Cohen and Hill (2007) and Loewenthal (2011) have further suggested that intrinsic religiosity may be of more benefit in individualistic cultures, especially predominantly Protestant ones, whereas extrinsic religiosity may give more health-and-well-being benefits in collectivistic cultures.

Ringdal (1996) further showed that in a group of cancer patients there was a 14% better survival rate in those with religious beliefs. Oxman *et al.* (1995) found that, in a group of 232 cardiac patients, 5% of those who regularly attended religious services died compared with 12% of those who rarely or never attended religious services. A meta-analysis of 29 studies by McCullough *et al.* (2000) concluded that there was a significant benefit from religious belief for survival rates in a range of physical illnesses. Again, the benefits of religion include improved health behaviors such as less smoking and lower alcohol intake, and increased social support. Drevenstadt (1998) in a study of 11 000 people in the United States found a positive correlation between church attendance and self-reported physical health, which, for the middle-aged whites, was primarily due to the social support that church-going offered. However, in this study the benefits of church-going were only found for young people if there was sufficient religious belief as well. The study shows that the benefits of church attendance for health may vary across the lifespan, with social support being a more major factor at some life stages than at others.

The buffering effect of religious belief is also clear from those coping with death of loved ones. McIntosh *et al.* (1993) followed up 124 people who had experienced the sudden death of a child. Those who attended church regularly reported being given more social support and finding more meaning in the loss, such that by 18 months following the loss they were less distressed. In a study reported by Loewenthal *et al.* (2000) a total of 126 participants from Protestant or Jewish backgrounds were interviewed. The participants had recently experienced stressful life events to do with finance and employment, illness, and family problems, and were selected to be either high or low on religiosity; those with intermediate religiosity were not interviewed. The results showed a possible causal model for both Jewish and Protestant participants in which religiosity leads to certain religious causal beliefs (for example, God is in control), which leads to positive mood, which in turn lowers reports of distress. The authors did not, however, run a simultaneous groups analysis to check if their stress coping model fitted both the high and the low religiosity groups equally well; thus, it seems unlikely that the low religiosity group would show the same coping mechanisms as the high religiosity group.

A recent study by McGregor *et al.* (2010) examined the general observation that under stress people often become more superstitious in their beliefs and behavior, which, when applied to religious ideals, may mean that people become more religious. This is an effect that was noted by William James in *The Varieties of Religious Experience* (1902). In their first study, McGregor *et al.* (2010) found that a mild academic threat to a group of undergraduate students significantly increased the students' ratings of their religious ideals. A replication in a second study further showed that such threats had more impact on those students with more monotheistic beliefs, especially for jingoistic items on superiority of one's own belief system and supporting war. In a third study, McGregor and co-workers tested the possible buffering effect of successful pursuit of worldly goals on religious idealism when under threat. As the authors note, more international aid is sometimes directed to parts of the world at risk for increased religious idealism in the hope that the support of everyday goals will ameliorate the tendency towards religious extremism under conditions of threat. In this third study, the authors used an interpersonal threat task in which the student participants were asked to think for two minutes about an important conflicted relationship in their lives. Again, as for Study 2, the results showed that the monotheistic students had higher religious zeal, the effects of goal engagement showing a significant impact of threat on religious zeal at low levels of engagement but not at high levels of engagement. The authors argue that these results, albeit with students, provide tentative support for policies that enable basic needs and other goals to be pursued in regions of the world that are vulnerable to religious extremism.

The relationship between stress and religious belief is of course a double-edged sword in that, whereas some people may benefit from religious belief at times of stress, others may find their religious beliefs weakened. A study by Chen and Koenig (2006) found that, in a group of 745 elderly patients admitted to Duke University Medical Center and followed up over three months, increases in severity of illness led to decreases in church attendance and in religious belief at follow-up. Although the church attendance reduction was mediated by reductions in physical activity, the reduction in belief was not mediated by reduced physical activity. A meta-analysis reported by

Ano and Vasconcelles (2005) that included a total of 13 512 participants
from 49 studies examined both the positive and negative links between
religious coping and stress. The authors found support, first, for positive
religious coping being associated with positive psychological adjustment;
second, for positive religious coping being associated with a reduction in
negative psychological adjustment; and, third, for negative religious coping
being associated with negative psychological adjustment. However, negative
religious coping did not seem to be associated with a reduction in positive
psychological adjustment. Ano and Vasconcelles defined negative religious
coping to include factors such as spiritual discontent, demonic reappraisal,
and belief in a punishing God. These findings highlight the complexity of the
relationship between religion, coping, and stress, in particular when stress
impacts negatively on the religious belief system (for example, if the person
comes to believe that a physical or mental health problem is a punishment
from God for previous wrong-doing (cf. Loewenthal, 2000)).

Miracles, Gurus, Relics, and Placebos

Jerome Frank in his classic book, *Persuasion and Healing* (1973), argued that
the modern work of psychotherapists and counsellors has been carried out
for thousands of years by priests and shamans and, in general, by people with
good interpersonal skills. Psychotherapists, priests, and shamans, according
to Frank, share a number of skills and methods that can be effective in the
treatment of psychological and some physical disorders. A summary of the
modern evidence base for psychotherapies can be found in *Handbook of
Evidence-Based Psychotherapies* by Freeman and Power (2007). What the
modern psychotherapies share in common with the earlier practices of
shamans and priests include rituals, sacred places, installation of hope, a
confiding relationship, and a rationale. These will now be considered in turn.

1. *Rituals.* The spectacular nature of rituals has become central to most
   religions, as we considered in detail in Chapter 4. These rituals are
   performed typically by men who believe that they have special powers and a special relationship to their gods, whose power they can
   channel to their followers. Religious healing is a common part of religions, in which people who are ill and suffering seek the healing power
   of those they believe have the power, or can channel the power in
   order to cure them or their loved ones. One of the observations that

Jerome Frank made about rituals and healing is that the religious healer, as with the traditional shaman, is usually able, in order to sustain their reputation, to discriminate between those illnesses that they can help versus those illnesses that they cannot. Those individuals chosen for healing may then participate in group ceremonies that are highly ritualized but emotionally evocative, even though they are highly familiar to the participants. We will return at the end of this chapter to consider how factors such as ritual are incorporated into modern medicine and psychotherapies, thereby revealing their origins in religious practices but also acknowledging the power of those religious rituals.

2. *Sacred places.* All religions have their sacred places, be they sacred springs or caves, mountain-tops, temples or cathedrals. These sacred places are imbued with special powers by the priests and shamans who practice there, and therefore those who attend and who seek healing believe that the places have healing powers. Indeed, there may well be some truth in these beliefs because a sacred spring may contain water that has special minerals and rare elements which are of benefit for health. For example, the Roman baths popular with visitors to Bath in south-west England began as a sacred spring to the Celtic goddess Sulis. During the Roman occupation of England, the spring was developed into Roman baths dedicated to the syncretic goddess, Sulis-Minerva, who among other things was goddess of wisdom and medicine. From the seventeenth century onwards the water has been a popular healing health drink, and chemical analysis has shown that it contains 43 different minerals (see www.romanbaths.co.uk). Of course, a cave, or church, or temple need not contain health-giving minerals as the waters of a spring may do, but, instead, custom and tradition can impart a belief in the healing powers of the place. Henri Ellenberger in *The Discovery of the Unconscious* (1970) considered that the ancient Greek practice of *incubation* was a precursor to modern psychotherapy. Incubation typically involved the sufferer spending a night in a sacred cave, where they would have evocative dreams that a priest-physician would interpret in the morning in order to resolve the conflict that was causing distress to the person. The Sanctuary of Asclepius, the Greek god of medicine (whose snake-entwined staff is still the symbol of modern medicine) in Pergamum combined a healing spring, a health sanctuary and an underground passageway and cave where incubation or dream interpretation was carried out along with a number of other health-related activities and practices.

3. *Installation of hope.* Jerome Frank examines the case of Lourdes, also considered here in Chapter 4. Despite the fact that the vast majority of the sick and the disabled who visit Lourdes are not cured of their illnesses and disorders, most of them nevertheless seem to experience a new sense of hope and often improved relationships with those around them who may have helped them with their trip to Lourdes. This more positive emotional state, of hope rather than hopelessness, can in some cases lead to a gradual improvement in functioning that can increase the chances of recovery from illness or improve processes of adaptation to chronic disorders. Those who develop a physical disorder or chronic illness and who become depressed are less likely to overcome the disorder and are at increased risk of further illnesses and disorders because depression, for example, reduces immune system functioning (see, for example, Power (2005), *Mood Disorders: A Handbook of Science and Practice*). Recent data from the World Health Organization's World Health Survey of almost a quarter of a million participants from 60 countries showed that depression had the worst impact of all disorders on subjective ratings of health, but depression combined with a chronic physical disease such as angina, arthritis, asthma or diabetes had the worst health ratings of all (Moussavi *et al.*, 2007).

Even in the absence of miracles, the installation of hope in the individual, whether through religious activity, new or different medical procedures, or psychotherapy, can reduce or eliminate the co-morbid depression and lead to better overall functioning and adaptation to a chronic illness or disorder, even, indeed, to the occasional "miracle" in which someone recovers from a chronic illness. However, as Jerome Frank notes, none of the documented "miracles" at Lourdes has ever involved something so clear-cut as the growth of an amputated limb. If God really wants to perform miracles, what stops him from performing such an obvious one? Frank also summarizes a study carried out by Rehder in Germany (see Frank, 1973, p.74) in which three severely ill bedridden women who had failed to respond to medical treatment were treated by a local faith healer. In the first phase of the study, the faith healer attempted to cure them at a distance but without the patients' knowledge. There was no effect of the faith healing. In the second phase of the study, the women were told about the faith healer and how he would be working to treat them at a certain time the following day, even though the faith healer was not actually working at that time. At the crucial time, all three women began to feel better, and one even became permanently cured. Hope and belief are crucial to the effectiveness of interventions and, as such studies demonstrate, may sometimes be sufficient and enable a permanent improvement in physical and mental functioning.

In medicine and psychology, the individual's positive expectations of help are often referred to as the "placebo effect." The word *placebo* is the Latin for "I shall please," and was first used in St. Jerome's translation of the Bible, the "Vulgate," in the phrase "I shall please the Lord." The word came to have a number of religious meanings before it was adopted in medicine. The placebo effect can be demonstrated by the prescription of an inert pill that contains only sugar or salt, but which the individual can nevertheless gain benefit from. A common research design for the testing of a new medicine or therapy is that it is compared with an inert placebo. The new medicine or procedure must perform better than the placebo condition in order to be of proven effectiveness. Many rituals and procedures used by shamans in traditional medicine have positive benefits because of this placebo effect. A recent study by Kaptchuk and colleagues (2008) in Harvard neatly demonstrated for a group of patients suffering with irritable bowel syndrome that a combination of assessment, a ritual that consisted of "sham acupuncture" (in which, unbeknownst to the patient, the needles retracted rather than penetrated the skin), plus warm clinical management all contributed to improved outcome and improved quality of life even though there was no active treatment at any point in the intervention.

4. *A confiding relationship.* Be it shaman, priest, or psychotherapist the person seeking help must develop trust in the person who is offering to help them. A shaman or priest is likely already to be known by the person seeking help because they are part of the same village or religious community. The relationship that is established between the healer and the sufferer depends in part on the personal qualities that each brings to the relationship, but in addition there are also dynamic features of that relationship. Again, if the priest or shaman is already known to the individual, the person may have a favorable positive attitude that is brought to the encounter. However, psychotherapists are unlikely to be known to their clients, so the quality of the therapeutic relationship develops through the initial interactions. We have summarized elsewhere the ongoing research on the therapeutic relationship and its importance for a positive therapeutic outcome (Freeman and Power (2007), *Handbook of Evidence-Based Psychotherapies*). This research generally

shows that, unless a good working relationship is established between the psychotherapist and the client, then the methods used to help the client are unlikely to be effective. It seems very likely, therefore, that the same principles apply in religious healing; namely, that the healer must establish a positive working relationship with the believer in order for the healing procedures to have any chance of being effective. A study by Conroy *et al.* (2000) with a sample of 200 general practice attenders in Dublin showed that about 10% of the sample had also seen a faith healer, but that GPs and faith healers were not seen as opposites but as being similar to each other. A study in Uganda where traditional healing is more widely used also showed that, in the case of attenders who had moderate to severe mental health problems, they were more likely to use both traditional and modern medicine rather than one or the other (Abbo *et al.*, 2009). Again, these results emphasize that users of services have positive views of the healers from both traditional and modern medicine, rather than seeing one as in some way opposite or contradictory to the other.

5. *A rationale.* One of the clear messages from the work of Jerome Frank (1973) and others is the importance of a *rationale* being given to the client, whether in traditional healing or in modern psychotherapy or medicine. Research on psychotherapy outcome shows that clients in therapy are less likely to drop out and will do better if they share a model or explanation similar to that of the therapist. For example, in a study of cognitive therapy, Melanie Fennell and John Teasdale (1987) found that a client's positive response to the *Coping With Depression* booklet handed out to depressed clients at the beginning of therapy was a good predictor of a positive outcome by the end of therapy. The booklet presents brief case examples and a straightforward summary of the cognitive therapy approach to depression. A client who agrees with the approach is more likely to improve with therapy than a client who does not understand or agree with this kind of therapy. This shared rationale is present for users of traditional medicine and religious healing approaches. The shaman and the patient share a world-view in which, for example, evil spirits are believed to have entered the patient and their removal depends on the skill and experience of the shaman. Jerome Frank presents a detailed analysis of the treatment of *espanto* (similar to agitated depression) in a Guatemalan Indian woman (Frank, 1973, pp. 59–62). The treatment took the form of a group healing ceremony that was attended not just by the patient, but also, as Frank

notes, by her husband, a male friend, and two anthropologists. In the initial meeting the shaman made the diagnosis of *espanto*. The group ceremony took place in the patient's house and lasted over 12 hours until late in the night. The shaman proceeded to make wax dolls of the evil spirits, then to massage the patient with eggs, which were believed to absorb the sickness from the body. At 2 a.m. the patient was taken outside semi-naked and sprayed with a "magic fluid" that had a high alcohol content so that she quickly became very cold. She also drank a pint of the magic fluid. She was taken back into her house, where she was massaged again with the eggs in order to absorb the remaining sickness. The shaman then broke the eggs into water one by one, eventually declaring that the *espanto* would be cured as the eggs fell to the bottom of the bowl. As it turned out, next day the patient developed a high fever, which the anthropologists treated with antibiotics, but within a few days she had recovered from both the fever and the *espanto* or depression.

Within Christianity the ritual of exorcism bears many similarities to some of the traditional healing ceremonies. The Christian tradition of exorcism begins in the Bible with Jesus famously casting out demons on several occasions such as in the case of the Gadarene swine when he cast devils out of a man from Gadarene into a herd of swine who then ran into the Sea of Galilee and drowned themselves:

> And they came over unto the other side of the sea, into the country of the Gadarenes . . . immediately there met him out of the tombs a man with an unclean spirit . . . He said unto him, Come out of the man thou unclean spirit. And he asked him, What is thy name? And he answered, saying, My name is Legion: for we are many . . . And forthwith Jesus gave them leave. And the unclean spirits went out, and entered into the swine; and the herd ran violently down a steep place into the sea, (they were about two thousand;) and were choked in the sea. (Mark 5:1–13)

By the third century CE, a special group of clerics had emerged in the Christian Church who were known as exorcists, and whose function was to cast out evil spirits from the afflicted. At that time, the ceremony of baptism included a ritual for exorcism because of the original sin with which every person was held to have been born. Ritual exorcism is still used in today's Christian churches to differing degrees; for example, a version of exorcism, the *deliverance ceremony,* is commonly used in the Charismatic Christian movement to help individuals overcome evil influences, a practice that became more common after the film *The Exorcist* was released in 1973. In Catholicism, the Roman Ritual is spelled out in the book *Of Exorcisms and Certain Supplications,* which was revised in 1998 for the first time since 1614. Exorcism is also carried out in other religions, including Hinduism, some forms of Buddhism, Islam, and Judaism. Indeed, the simple act of sneezing which from medieval times onwards has been followed by the statement "Bless you!" can be considered a mini-exorcism in which the evil spirit expunged by the sneeze is prevented from returning back into the person's body with the blessing statement.

The take-home message from studies of shamanism, exorcism, psychotherapy, and the placebo effect in medicine is that people's world beliefs have a major impact on their understanding of health and illness. Therefore, curative rituals that are consistent with those world views may have a positive health-enhancing and spiritually uplifting effect for those people when they have engaged in ritual practices led by a shaman, a priest, a psychotherapist, or a medical doctor. Jerome Frank made these links explicit in *Persuasion and Healing* in a way that helps us to understand why religious healing practices can clearly benefit some of the people who seek help, though it is likely that the mechanisms of such benefits include the placebo effect, and other responses that belief can engender.

Pilgrimage and Purpose

Throughout this chapter and earlier chapters, a common thread has been that religion provides meaning and purpose in people's lives. Sometimes, as we have seen, the sense of purpose can come from a traumatic period in life which leads the person to become more religious, or to reinvest in religious beliefs that might have stagnated. Such periods can lead to conversion to a different or new religious belief, as William James discussed in detail in *The Varieties of Religious Experience* (1902). A common theme or metaphor that runs through many religions is that life is a pilgrimage in which we pilgrims must struggle and suffer but eventually we discover truth and purpose through that pilgrimage. The metaphor of life as pilgrimage is extremely powerful such that many people engage in difficult or hazardous pilgrimages to remote or sacred places that are associated with a particular religion. The writer David Lodge captured this sense of pilgrimage in his novel *Therapy* (1995) in which a successful sitcom writer experiences a sense of despair in mid-life following a failed marriage. The protagonist then walks the medieval pilgrimage to Santiago de Compostela in Galicia in Spain. This helps him to rediscover purpose and meaning in his life as well as re-establishing his relationship with his first girlfriend whom he had abandoned. The pilgrimage to Santiago, known as the Way of St. James in English or the *Camino* in Spanish, has existed since the ninth century CE, and is still walked by tens of thousands of pilgrims every year with starting points as far away as Paris, Vezelay, and Le Puy in France. It includes an onerous trek over the Pyrenees traditionally via Saint Jean Pied de Port. As someone who has cheated and only driven by car along the Camino to Santiago with just a few days of travel, I have to admire those pilgrims who have spent many months walking the whole route.

There are of course even more famous pilgrimages that are essential to religions other than Christianity. Perhaps the most famous of all is the pilgrimage to Mecca, the *hajj*, which all Muslims are meant to undertake at least once during their lifetime. The *hajj* is the world's largest pilgrimage: a total of 2 million pilgrims attended Mecca during the seven-day period in 2009. The *hajj* includes specified ritual actions such as walking counterclockwise seven times around the Kaaba central shrine, drinking from the Zamzam well, throwing stones at the devil, and shaving the head.

What can modern studies of pilgrims and pilgrimages tell us about the purpose of the pilgrimage? Detailed studies of Dutch pilgrims are summarized in a book by Paul Post and colleagues, *The Modern Pilgrim: Multidisciplinary Explorations of Christian Pilgrimage* (1998). The studies were focused on pilgrims to Catholic pilgrimage sites such as Wittem, Lourdes, and Banneux. The majority of pilgrims tend to be older, though Lourdes also has a younger (below 35 years, as defined by the researchers) group of pilgrims who often accompany older family members. Analysis of questionnaires completed by Dutch pilgrims showed that the main reasons for going on the pilgrimage were as follows: 73% went on the pilgrimage primarily for help and assistance, 60% went in order to deepen their faith, 54% went for spiritual reflection, and 44% went because of the healing tradition of the place of pilgrimage. Overall, the pilgrimage is experienced as a transforming ritual that deepens religious values and provides hope and improved well-being for pilgrims. Nordin (2009) further analyses psychological reasons for pilgrimage based on a study of Hindu pilgrims in Nepal and Tibet. Nordin found that pilgrims' journeys also involve the transfer of material and spiritual substances to the pilgrimage site, typically connected with the management of sin, illness, disability, and evil. The journey to the pilgrimage site and the ritual interaction there serve to unburden the individual of badness, and thereby the person takes something away from the pilgrimage site centered around the blessing of the divine agency connected to the site. The pilgrimage can therefore serve as a ritual penance for past sin and evil or questioning of faith, such that the pilgrim is then renewed in faith and cleansed through the pilgrimage ritual.

To return to the metaphor of life as a pilgrimage, the rise of psychotherapies over the last hundred years may reflect the need for spiritual pilgrimage in which the pilgrim-patient endures hardship in order to visit a psychotherapist who has the spiritual powers to cleanse and restore the person, to take away the feeling of malaise and purposelessness, and enable them to continue life's pilgrimage at a more optimal level of functioning.

Suicide and Religion

Mariam Sharapova was a 28-year-old married teacher from Dagestan in the south of the Russian Federation. On the morning of Monday March 29, 2010, she travelled on the Moscow Metro, which is the world's busiest subway system and carries upwards of 10 million passengers per day. When the train entered Lubyanka station in the centre of Moscow and was almost directly underneath the headquarters of the FSB (the new name for the KGB), she waited for the carriage doors to open and then, at 7.56 a.m., she detonated the explosive vest that she was wearing, which triggered a blast equivalent to 1.5 kg of TNT. Fifteen passengers on board the train and a further 11 people who had been waiting on the platform were killed by the explosion. A little later, at 8.38 a.m., further along the same metro line, Dzhanet Abdullayeva, a 17-year-old widow also from Dagestan, waited for the train she was on to enter Park Kultury Station and, as the doors opened, she detonated her explosive vest, which killed a further 12 people. Mariam and Dzhanet, now known as "black widows," were members of an Islamic separatist movement from the North Caucasus region in Russia that includes Dagestan and Chechnya.

Suicide bombing carried out by Islamic extremists has until recently been carried out mostly by young men, who seem to have been promised hero status for themselves and their families here on Earth, plus the eternal ministrations of 72 ever-willing dark-eyed virgins on their ascent to heaven. Unfortunately for the high-testosterone martyrs, a German scholar,

Christoph Luxenberg, has recently suggested that the relevant phrases in the Koran and the Hadith should be read in Syriac rather than Arabic, in which case there will be 72 "white raisins of crystal clarity" rather than "dark-eyed virgins" awaiting the young male martyrs. Do people in heaven ever experience disappointment, or can the raisins be that good? Many Muslim theologians condemn suicide and state that it is prohibited by the Koran, though the Muslim communities see these acts as "martyrdom" for the sake of a *jihad*, a holy war, as Sam Harris (2004) summarizes in his book, *The End of Faith: Religion, Terror, and the Future of Reason*.

In contrast to the positive view of the "martyr" in religions such as Islam, Hinduism, and Buddhism, the view of suicide among the Christian religions, even the noble suicide of the martyr, has been far more negative. In the UK, suicide was seen as a criminal act until 1961, when Parliament passed the Suicide Act. Previously anyone who attempted suicide but failed could be prosecuted and imprisoned. Even the families of those who completed suicide were at risk of prosecution. This view of suicide reflected religious ideas of suicide as self-murder that were formulated by the early Church Fathers. St. Augustine and St. Thomas Aquinas had stated that anyone who committed suicide had shown disregard for the will and authority of God such that the Church came to treat suicide as a sin. The person who committed suicide was traditionally not allowed to be buried in a Catholic churchyard; indeed many older churches have an area just outside the walls of the churchyard for the burials of suicides, though there has been some relaxation of this rule in recent years.

At a simplistic level of analysis, therefore, and with the exception of the suicide bombers, if religion is good for health and longevity, then it ought also to protect against the extremes of depression and suicide. However, the story is far more complex. We discussed earlier in the chapter how religiosity, especially if it is intrinsic, may have general health benefits, and a similar picture emerges for suicide and suicidal ideation with religiosity. For example, the US National Longitudinal Survey of Adolescent Health showed that private (intrinsic) religiosity was protective against use of cigarettes, alcohol and marijuana, lower use of violence, and lower likelihood of suicidal ideation and attempted suicide (Nonnemaker *et al.*, 2003). Interestingly, religiosity does not appear to be protective against suicide in China; thus, Zhang *et al.* (2010), in their psychological autopsy study of suicide in young rural Chinese, reported that religiosity was not protective but increased risk of suicide. These contrasting findings highlight the fact that different religions are associated with different degrees of risk for suicide and for a variety of reasons such as the issue of individualist versus collectivist cultures that we noted earlier. From Emile Durkheim's classic work *Suicide* (1897) onwards, it has been clear that suicide is higher in Protestant groups than in Catholics. Gearing and Lizardi (2009) summarized studies published on suicide and religion over the period 1980 to 2008 in order to examine trends in suicide rates between the four main religions of Christianity, Judaism, Islam, and Hinduism. The lowest rates of suicide appear to be in Islamic and Jewish individuals because both religions prohibit suicide. Within Christian faiths there are higher rates among Protestants than Catholics, with the exception of Evangelical Baptists who have low rates comparable to those of Catholics. Although the figures on suicidality in Hindus are limited, the tolerance of suicide and views on reincarnation and karma tend to show that higher rates of suicide occur among Hindu groups; for example, the ritual practice of suttee (sati) in which a newly widowed Hindu woman self-immolates on her husband's funeral pyre, is still occasionally practiced in some Hindu communities although it is now illegal. Data collected by the World Health Organization at national levels also provide some crude indications about trends across different countries where these can be grouped by a predominant religion or absence of religion (see, for example, Bertolote and Fleischmann, 2002). The WHO figures show that many Islam countries have very low suicide rates close to zero (e.g. in Kuwait) at about 0.1 per 100 000 of population. In contrast, in Buddhist countries such as Japan the rate is much higher at 17.9 per 100 000, whereas Hindu and Christian countries have intermediate rates at around 10 per 100 000. The bad news is that the "atheist" countries of the former Soviet Bloc and China have the highest suicide rates at 25.6 per 100 000 population, though, as we saw from the Chinese study by Zhang *et al.* (2010), labelling these countries as "atheist" is extremely misleading given that the suicide rates were higher in the more religious people in rural China whom Zhang and colleagues studied. What is clear, however, is that suicide rates in males in "atheist" countries are much higher than those for males in "religious" countries, whereas the rates for females are roughly similar between atheist and religious countries with the exception of the Islamic countries, where, as we noted above, the rates for both men and women are close to zero. Better epidemiology is needed to disentangle these effects of gender and religion, and to understand why men in countries such as Russia, Lithuania, Kazakhstan, and China have such high rates of suicide.

To return to Durkheim's observation that suicide rates seemed to be higher in primarily Protestant European countries than in countries that are primarily Catholic, an interesting analysis of European suicide and traffic accident fatality data was carried out by Melinder and Andersson (2001). They calculated death rates per 100 000 inhabitants for 12 western European countries. The researchers found that one group of Catholic countries (Portugal, Spain, and Ireland) are high on traffic fatalities but low on suicides (with a range of 7.1 to 10.7 suicides per 100 000). In contrast there is an opposite group of primarily Protestant countries (Denmark, Finland, Norway, Sweden) that are low on traffic fatalities but high on suicide rates (a range of 15.1 to, in Finland, 29.1 cases per 100 000). The figures demonstrate clearly the impact of the Protestant religions on the rate of suicide, with the figures for Finland being at a level comparable to the "atheist" countries discussed above. As an aside, we might also note that many of the high suicide countries are above a latitude of 50 degrees North, the point above which the winter sun is too weak for the body to manufacture vitamin D. But there is a whole other book to be written about the relationship between geography and longevity.

Meditation and the Psychotherapies

As a clinical psychologist and practising psychotherapist (my most recent book was *Emotion Focused Cognitive Therapy*, 2010) one of the interesting developments in the past 20 years or so has been the incorporation of Eastern religious practices such as meditation into psychological therapies, along with concepts such as compassion and forgiveness which are emphasized in Buddhism in particular. It is especially interesting that the hard-nosed "scientific" end of the psychotherapy spectrum seems to have been most vulnerable to the creeping religiosity that includes many friends and colleagues in clinical psychology in the United Kingdom such as Paul Gilbert (e.g. *The Compassionate Mind*, 2010), Willem Kuyken, John Teasdale, and Mark Williams (e.g. Segal *et al.* (2001), *Mindfulness-Based Cognitive Therapy*). All of them come from within the scientific cognitive-behavioral tradition, some of them are also Christian and some are Buddhist in their religions, but they have all moved to incorporate religious ideas and practices into so-called "third wave" cognitive-behavioral therapies. These developments illustrate both the positive and the negative aspects of religious practices that we have tried to highlight throughout this chapter. As Jerome Frank (1973) emphasized, the psychotherapist, the priest, and the shaman have much in common and when their techniques are effective in providing relief and healing, factors such as shared belief systems, immersing rituals, and a trusting relationship are common to all. Perhaps it should be no surprise then that cognitive-behavioral therapies are now borrowing heavily from the religions. Indeed, Freud's original psychoanalytic method can be seen as a variation and continuation of the Catholic confessional in which God is believed to forgive sinners for their sins and send them out into the world renewed (see Henri Ellenberger, *The Discovery of the Unconscious*, 1970). The important difference is that, despite his interest in religion and its origins, Freud was an atheist because he understood the psychological functions of religion in the way that we have summarized in this book. The problem for my friends and colleagues, the religious scientists, is that they do not share Freud's atheism, because, it could be argued, to date cognitive-behavioral therapies have been directed at a more superficial level (the relief of symptoms in short-term interventions) than have the psychoanalytic therapies. This "superficiality" works well if you have a problem with panic attacks, you want to manage your anxiety better, or you feel depressed following a major life event. However, the cognitive-behavioral therapies are silent when it comes to existential issues, the meaning of life, purpose, and everything. So I do not blame my colleagues, these world-leading cognitive-behavioral therapists, for wanting to go beyond the constraints of a short-term therapy that says nothing about existential problems. However, the warning to be made is that, as we have argued throughout this book, the world's religions provide a comforting illusion that they have the answers, that they can solve all existential problems, but the truths they offer, and the words of gods that they have claimed to document, are a collection of fairytales, some of which may still be believable and some of which are definitely not. Cognitive-behavioral therapies are letting religion enter through the back door. Beware!

Summary and Conclusions

This review of religion and health shows a mix of pluses and minuses for religion in general, with some religions performing better than others, and some people clearly doing well with some religions some of the time. On the plus side, religion can help believers cope with significant stressors and can buffer adversity when it occurs. We saw, for example, that people with *intrinsic* religiosity tend to show the most health benefits from their religiosity, but these benefits probably only occur in some individualistic cultures and at some stages of the lifespan.

These positive effects of religion clearly work through a variety of mechanisms. For example, one benefit is that health behaviors may be more positive because most religions constrain or even prohibit the use of substances such as alcohol and cigarettes, which create significant health problems especially in mid- to later life. A second benefit is the sense of community that can be created by membership of a local religious group and through regular attendance at a church, mosque, or synagogue. This membership provides important sources of social support, both practical and emotional, which contribute to health and longevity. We saw in the previous chapter that membership of some religious groups is increasing rapidly, especially among oppressed and formerly oppressed groups; thus, African-Americans, who have only recently achieved equality in the United States but who still suffer extremes of poverty, deprivation, and unemployment, have turned in large numbers to the Protestant Evangelical movements; and low-caste "Untouchable" Hindus in India have converted in significant numbers to religions such as Buddhism and Christianity, which are less oppressive and not caste-based. Undoubtedly, there will be health and longevity benefits from membership of these religions for these oppressed individuals.

However, the positive effects of religion are not simply reducible to improved health behaviors, social support, and stress buffering during adversity. For those people with a sincere and deep belief in their religious system, there is also an existential benefit, because their religions give them a sense of purpose and meaning in life. It is known that, without these, the feelings of negativity and hopelessness that ensue increase the risk of physical and psychological disorders. We have seen that country-level statistics, even though crude, give a sense of how religious beliefs can protect against, for example, the extremes of depression and suicide; thus, the Islamic countries have near-zero levels of suicide because it is prohibited within the religion (though the high-media profile of the Islamic suicide bomber "martyrs" could mistakenly lead people to believe that suicide rates are higher in Islamic countries).

Humans need a sense of meaning and purpose, and one of the criticisms of science is that it only addresses the "how" questions but not the "why" questions. In fact, the situation with science is even worse. It is not true that science fails to address the "why" questions, because what modern science has actually done is undermine and disprove many of the "why" answers that have been proposed and believed for thousands of years. For example, based on the biblical records in 1650, Bishop Ussher declared that the world was created in 4004 BCE, whereas science has shown that the present universe in fact began about 13.75 billion years ago. However, this scientific fact does not simply replace Bishop Ussher's mistaken calculation, but it also undermines the whole biblical cosmogony, or, as Hawking and Mlodinow (2010) have put it, "It is not necessary to invoke God to light the blue touch paper and set the universe going" (*The Grand Design: New Answers to the Ultimate Questions of Life*, p. 180). The problem for science and our modern scientific age is that science rejects many of the "why" answers that have been proposed, but science can seem to many people to offer little in the way of purpose and meaning. For this reason alone, religions will continue to exist and will continue to be believed because of the human need for meaningfulness.

Before it can be concluded that religions only have positive benefits, it should be noted that we have tried to provide a balanced overview in this chapter of the negatives of religion for health and longevity also. One need only be reminded of the Catholic Church's archaic and punitive views on sexuality that have led to the unnecessary deaths of thousands of people in Africa from AIDS because the Catholic Church opposes the use of condoms with the bizarre view that contraception is "against the will of God." The Catholic Church has really got itself in a mess with its oppressive views on sexuality; sex is prohibited among its elite male clergy, who, as we now know, have caused untold damage to generations of children through widespread child sexual abuse around the world. The negatives of religion include a long list of bizarre beliefs that impact on health and longevity, whether through sexuality, through an unwillingness to use medical interventions (e.g. Jehovah's Witnesses' opposition to blood transfusions), through a promotion of religious terror and war (e.g. the Christian Crusades, the Islamic jihads), and through superiority, patriarchy and misogyny. The health and longevity consequences for some religious believers, in particular the male elite who form religion's patriarchies, are clearly there to be seen and to be measured. However, hidden behind the group statistics that show that on average there may be benefits for religion and religious belief, there are far more complex stories that need to be told. Just as history is written by the victors, religion is the account provided by the patriarchs. In order to get the full picture, we need also to consider history as told by the vanquished and the accounts of the victims of religion.

Finally, we must note again, despite danger of repetition, that the thousands of religions that have existed cannot all be right because they offer such contrasting and contradictory views on life, the supernatural, and the universe. Many religions deal with this panoply of belief systems by believing that they are right and everyone else is wrong. This institutional narcissism points to one conclusion: despite all the benefits of religion for many people, ultimately, all religions have to be wrong. However, the challenge is to learn from the prevalence and level of belief in religion about what must be put in its place, a bit like the recovered alcoholics who cannot simply have alcohol taken out of their lives but need something to be added in so as to replace what alcohol gave them. Similarly, if, as Karl Marx claimed, religion is the opium of the people, we cannot simply take away the opium, but we must replace it with something healthier that can offer similar benefits. This challenge we will endeavour to pursue in the next chapter.

7

How to Be a Healthy Atheist

You can't fool me, there ain't no Sanity Clause.

Chico Marx

Overview

The purpose of this book has not been to state that all religion is bad and therefore that all religions should be banned, in contrast to other recent books. Nor do we predict the demise of religion in the face of the onslaught of science as many sociologists have predicted. Instead, this book has taken a different starting point and asked the question: why, in the face of all the scientific evidence to the contrary, do religions continue to grow in strength and numbers in some parts of the world and in some cultural groups? Drawing primarily on work in psychology, but also with input from philosophy, sociology, and anthropology, we can begin to understand that, although science has now disproved the existence of gods and the supernatural, at least for those who are open to such disproof, we can also understand that belief in gods and the supernatural, especially in the form of organized religions, will persist because of the attraction of understanding, explanation, and benefits that such beliefs offer their followers.

In Chapter 1 we summarized how it is that, at least since Neolithic times, all cultures and groups seem to have had supernatural belief systems. Part of the explanation for the prevalence of such beliefs must be in attempts to explain, understand, and predict *external* cycles and one-off events, such as the progression of the seasons, cycles of birth, life, and death, and events such as thunder and lightning, volcanoes, earthquakes, and the like. These

Adieu to God: Why Psychology Leads to Atheism, First Edition. Mick Power.
© 2012 Mick Power. Published 2012 by John Wiley & Sons, Ltd.

powerful life-threatening cycles and events are beyond the control of humanity. Belief in human-like gods provided an intermediary through which the consequent fear could be managed. Humans believed that they could influence such forces through rituals in which they pleaded with the gods to intervene on their behalf

In Chapter 1 we also emphasized that part of what must have been mysterious to our ancestors was not just these puzzling external events and cycles but also *internal* events and cycles. We examined in detail in Chapter 2 what some of these internal phenomena are most likely to be. First and foremost has to be the unique human experience of consciousness and self-consciousness, which, understandably, can lead to what we have called the "immortality illusion." That is, the experience of consciousness places each experiencer at the center of a unique personal universe, in which that person can experience at least some degree of omnipotence and omniscience and the illusion that the experience should continue eternally. Only under certain circumstances does the immortality illusion become challenged, such as after traumatic life-threatening experiences. For example, people suffering from post-traumatic stress disorder experience a sense of vulnerability and impermanence because of the trauma they have undergone. The emergence of consciousness is, however, one of the notorious "gaps" in scientific explanation into which religious explanations easily fit; thus, it is unclear why complex multicellular organisms such as ourselves should ever develop consciousness. One possible explanation is that the primary driver for consciousness may have been the *social* nature of higher primates such as ourselves for whom an advantage is obtained through being able to model, understand, and predict the mental states of other conspecifics. In the process of the development of this social capacity, we have by default become able to model ourselves as the objects of our own consciousness and, equally, have become able to model ourselves as others see us. Whatever the origin of our capacity for consciousness, one can still marvel at its moment-to-moment experience and the fact that it ever emerged at all from an evolutionary system of biochemicals that grouped together to form simple organisms that then grouped together to form complex multicellular organisms. It is not at all clear that conscious organisms ever needed to emerge from this evolutionary sequence, so it is easy to understand how religious explanations have arisen in which consciousness is equated with a non-physical eternal soul (and variants of this theme).

In Chapter 2 we also considered other common experiences such as dreaming, grief, the loss of significant others, the search for meaning, and mystical experience. For example, the experience of dreaming can be viewed as an entry point into other worlds in which the normal physical laws are no longer viable, in which people who have died or disappeared mysteriously re-emerge, and in which people and animals can fuse with each other. It is therefore no surprise that many religions have viewed dreams with special significance. In the example of the Australian Aboriginal belief system, the Dreamtime is the eternal place occupied by the ancestors to which all will return; thus, dreams are seen to connect a temporary here-and-now earthly state with the eternal Dreamtime state. In many other religions, dreams have been interpreted as revelations from the gods who communicate through the dreamer. We also noted that the common experience of grief at the loss of a loved one is typically accompanied by a range of phenomena which appear to deny the death of that loved one. For example, in Agneta Grimby's (1993) study of grieving people in Sweden, many of them reported experiencing the presence of the deceased person, of having conversations with the person, and of experiencing visual and auditory hallucinations of them. Again, it is no surprise that such psychological phenomena easily lead to the quasi-religious conclusion that the deceased has not actually died but has passed from an earthly state into some form of supernatural state. The important belief is that the deceased person appears to continue to exist in a state to which the grieving person will eventually transform and will then be reunited with the loved one. We suggested that such powerful grieving phenomena could underlie supposed religious miracles such as the resurrection of Jesus through grief-related hallucinations experienced by his possible wife, Mary Magdalene, and his mother, Mary.

Perhaps the most significant experiences that have been considered both by individuals and by religions as proof of the existence of gods and the supernatural have been the so-called mystical or religious experiences. In Chapter 2 we examined a common range of mystical experiences, and in Chapter 3 we looked at some of the more abnormal experiences such as the religious visions that people have also taken as proof of the supernatural. St. Teresa of Avila has been considered by many, including William James, to be the most authoritative documenter of the variety of such mystical experiences that ranged from the more commonplace to the most extraordinary visions of interactions with the supernatural. Religious mystics such as St. Teresa achieve their appeal in part through their complete belief in experiences that other believers are prepared to take at face value. However, despite the beauty and conviction of the experiences of mystics such as Saint Teresa, we must avoid the danger of being lulled into their extraordinary personal universes as if such universes were a reality. Hallucinations and delusional systems built around hallucinations are the bread-and-butter of psychiatry, and whereas few have the beauty and narrative conviction of a St.Teresa, it is a mistake for the rest of us to equate the certainty of the experiencer with truth. In addition to hallucinations and delusions, Saint Teresa describes the types of mystical experiences that many people report and that therefore provide fuel for their religious beliefs. Such experiences typically seem to include a loss of sense of self, a fusion with the surroundings, and a feeling of euphoria or even ecstasy. We suggested that such experiences share much in common with sexual orgasm in that they too involve a sense of union and of ecstasy such as mystics can induce through deprivation of food and sleep and through drug-enhanced induction as seen in many traditional healers or shamans. Again, we must caution against taking the conviction of the experiencer as the truth of the origins of such ecstatic experiences, and look to more commonplace psychological interpretations for their occurrence.

Chapters 4 and 5 considered the social structures and processes of religion and religious organizations and how these provide important social validation for their followers. A summary chronology of the development of religions shows that, as Emile Durkheim (1912) and subsequent sociologists have argued, the social structures imposed on the gods have been reflections of the predominant extant social structures among people themselves. Earlier polytheistic religions with multiple gods and goddesses reflected small nomadic social structures of hunter-gatherer groups. However, the development of larger agriculturally based chiefdoms such as those along the Nile and other Middle Eastern rivers, saw the increased importance of the fertility goddesses and ritual practices that were designed to ensure seasonal fertility cycles and successful crop production. At these times the female goddesses were dominant, though the male gods played essential roles in the fertilization of the earth goddesses. A complex and interacting set of cultural changes that included the development of large urban communities and the capture of female and child slaves in battles, who were then forced into labour and sexual slavery, saw the emergence of patriarchal societies that were dominated by a single male and his offspring, who then established dynastic control over those societies. In what is perhaps the single most important event in religious history, the Egyptian pharaoh, Amenhotep IV, changed his name to Akhenaten and abandoned the polytheistic religion of his predecessors in order to establish the world's first monotheistic religion, which worshipped the sun-god Aten. Although this religion appears to have been rejected early in the reign of his son Tutankhaten, who changed his name to Tutankhamun, there is every possibility that the

Aten-based religion may have survived and then re-emerged in the Egyptian province of Canaan, where it subsequently developed into the religion of Yahweh and Judaism, the starting point for the other great monotheisms of Christianity and Islam. The important point to note, however, is that it is no surprise that the male-dominated societies such as those of the Egyptian pharaoh Akhenaten, who ruled vast empires, not only proposed that the supernatural was arranged with a social structure that was dominated by one male god, but even that they themselves had a special relationship to that god, such that they ruled their subjects as god-kings.

One of the interesting consequences of following this sociological analysis through to the present day is that the age of the god-king and of patriarchal monotheism has mostly now passed and modern social structures are more complex and pluralistic. The prediction could therefore be made that the male monotheisms should be weakened by the demise of the god-king-based dynasties as many societies develop democratically elected, fast-changing, non-hereditary groups, many of whom are increasingly likely to have female leaders (for example Germany, Brazil, the United Kingdom, the United States eventually). Following this argument, the monotheisms should be forced to maintain their popularity with attempts to modify their alpha-male god structure. Pressures of this nature are clear within Catholicism, in which recent centuries have witnessed the promotion of the worship and status of the Virgin Mary through papal pronouncements about her Immaculate Conception and her bodily Assumption into heaven. Her elevation as the "Mother of God" must in part reflect changing societal structures in which women are no longer merely the consorts of male god-kings but are leaders in their own right. So watch out, male monotheisms: as strong as you think you are, your time may have come.

To summarize this overview of the arguments presented in Chapters 1 to 5, we can conclude that there is no puzzle as to why people have always believed in religions and why they will continue to do so. Sociology has been wrong to predict the death of religion because religions provide people with powerful and convincing explanations of common everyday experiences such as the nature of consciousness, and give explanations for unique experiences that may be beyond the commonplace but which may be presented as authentic and with great conviction. Religions offer reward in exchange for belief; they offer freedom to the oppressed, if not in this life, then perhaps in the next. In the promised paradise, the last become first, the crops are always plentiful, the rains never fail, and your enemies have been consigned to eternal hell. Who could resist such an offer? As we reviewed in Chapter 6, religions can also be good for your health, they can lengthen life, they offer purpose and meaning, and they offer a sense of support and belonging. Religions provide off-the-shelf answers to existential issues that may otherwise be too painful to contemplate. It takes courage therefore not to be convinced and manipulated by their promises of paradise, especially given that there is evidence of their possible benefits. In the next section we therefore turn to a detailed analysis of what these benefits are for health, meaning, and longevity, and how such benefits can be obtainable without buying into a religious ideology.

Health, Religion, and Atheism

There are undoubted benefits for many people that result from religious belief systems. As we reviewed in Chapter 6, the benefits include a sense of meaning and purpose, improved health-related behaviors, improved longevity, stress-buffering such as a reduction in the long-term impact of grief following loss of a loved one, and a sense of support through membership of a community-based organization. There are other benefits too that can arise occasionally, such as the receipt of practical help and advice from the religious community, possible religion-based careers, the feeling of superiority and increased self-esteem, and a long-term perspective in the face of adversity. Of course, the story of religion is not a one-sided account of positive achievement and happiness, because there are as many casualties among the followers of religion as there are beneficiaries. Writers such as Christopher Hitchens and Sam Harris have written extensively about the casualties of religion, and we have referred to its adverse effects here. However, this book does not set out to be another Harris or Hitchens volume, but, rather, to attempt to draw from religion a sense of what the multiple benefits might be, and then to begin to sketch what an alternative atheism must look like in order to possess these same benefits for health, happiness, and longevity. In this section, therefore, we will briefly enumerate what these benefits are and consider how the healthy atheist might achieve something similar. We begin with the most challenging existential topic of all, that of achievement of a sense of purpose and meaning.

A Sense of Purpose and Meaning

The primary strength of the religions has to be that they face head-on the crucial existential questions that we all have to deal with. The religions answer these questions of origin, purpose, and cause with a definiteness and confidence such that if you can accept and believe in the answers that a particular religion offers, then you are likely to benefit in multiple ways from that acceptance. However, the first problem that arises from what superficially might sound like an easy and straightforward task is: which one of the many, varied, and contradictory statements of religious purpose and meaning should you subscribe to? The great strength of the religions, in that they all answer the fundamental existential questions, is also their great weakness. One could point to the growth of the monotheisms in the last two millennia and argue that they offer something roughly equivalent in terms of answers. As we argued above, however, the monotheisms are actually anachronisms from the time of the patriarchal and feudal god-king social structures that have been replaced with more complex democratic modern political systems. The absence of the feminine from the monotheisms, both in terms of their supernatural structures and in terms of their patriarchal and hierarchical structures here on Earth, can only become increasingly problematic. But which of the polytheisms and animisms could replace them? Or, more likely, how will the monotheisms evolve to reflect modern society? As we have stated, the answers that religions provide are only a strength if you can buy into them. Otherwise, the answers they offer seem at best to consist of a set of idiosyncratic if sometimes amusing fairytales.

As a consequence, atheism begins with a disadvantage when compared with the religions on the issue of purpose and meaning. At first sight, and especially to those from a religious background, atheism seems to offer a nihilism, or a set of vague answers intended to respond to our need to find meaning and purpose in our existence. The advances of science, summarized briefly in Chapter 1, have challenged most of the religions in significant ways and forced their adherents to take counter-measures or to adapt their belief-systems in important ways. The problem is that many people do not see the methods and answers of science as sufficient, because they wish still to be at the center of a narcissistic universe. However, science tells us that, contrary to what the Bible says, we are not even at the center of our own solar system; that Earth is one among millions of planets that might contain other life-forms; that we are not the end-point of evolution, but we are part of a local process of increased chemical, biochemical, and cellular forms that will continue as long as our universe exists, and then may start again in future universes. Again, the religious believer will point to these statements as a form of nihilism that denies the divine purpose that the gods put humans on the Earth to achieve.

The answer that the atheist must offer the religious believer is that systems based on false beliefs, as superficially attractive as they might seem, are systems that are built like a house of cards and so are nothing to boast about. What atheism has to offer in place of religious delusions are some hard-nosed truths on the one hand, but on the other a realistic sense of the importance of psychological, social, and political values in the provision of a solid base for our belief systems. Although such goal- and value-based systems sound more mundane, they show that a sense of meaning and purpose is possible without necessitating the introduction of imaginary gods into the solution. One need only point to the atheist cultures of the past 100 years to see that a sense of purpose and meaning is just as possible within such societies as it is within a theocracy. Those who have their own religious values might see their absence as the fundamental problem for the Soviet Union, but the Soviet Union collapsed not because of its atheism but because of its internal economic and political instability. To argue that life becomes empty if you take away God is equivalent to saying that life becomes meaningless for children if you take away Santa Claus. We know that, in the story of Santa Claus, we are participating in an enjoyable fantasy game, but we also know and accept that it is a fantasy. Life does not become meaningless without Santa Claus: we simply become more grown-up in our outlook. The first step towards a healthy atheism is to give up these false-god beliefs, and to have the courage to face up to our understanding of the universe and our place in it. Our life beliefs and values need to incorporate these truths and then build our values around the social systems with which we identify, as we will outline in the following sections.

A Sense of Belonging and Community

The importance of social capital has been emphasized by sociologists such as Robert Putnam (2003) in his well-known book *Bowling Alone*. Community involvement and participation have been on the decline over the past 50 years in places such as the United States because of the impact of television on such activities. Yet it is clear from the research that we summarized earlier that one of the clear benefits of religion is the sense of community and belongingness that active membership of a religious group bestows. Regular church attendance can enhance this sense of community and would appear to offer benefits for health and longevity. The evangelical Protestant movements of the southern United States and of South Korea have sought to capitalize on community in their establishment of mega-churches;

similarly, many of the New Religious Movements have sought to establish their own religious communities that work along the lines of the earlier monastic movements established in religions such as Christianity and Buddhism. Putnam (2003) and other sociologists have shown the importance of *volunteering*, that is, the value of engagement in activities that aim to help others such as the young, the elderly, or the disabled. Activities like these are often a normal or expected part of being a member of a religious community, and they bring benefits not only to the recipients of volunteering, but to the volunteers as well.

Perhaps one of the most difficult challenges for atheists is to obtain a sense of community and participation that is equivalent to that obtained by many members of religious groups. There are no obvious equivalents to the sense of community that is obtained from regular church attendance, from the celebration of saints' days and other feast days, and from visits of religious clergy to their communities. Of course, membership of political parties and of pressure groups such as Greenpeace and Amnesty International, and the celebration of family and cultural events, can go some way towards establishing some sense of community for atheists. Indeed, the increased importance of social network groups via the internet may be of particular benefit for atheists. However, there is still a real need for atheists to have a *local* sense of social involvement and participation, which may need to be structured around more mundane hobbies and interests but which require local participation, in order to capture something of the sense of community and belongingness that members of religious groups can obtain very readily.

At this point, however, we also need to remind ourselves once more that not everything is greener and better on the side of religion than on that of atheism. The claimed superiority of each of the monotheisms over everything else, the drive for expansion and conversion within Christianity and Islam, the feuding that has led to the splits that have occurred within Christianity and Islam—all of these factors bring with them a risk to global stability. The global split between Christianity and Islam provides the highest risk of a future world war, especially if the tensions between Judaism and Islam are added into the equation. In sum, between them, the three great monotheisms, although they share beliefs and scriptures, could yet bring about their own great end of days. None of the individual and local benefits that accrue from the monotheisms is worth the exchange for the risk that these religions create for the rest of us. It is attendant on all atheists, who are not burdened with religious prejudices, to step into the void between the religions and lead the way forward. So, even though our starting point in this section was to praise religions for the sense of community that they offer their followers, in the end they must be damned because they view those outside that community as the heathen enemy. The simple splitting that the monotheisms offer as their view of good and evil, in which God and his followers are all good but those who do not follow are all bad, is a crucial part of the global risk of war and misery that they present and that atheism must strive hard to overcome. But what we need is a tolerant atheism that can step into the breach.

A Set of Personal Goals and Values

One of the goals of the movement towards universal education for children has been to offer skills and opportunities to them according to their needs and abilities. Freud identified work and love as the two key factors in well-being, such that finding the right work has to be part of the social opportunities that a society must offer individuals in order to promote the well-being and happiness of its citizens. The opportunities provided by universal education enable the individual to maximize his or her achievable goals and values throughout the lifespan. We have reviewed elsewhere the importance of a range of goals and values in different domains (see Power and Dalgleish, 2008), so we will just examine a couple of relevant issues here. The first issue is to reiterate the importance of education; as we summarized in our review of the nuns study in Chapter 6 (Snowdon, 2001), one of the important factors found in this longitudinal study, and other longitudinal studies of health, is that there is some benefit for longevity from greater length of education. Whatever the mechanisms of this effect on longevity, part of the benefit is likely to be from a continuing positive attitude to learning throughout the lifetime, not simply the more university degrees the better. One suspects that those who value education the most through a prolonged engagement in it during their adolescence and early adulthood maintain this positive view throughout their lifetimes. Such people are the ones who are likely, for example, to see retirement from work as an opportunity for new learning, such as to learn a new language, or to do adult learning courses on computing, or history of art or whatever. The engagement of the brain in new learning throughout the life course seems protective and seems to enhance longevity.

One of the important factors for health, quality of life, and well-being that we have found from work with older adults (Power *et al.*, 2005) is what can be labelled *generativity*. A consistent theme in focus groups with older adults in countries as diverse as China, Japan, Hungary, Norway, Brazil, the United Kingdom and the United States was the need to have made a contribution to society and to the next generation. Such generativity could be through a contribution to children and grandchildren, or it could be achieved through more abstract activities such as the arts, literature, a contribution to sports or hobbies, or knowledge and expertise in a new area. Of course, one of the great and continuing contributions of religion has been its generativity in construction of works of beauty and grandeur, be it the Sagrada Familia Church in Barcelona, the Buddhist and Shinto temples of Kyoto, or the Blue Mosque in Istanbul. Religion has fostered some of the most beautiful works within the arts, though we should now be grateful that present-day popes have abandoned the practice of the castration of choirboys in order to preserve their angelic soprano voices into adulthood as *castrati*. Religions have always had the capacity to go a step too far with human sacrifice. The important point is that we all need to have achieved a sense of generativity, on whatever scale we value such activity. For many people it will simply consist of involvement in the growth and well-being of children and grandchildren. In the context of a close, loving and intimate relationship, most people can achieve a sense of completeness in their lives that does not require the illusory promises of religion.

A Healthy Lifestyle

One of the clear benefits of religions is in their promotion of positive health-related behaviors, though there is the occasional downside as we saw with the Catholic Church's confused and misogynistic views on sexuality that have contributed to the AIDS crisis in Africa and to worldwide sexual abuse of children by its clergy. But let us leave these obvious negatives aside for a moment in order to focus on the positive contribution that religions make towards health behaviors among their followers. As we saw in Chapter 6, religions generally discourage drug and alcohol abuse, smoking and gluttony, and encourage a balanced lifestyle with exercise and respect for oneself and one's body. From the studies that we reviewed, the least religious people seem to be most at risk for excesses or problems in one or more of these areas, though what is cause and what is effect is unclear. As we stated in Chapter 6, we are not here to write a book about the details of what a healthy lifestyle should be. We have, however, tried to highlight what is, in the main, the positive contribution of religious belief to health and longevity, although it does not in itself explain away all the benefits of religion. The challenge for atheists therefore is to take what is good from religion while avoiding that which is bad.

One interesting area of work in relation to religious practices concerns the examination of the possible benefits of meditation and prayer. The benefits of meditation have become so clear that many Western psychotherapies have even begun to include it in their practice for people with a range of psychological and physical problems. The actual practice of meditation encourages the development and use of a mode of consciousness in which the individual steps back from an immersion in experience in order to become an observer of the self that is undergoing that experience. Such a capacity provides a high-level emotion regulation strategy that may be particularly useful when the individual is experiencing times of stress (Power, 2010). However, as we saw in Chapter 6, the evidence to date on the claims for the benefit of prayer are much more mixed. Some of the research seems to have verged on the fraudulent, but then religions have always been vulnerable—as we have seen throughout this book—to the fraudulent if charming psychopath of the Joseph Smith and the origins of Mormonism variety. In the case of prayer, the most reliable and credible studies do not show that petitionary or intercessory prayer is of any proven benefit. This is not to doubt the claims of religious individuals that prayer is of personal benefit to them, only to point out that the mechanisms of that benefit are not from the intercession of the supernatural, but through a psychological process of emotion regulation and narrative construction which helps to induce meditation and prayer, the benefits of which are not of supernatural origin but take a more psychological form. The practice of meditation does not require the purchase of a lorry-load of religious beliefs, but can be part of the day-to-day lifestyle practices of any atheist.

Conclusion

Reports of the death of religion are clearly premature. An examination of the psychological and social benefits of religions generally shows that these are numerous and not easily replaced for many individuals. The benefits and believable explanations range across unique but puzzling everyday experiences such as personal consciousness, dreaming, and the search for meaning and purpose. Religions also offer a powerful sense of community and belongingness that often covers not only one's earthly existence but perhaps also one's eternal existence in a paradisiacal afterlife. The advances in the physical and biological sciences have proven that there are no gods and no supernatural forces, so the puzzle is why religions continue and even grow in strength. The answer that we have offered in this book is that religions must also be viewed in terms of the psychological and social benefits that they offer their followers. This is why advances in the physical and biological sciences will not be sufficient in themselves to lead to the demise of religious belief. We have seen how many of the religions have come to adapt their belief systems, albeit reluctantly, to developments in the sciences, for example through the acceptance of the metaphorical nature of books such as the Bible, and the acceptance of processes such as evolution and the scientific origins of the universe. Religions are not going to roll over that easily to science, and may even be beginning to gain a new confidence because they retain and increase their following in many parts of the world despite the advances in science. However, the psychological and social sciences offer a different level of understanding as to why religions persist. It takes courage to face up to the truths about existence and the infinitesimally small part that we play in the universe. To face up to those truths without falling into nihilism or despair is what a humanistically based atheism must offer. In the end, there are no gods. There are only despots who would have you follow them for their own purposes.

References

Abbo, C., Ekblad, S., Waako, P., *et al.* (2009). The prevalence and severity of mental illnesses handled by traditional healers in two districts in Uganda. *African Health Sciences*, 9, Supplement 1, 516–522.

Allan, K. and Burridge, K. (2006). *Forbidden Words: Taboo and the Censoring of Language.* Cambridge: Cambridge University Press.

Allport, G.W. and Ross, J.M. (1967). Personal religious orientation and prejudice. *Journal of Personality and Social Psychology*, 5, 432–443.

American Psychiatric Association (1994). *Diagnostic and Statistical Manual of Mental Disorders*, 4th edn. Washington, DC: APA.

Ano, G.G. and Vasconcelles, E.B. (2005). Religious coping and psychological adjustment to stress: A meta-analysis. *Journal of Clinical Psychology*, 61, 461–480.

Argyle, M. (2000). *Psychology and Religion: An Introduction.* London: Routledge.

Armstrong, K. (2005). *A Short History of Myth.* Edinburgh: Canongate.

Armstrong, K. (2007). *The Bible: The Biography.* London: Atlantic Books.

Avila, St. T. (1957). *The Life of Saint Teresa of Avila by Herself.* London: Penguin Books.

Baetz, M. and Toews, J. (2009). Clinical implications of research on religion, spirituality, and mental health. *Canadian Journal of Psychiatry*, 54, 292–301.

Bahr, H.M. and Albrecht, S.L. (1989). Strangers once more: Patterns of disaffiliation from Mormonism. *Journal for the Scientific Study of Religion*, 28, 180–200.

Baigent, M., Leigh, R., and Lincoln, H. (1983). *Holy Blood, Holy Grail.* New York: Bantam Dell.

Baker, J. (2008). An investigation of the sociological patterns of prayer frequency and content. *Sociology of Religion*, 69, 169–185.

Banville, J. (1999). *Doctor Copernicus.* London: Picador.

Barrow, J.D. and Tipler, F.J. (1988). *The Anthropic Cosmological Principle.* New York: Oxford University Press.

Benson, H., Dusek, J.A., Sherwood, J.B., *et al.* (2006). Study of the therapeutic effects of intercessory prayer (STEP) in cardiac bypass patients: A multicenter randomized trial of uncertainty and certainty of receiving intercessory prayer. *American Heart Journal*, 151, 934–942.

Bentall, R.P. (2003). *Madness Explained: Psychosis and Human Nature*. London: Allen Lane.

Bertolote, J.M. and Fleischmann, A. (2002). A global perspective in the epidemiology of suicide. *Suicidology*, 7, 6–8.

Blair, J., Mitchell, D. and Blair, K. (2005). *The Psychopath: Emotion and the Brain*. Oxford: Blackwell.

Bloch, M. (1989). The disconnection between power and rank as a process: an outline of the development of kingdoms in central Madagascar, in *Ritual, History and Power: Selected papers in Anthropology*. Oxford: Berg Publishers.

Bocaccio, G. (1353/2003). *The Decameron*. London: Penguin.

Bonanno, G.A., Wortman, C.B., and Nesse, R.M. (2004). Prospective patterns of resilience and maladjustment during widowhood. *Psychology and Aging*, 19, 260–271.

Bowlby, J. (1980). *Attachment and Loss. Vol. 3: Sadness and Depression*. London: Hogarth Press.

Boyce, M. (2001). *Zoroastrians: Their Religious Beliefs and Practices*. London: Routledge.

Brown, D. (2004). *The Da Vinci Code*. London: Corgi.

Byrd, R.C. (1988). Positive therapeutic effects of intercessory prayer in a coronary care unit population. *Southern Medical Journal*, 81, 826–829.

Carrico, A.W., Ironson, G., Antoni, M.H., *et al.* (2006). A path model of the effects of spirituality on depressive symptoms and 24-h urinary-free cortisol in HIV-positive persons. *Journal of Psychosomatic Research*, 61, 51–58.

Carter, B. (1974). Large number coincidence and the anthropic principle in cosmology, in *Confrontation of Cosmological Theories with Observational Data* (ed. M.S. Longair). Dordrecht: Reidel.

Cavalli-Sforza, L.L., Feldman, M.W., Chen, K.H., *et al.* (1982). Theory and observation in cultural transmission. *Science*, 218, 19–27.

Cha, K.Y., Wirth, D.P., and Lobo, R.A. (2001). Does prayer influence the success of in vitro fertilization-embryo transfer? Report of a masked, randomized trial. *Journal of Reproductive Medicine*, 46, 781–787.

Chen, Y.Y. and Koenig, H.G. (2006). Do people turn to religion in times of stress? An examination of change in religiousness among elderly, medically ill patients. *Journal of Nervous and Mental Disease*, 194, 114–120.

Cohen, A.B. and Hill, P.C. (2007). Religion as culture: religious individualism and collectivism among American Catholics, Jews and Protestants. *Journal of Personality*, 75, 709–742.

Conroy, R.M., Siriwardena, R., Smyth, O., *et al.* (2000). The relation of health anxiety and attitudes to doctors and medicine to use of alternative and complementary treatments in general practice patients. *Psychology, Health and Medicine*, 5, 203–212.

Crick, F. (1994). *The Astonishing Hypothesis: The Scientific Search for the Soul*. New York: Simon and Schuster.

Crockett, A. and Voas, D. (2006). Generations of decline: Religious change in 20th-century Britain. *Journal for the Scientific Study of Religion*, 45, 567–584.

Darwin, C. (1859/1996). *On the Origin of Species*. Oxford: Oxford University Press.

Darwin, C. (1871/2004). *The Descent of Man*. London: Penguin.

David, R. (1998) *The Ancient Egyptians: Beliefs and Practices*. Brighton: Sussex Academic Press.

Davies, G.M. and Dalgleish, T. (2001) (Eds). *Recovered Memories: Seeking the Middle Ground*. Chichester: Wiley.

Dawkins, R. (1976). *The Selfish Gene*. Oxford: Oxford University Press.

Dawkins, R. (2006). *The God Delusion*. London: Bantam Press.

Dennett, D. (1991). *Consciousness Explained*. Boston: Little Brown.

De Roos, S.A., Iedema, J. and Miedema, S. (2004). Influence of maternal denomination, god concepts, and child-rearing practices on young children's god concepts. *Journal for the Scientific Study of Religion*, 43, 519–535.

Dickie, J.R., Eshleman, A.K., Merasco, D.M., *et al*. (1997). Parent-child relationships and children's images of god. *Journal for the Scientific Study of Religion*, 36, 25–43.

Domhoff, W. (2003). *The Scientific Study of Dreams: Neural Networks, Cognitive Development, and Content Analysis*. Washington, DC: American Psychological Association.

Drevenstadt, G.L. (1998). Race and ethnic differences in the effects of religious attendance on subjective health. *Review of Religious Research*, 37, 19–32.

Durkheim, E. (1897). *Suicide*. London: Routledge and Kegan Paul.

Durkheim, E. (1912). *The Elementary Forms of Religious Life*. New York: Free Press.

Ehrsson, H.H. (2007). The experimental induction of out-of-body experiences. *Science*, 317, 1048.

Ellenberger, H. (1970). *The Discovery of the Unconscious: The History and Evolution of Dynamic Psychiatry*. New York: Basic Books.

Erickson, J.A. (1992). Adolescent religious development and commitment: a structural equation model of the role of family, peer group, and educational influences. *Journal for the Scientific Study of Religion*, 31, 131–152.

Fenix, J.B., Cherlin, E.J., Prigerson, H.G., *et al*. (2006). Religiousness and major depression among bereaved family caregivers: a 13-month follow-up study. *Journal of Palliative Care*, 22, 286–292.

Fennell, M.J.V. and Teasdale, J.D. (1987). Cognitive therapy for depression: individual differences and the process of change. *Cognitive Therapy and Research*, 11, 253–271.

Festinger, L., Riecken, H.W., and Schachter, S. (1956). *When Prophecy Fails*. Minneapolis: Minnesota University Press.

Field, N.P. and Filanosky, C. (2010). Continuing bonds, risk factors for complicated grief, and adjustment to bereavement. *Death Studies*, 34, 1–29.

Frank, J.D. (1973). *Persuasion and Healing: A Comparative Study of Psychotherapy.* New York: Schocken Books.

Franklin, S.B. (1991). *Promise of Paradise: A Woman's Intimate Story of the Perils of Life with Rajneesh.* New York: Station Hill Press.

Freeman, C. and Power, M.J. (2007) (Eds). *Handbook of Evidence-Based Psychotherapies.* Chichester: Wiley.

Freud, S. (1900). The Interpretation of Dreams. London: Hogarth Press.

Freud, S. (1914). On Narcissism. London: Hogarth Press.

Freud, S. (1927). The Future of an Illusion. London: Hogarth Press.

Freud, S. (1937). Moses and Monotheism. London: Hogarth Press.

Garcia-Albea, E. (2003). The ecstatic epilepsy of Teresa of Jesus. *Revista de Neurologia*, 37, 879–887.

Gearing, R.E. and Lizardi, D. (2009). Religion and suicide. *Journal of Religion and Health*, 48, 332–341.

Geertz, C. (1966). Religion as a Cultural System, in Anthropological Approaches to the Study of Religion (ed. M Banton). London: Tavistock.

Geertz, C. (1973). *The Interpretation of Cultures.* New York: Basic Books.

Gilbert, P. (2010). *The Compassionate Mind.* London: Constable.

Green, M. and Elliott, M. (2010). Religion, health, and psychological well-being. *Journal of Religion and Health*, 49, 149–163.

Greyson, B. (1990). Near-death encounters with and without near-death experiences: Comparative NDE Scale profiles. *Journal of Near Death Studies*, 8, 151–161.

Grimby, A. (1993). Bereavement among elderly people: grief reactions, post-bereavement hallucinations and quality of life. *Acta Psychiatrica Scandinavica*, 87, 72–80.

Harris, S. (2004). *The End of Faith: Religion, Terror, and the Future of Reason.* London: Free Press.

Hawking, S. and Mlodinow, L. (2010). *The Grand Design.* London: Bantam Press.

Hayes, B.C. and Pittelkow, Y. (1993). Religious belief, transmission, and the family: an Australian study. *Journal of Marriage and the Family*, 55, 755–766.

Headley, M. (2010). *Blown for Good: Behind the Iron Curtain of Scientology.* Burbank: BFG Books.

Hidalgo, M. (2007). *Sexual Abuse and the Culture of Catholicism: How Priests and Nuns Become Perpetrators.* New York: Haworth Press.

Higham, C. (2001). *The Civilization of Angkor.* London: Phoenix.

Hitchens, C. (2007). *God Is Not Great: How Religion Poisons Everything.* London: Atlantic Books.

Horsfall, S. (2000). The experience of Marian apparitions and the Mary cult. *The Social Science Journal*, 37, 375–384.

Hubbard, L.R. (1950). *Dianetics: The Modern Science of Mental Health.* New York: Bridge Publications.

Hume, D. (1748/2007). Of Miracles. In An Enquiry Concerning Human Understanding. Oxford: Oxford University Press.

Hummer, R.A., Ellison, C.G., Rogers, R.G., *et al.* (2004). Religious involvement and adult mortality in the United States: Review and perspective. *Southern Medical Journal,* 97, 1223–1230.

Humphrey, N. (2008). *The Mind Made Flesh: Essays from the Frontiers of Psychology and Evolution.* Oxford: Oxford University Press.

Hutton, J. (1795/2010). *A Theory of the Earth with Proofs and Illustrations.* Amazon: Kindle Edition.

Idler, E.L. and Kasl, S.V. (1992). Religion, disability, depression and the timing of death. *American Journal of Sociology,* 97, 1052–1079.

James, W. (1902). *The Varieties of Religious Experience.* New York: Longman Green.

Janoff-Bulman, R. and Frantz, C.M. (1997). The impact of trauma on meaning: From meaningless world to meaningful life, in *The Transformation of Meaning in Psychological Therapies: Integrating Theory and Practice* (eds M.J. Power and C.R. Brewin). Chichester: Wiley.

Jay, T. (2000). *Why We Curse: A Neuro-Psycho-Social Theory of Speech.* Philadelphia: John Benjamins.

John Jay College (2004). *The Nature and Scope of the Problem of the Sexual Abuse of Minors by Catholic Priests and Deacons in the United States.* Washington: US Conference of Catholic Bishops.

Johnson, S.C. and Spilka, B. (1991). Outcome research and religious psychotherapies: Where are we and where are we going? *Journal of Psychology and Theology,* 21, 297–308.

Johnson, W.B. and Eastburg, M.C. (1992). God, parent and self concepts in abused and nonabused children. *Journal of Psychology and Christianity,* 11, 235–243.

Johnson-Laird, P. (1988). *The Computer and the Mind: An Introduction to Cognitive Science.* London: Fontana.

Johnson-Laird, P. (2008). *How We Reason.* Oxford: Oxford University Press.

Kant, I. (1795/2007). *Perpetual Peace.* London: Penguin.

Kaptchuk, T.J., Kelley, J.M., Conboy, L.A., *et al.* (2008). Components of placebo effect: randomised controlled trial in patients with irritable bowel syndrome. *British Medical Journal,* 336, 999–1007.

Kenez, P. (2006). *A History of the Soviet Union from the Beginning to the End,* 2nd edn. Cambridge: Cambridge University Press.

Kern, U., Busch, V., Rockland, M., *et al.* (2009). Prevalence and risk factors of phantom limb pain and phantom limb sensations in Germany. A nationwide field survey. *Schmerz,* 23, 479–488.

Knight, C. and Lomas, R. (1997). *The Hiram Key: Pharaohs, Freemasons and the Discovery of the Secret Rolls of Christ.* London: Arrow.

Koenig, H.G. (2009). Research on religion, spirituality, and mental health: a review. *Canadian Journal of Psychiatry*, 54, 283–291.

Koenig, H.G., McCullough, M.E., and Larson, D.B. (2001). *Handbook of Religion and Health*. Oxford: Oxford University Press.

Kohlberg, L. (1969). *Stages in the Development of Moral Thought and Action*. New York: Holt, Rinehart and Winston.

Kopp, S.B. (1986). *If You Meet The Buddha On The Road, Kill Him: The Pilgrimage of Psychotherapy Patients*. Toronto: Bantam Books.

Kramer, H. and Sprenger, J. (1487/1951). *Malleus Maleficarum [The Witches Hammer]*. London: Hogarth Press.

Krucoff, M.W., Crater, S.W., Gallup, D., *et al.* (2005). Music, imagery, touch, and prayer as adjuncts to interventional cardiac care: The monitoring and actualization of noetic trainings (MANTRA) II randomized study. *Lancet*, 366, 211–217.

Lambek, M. (1981). *Human Spirits: A Cultural Account of Trance in Mayotte*. New York: Cambridge University Press.

Lawton, L.E. and Bures, R. (2001). Parental divorce and the "switching" of religious identity. *Journal for the Scientific Study of Religion*, 40, 99–111.

Lenggenhager, B., Tadi, T., Metzinger, T., *et al.* (2007). Video ergo sum: Manipulating bodily self-consciousness. *Science*, 317, 1096–1099.

Lerner, G. (1986). *The Creation of Patriarchy*. Oxford: Oxford University Press.

Leslie, A.M. (1994). ToMM, ToBY and agency: core architecture and domain specificity, in *Mapping the Mind* (eds L.A. Hirschfield and S.A. Gelman). New York: Cambridge University Press.

Lewis-Williams, D. (2010). *Conceiving God: The Cognitive Origin and Evolution of Religion*. London: Thames and Hudson.

Levav, I., Kohn, R., Golding, J.M., *et al.* (1997). Vulnerability of Jews to affective disorders. *American Journal of Psychiatry*, 154, 941–947.

Levi-Strauss, C. (1962) *The Savage Mind*. Chicago: University of Chicago Press.

Lindsay, M.D. (2008). Mind the gap: Religion and the crucible of marginality in the United States and Great Britain. *The Sociological Quarterly*, 49, 653–688.

Lodge, D. (1995). *Therapy*. London: Viking Press.

Loewenthal, K.M. (2000). *The Psychology of Religion: A Short Introduction*. Oxford: Oneworld.

Loewenthal, K.M. (2008). The alcohol–depression hypothesis: gender and the prevalence of depression among Jews, in *Comorbidity of Depression and Alcohol Use Disorders* (ed. L. Sher). New York: Nova Science Publishers.

Loewenthal, K.M. (2011). Religion, spirituality and culture, in *APA Handbook of Psychology, Religion, and Spirituality* (K.I. Pargament *et al.* eds). in press.

Loewenthal, K.M., MacLeod, A.K., Goldblatt, V., *et al.* (2000). Comfort and joy? Religion, cognition, and mood in Protestants and Jews under stress. *Cognition and Emotion*, 14, 355–374.

Long, J. (2005). *Biblical Nonsense: A Review of the Bible for Doubting Christians.* New York: iUniverse.

MacCulloch, D. (2009). *A History of Christianity.* London: Allen Lane.

Machiavelli, N. (1532/2003). *The Prince.* London: Penguin.

Mah, K. and Binik, Y.M. (2002). Do all orgasms feel alike? Evaluating a two-dimensional model of the orgasm experience across gender and sexual context. *Journal of Sex Research*, 39, 104–113.

McCullough, M.E., Hoyt, W.T., Larson, D.B., *et al.* (2000). Religious involvement and mortality: a meta-analytic review. *Health Psychology*, 19, 211–222.

McGregor, I., Nash, K., and Prentice, M. (2010). Reactive approach motivation (RAM) for religion. *Journal of Personality and Social Psychology*, 99, 148–161.

McHugh, P.R., Lief, H.I., Freyd, P.P., *et al.* (2004). From refusal to reconciliation: family relationships after an accusation based on recovered memories. *Journal of Nervous and Mental Disease*, 192, 525–531.

McIntosh, D.N., Silver, R.C. and Wortman, C.B. (1993). Religion's role in adjusting to a negative life event: coping with the loss of a child. *Journal of Personality and Social Psychology*, 65, 812–821.

Melinder, K.A. and Andersson, R. (2001). The impact of structural factors on the injury rate in different European countries. *European Journal of Public Health*, 11, 301–308.

Milne, H. (1986). *Bhagwan: The God That Failed.* London: St Martin's Press.

Morris, J.C. and Whitcomb, H.M. (1961). *The Genesis Flood.* New York: The Presbyterian and Reformed Publishing Co.

Moussavi, S., Chatterji, S., Verdes, E., *et al.* (2007). Depression, chronic diseases, and decrements in health: results from the World Health Surveys. *Lancet*, 370, 851–858.

Newman, L.S. and Baumeister, R.F. (1998). Abducted by aliens: spurious memories of interplanetary masochism, in *Truth in Memory* (S.J. Lynn and K.M. McConkey, eds). New York: Guilford.

Nonnemaker, J.M., McNeely, C.A. and Blum, R.W. (2003). Public and private domains of religiosity and adolescent health risk behaviours: evidence from the National Longitudinal Study of Adolescent Health. *Social Science and Medicine*, 57, 2049–2054.

Nordin, A. (2009). Ritual agency, substance transfer and the making of supernatural immediacy in pilgrim journeys. *Journal of Cognition and Culture*, 9, 195–233.

Oxman, T.E., Freeman, D.H. and Manheimer, E.D. (1995). Lack of social participation or religious strength and comfort as risk factors for death after cardiac surgery in the elderly. *Psychosocial Medicine*, 57, 5–15.

Pargament, K.I. (1997). *The Psychology of Religion and Coping: Theory, Research, Practice.* New York: Guilford Press.

Piaget, J. (1954). *The Construction of Reality in the Child.* London: Routledge and Kegan Paul.

Pope Paul VI (1968). *Humanae Vitae.* Vatican: Catholic Truth Society.

Post, P., Pieper, J., and van Uden, M. (1998). *The Modern Pilgrim: Multidisciplinary Explorations of Christian Pilgrimage.* Leuven: Uitgeverij Peeters.

Power, M.J. (1997). Conscious and unconscious representations of meaning, in *The Transformation of Meaning in Psychological Therapies.* (eds M.J. Power and C.R. Brewin). Chichester: Wiley.

Power, M.J. (2001). Memories of abuse and alien abduction: close encounters of the therapeutic kind, in *Recovered Memories: Seeking the Middle Ground* (eds G.M. Davies and T. Dalgleish). Chichester: Wiley.

Power, M.J. (2005) (Ed.). *Mood Disorders: A Handbook of Science and Practice.* Chichester: Wiley.

Power, M.J. (2010). *Emotion Focused Cognitive Therapy.* Chichester: Wiley.

Power, M.J. and Dalgleish, T. (2008). *Cognition and Emotion: From Order to Disorder,* 2nd Edn. Hove: Erlbaum.

Power, M.J., Quinn, K., Schmidt, S., *et al.* (2005). Development of the WHOQOL-OLD module. *Quality of Life Research,* 14, 2197–2214.

Pullman, P. (2010). *The Good Man Jesus and the Scoundrel Christ.* Edinburgh: Canongate.

Putnam, R. (2003). *Bowling Alone: The Collapse and Revival of American Community.* New York: Simon and Schuster.

Radcliffe-Brown, A.R. (1922). *The Andaman Islanders.* New York: Free Press.

Rappaport, R.A. (1999). *Ritual and Religion in the Making of Humanity.* Cambridge: Cambridge University Press.

Ringdal, G.I. (1996). Religiosity, quality of life, and survival in cancer patients. *Social Indicators Research,* 38, 193–211.

Rizzutto, A.M. (1979). *The Birth of the Living God: A Psychoanalytic Study.* Chicago: University of Chicago Press.

Rushdie, S. (1988). *The Satanic Verses.* London: Vintage.

Ruthven, M. (2000). *Islam: A Very Short Introduction,* 2nd edn. Oxford: Oxford University Press.

Samarin, W.J. (1972). *Tongues of Men and Angels: Religious Languages of Pentecostalism.* New York: Collier Macmillan.

Saroglou, V. and Fiasse, L. (2003). Birth order, personality, and religion: a study among young adults from a three-sibling family. *Personality and Individual Differences,* 35, 19–29.

Searle, J. (1997). *The Mystery of Consciousness.* London: Granta.

Segal, Z.V., Williams, J.M.G., and Teasdale, J.D. (2001). *Mindfulness-Based Cognitive Therapy for Depression: A New Approach to Preventing Relapse.* New York: Guilford.

Shermer, M. (2003). *How We Believe: Science, Skepticism, and the Search for God*, 2nd edn. New York: Freeman.

Shushan, G. (2009). *Conceptions of the Afterlife in Early Civilizations*. London: Continuum International Publishing Group.

Smart, J.J.C. and Haldane, J.J. (2003). *Atheism and Theism*, 2nd edn. Oxford: Blackwell.

Smith, T.B., McCullough, M.E., and Poll, J. (2003). Religiousness and depression: evidence for a main effect and the moderating influence of stressful life events. *Psychological Bulletin*, 129, 614–636.

Snowdon, D. (2001). *Aging with Grace*. London: Fourth Estate.

Solomon, S., Greenberg, J., and Pyszczynski, T. (1991). A terror management theory of social behaviour, in *Advances in Experimental Social Psychology*, 24 (ed. M.P. Zanna). New York: Academic Press.

Stokes, C.E. and Regnerus, M.D. (2009). When faith divides family: religious discord and adolescent reports of parent–child relations. *Social Science Research*, 38, 155–167.

Stork, J. (2009). *Breaking the Spell: My Life as a Rajneshee and the Long Journey Back to Freedom*. Sydney: Pan Macmillan.

Storr, A. (1996). *Feet of Clay: A Study of Gurus*. London: Harper Collins.

Stroebe, M.S., Hansson, R.O., Stroebe, W., *et al.* (2001) (Eds). *Handbook of Bereavement Research*. Washington: American Psychological Association.

Swanson, G.E. (1960). *The Birth of the Gods*. Michigan: University of Michigan Press.

Terry, K.J. (2008). Stained glass: The nature and scope of child sexual abuse in the Catholic Church. *Criminal Justice and Behavior*, 35, 549–569.

Van de Port, M. (2005). Candomblé in pink, green, and black: Re-scripting the Afro-Brazilian religious heritage in the public sphere of Salvador, Bahia. *Social Anthropology*, 13, 3–26.

Van Lommel, P., van Wees, R., Meyers, V., *et al.* (2001). Near-death experience in survivors of cardiac arrest: A prospective study in the Netherlands. *Lancet*, 358, 2039–2045.

Vergote, A. and Tamayo, A. (1980). *The Parental Figures and the Representation of God*. The Hague: Mouton.

Voas, D. and Crockett, A. (2005). Religion in Britain: Neither believing nor belonging. *Sociology*, 39, 11–28.

Vossler, M.T. (2009). *Jedi Manual Basic—Introduction to Jedi Knighthood*. New York: Dreamz-Work Productions.

Wallace, D. (2010). *The Jedi Path: A Manual for Students of the Force* (Vault Edition). New York: Becker and Meyer.

Watts, F. and Williams, J.M.G. (1988). *The Psychology of Religious Knowing*. Cambridge: Cambridge University Press.

Weber, M. (1922/1947). *The Sociology of Religion.* Boston: Beacon Press.

Western Shugden Society (2010). *A Great Deception: The Ruling Lama's Policies.* London: Western Shugden Society.

Wolf, E.R. (1958). The Virgin of Guadalupe: a Mexican national symbol. *Journal of American Folklore,* 121, 34–39.

Woods, B. (2009). *Deceived: One Woman's Stand Against the Church of Scientology.* Worthing: Bonnie Woods.

Wright, R. (2009). *The Evolution of God.* New York: Little Brown.

Zhang, J., Wieczorek, W., Conwell, Y., *et al.* (2010). Characteristics of young rural Chinese suicides: a psychological autopsy study. *Psychological Medicine,* 40, 581–589.

Author Index

Abbo, C., 154
Albrecht, S.L., 49
Allan, K., 131
Allport, G.W., 144, 148
American Psychiatric Association, 121
Andersson, R., 161
Ano, G.G., 150
Applewhite, M., 128
Argyle, M., 47
Aristotle, 21–2
Armstrong, K., 5, 7, 44
Arnada, E., 132
Athanasius, 100

Baetz, M., 143–144
Bahr, H.M., 49
Baigent, M., 45
Baker, J., 109, 147
Banville, J., 22
Barrow, J., 25
Baumeister, R.F., 79–80
Benson, H., 146
Bentall, R., 67
Bertolote, J.M., 160
Binik, Y., 56
Blair, J., 53
Blanke, O., 71

Bloch, M., 107
Bocaccio, G., 60
Bonanno, G., 46
Bowlby, J., 43, 98
Boyce, M., 12
Brown, D., 45, 136
Bures, R., 49
Burns, R., 36–7
Burridge, K., 131
Byrd, R.C., 145

Carrico, A.W., 144
Carter, B., 25
Cavalli-Sforza, L.L., 101
Cendrars, B., 46
Cervantes, M., 54
Cha, K.Y., 146–7
Chen, Y.Y., 149
Cho, D.Y., 103–4
Christie, A., 73
Clarke, A.C., 124
Cohen, A.B., 148
Conroy, R.M., 154
Copernicus, N., 22, 26, 124
Crick, F., 41, 43
Crockett, A., 101
Cromwell, O., 91–2

Adieu to God: Why Psychology Leads to Atheism, First Edition. Mick Power.
© 2012 Mick Power. Published 2012 by John Wiley & Sons, Ltd.

Dalgleish, T., 36, 63, 79, 176
Darwin, C., 23–4, 58
David, R., 8, 58
Davies, G., 79
Davies, P., 20
Dawkins, R., 25, 30, 37, 49–50, 99, 102, 146
Dennett, D., 35
De Roos, S.A., 48
Descartes, R., 35, 77
Dickie, J.R., 48, 98
Domhoff, W., 41, 43
Drevenstadt, G.L., 148
Durkheim, E., 4, 89, 95, 97, 102, 160, 170

Eastburg, M.C., 48
Ehrsson, H.H., 71
Ellenberger, H., 151, 162
Elliott, M., 143
Erickson, J.A., 101
Evans-Pritchard, E., 4
Ewing, J., 85

Fenix, J.B., 46, 142
Fennell, M., 154
Festinger, L., 129
Fiasse, L., 101
Field, N.P., 44
Filanosky, C., 44
Fleischmann, A., 160
Frank, J., 150–152, 154, 156, 161
Franklin, B., 138
Franklin, S.B., 114
Frantz, C.M., 69
Freeman, C., 150, 153
Freud, S., 4, 14–15, 38, 40–41, 43, 47, 55, 57, 69, 97–98, 162, 176

Galileo, G., 22–24, 124
Garcia-Albea, E., 63
Gearing, R.E., 160

Geertz, C., 98, 107
Gilbert, P., 161
Green, M., 143
Greenberg, J., 69
Greyson, B., 71
Grimby, A., 43–45, 169

Haldane, J., 50
Harris, S., 106, 159, 172
Hawking, S., 164
Hayes, B.C., 101
Headley, M., 125
Hidalgo, M., 135–6
Higham, C., 28
Hill, P.C., 148
Hitchens, C., 64, 172
Horney, K., 97
Horsfall, S., 67
Hubbard, L.R., 124–5, 129
Hume, D., 83–4
Hummer, R.A., 143
Humphrey, N., 37
Hutton, J., 23

Idler, E.L., 143

James, C., 114
James, W., 3, 33, 54, 82, 89, 149, 156, 169
Janoff-Bulman, R., 69
Jay, T., 131
Johnson, S.C., 147
Johnson, W.B., 48
Johnson-Laird, P., 35, 129
Jung, C.G., 55

Kasl, S.V., 143
Kant, I., 107
Kaptchuk, T.J., 153
Kelly, G., 3
Kelvin, L., 24
Kenez, P., 38

Kern, U., 47
Knight, C., 137
Knox, J., 53
Koenig, H.G., 143, 145, 149
Kohlberg, L., 51
Kopp, S., 123
Kramer, H., 117
Krucoff, M.W., 145
Kuyken, W., 161

Lambek, M., 73
Larson, D., 145
Lawton, L.E., 49
Lenggenhager, B., 71
Lerner, G., 97, 115–6
Leslie, A., 40
Levav, I., 143
Levi-Strauss, C., 4, 28, 40
Lewis-Williams, D., 29, 55
Lindsay, M.D., 102
Lizardi, D., 160
Lobo, R., 147
Lodge, D., 157
Loewenthal, K., 48, 83, 108, 143,
    148–150
Lomas, R., 137
Long, J., 29
Lucas, G., 125
Luther, M., 53, 102, 110
Luxenberg, C., 159
Lyell, C., 23

MacCulloch, D., 22, 58, 65, 78, 91,
    134
Machiavelli, N., 37
Mah, K., 56
Marx, K., 165
McCullough, M., 145, 148
McGregor, I., 149
McHugh, P.R., 79
McIntosh, D.N., 148
Melinder, K.A., 161

Miller, W., 127
Milne, H., 114
Mlodinow, L., 164
Morris, H., 25
Moussavi, S., 152

Nettles, B., 128
Newman, L.S., 79–80
Newton, I., 22, 136
Nonnemaker, J.M., 159
Nordin, A., 157

Owen, R., 24
Oxman, T.E., 148

Pargament, K.I., 144
Pascal, B., 30–31
Piaget, J., 39–40, 51
Pittelkow, Y., 101
Poe, E.A., 62
Pope Benedict XVI, 23, 53, 90, 94, 136
Pope Gregory IX, 117
Pope John Paul II, 66
Pope Leo XIII, 24, 136
Pope Paul VI, 134
Pope Pius IX, 65, 100
Pope Pius X, 85
Pope Pius XI, 134
Pope Urban II, 110
Popper, K., 3
Post, P., 157
Power, M.J., 38, 63, 79, 150, 152–3, 176,
    178
Ptolemy, 22
Pullman, P., 44
Putnam, R., 174–5
Pyszczynski, T., 69

Radcliffe-Brown, A.R., 42
Rappaport, R., 107
Regnerus, M.D., 101
Ringdal, G.I., 148

Rizzutto, A.-M., 48
Ross, J.M., 144
Rushdie, S., 131
Russell, C.T., 125
Russell, W., 66, 127
Rutherford, J.F., 128
Ruthven, M., 130

St. Augustine, 53, 115, 159
St. Basil, 76–7
St. Bernadette, 65, 100
St. Jerome, 153
St. John The Divine, 124–5
St. Paul, 58, 63, 70, 83, 115, 133
St. Teresa of Avila, 60, 107, 169
St. Thomas Aquinas, 159
Samarin, W., 76
Saroglou, V., 101
Schirmer, H., 80
Searle, J., 35
Segal, Z., 161
Shaw, G.B., 139
Shermer, M., 102, 128
Shushan, G., 72
Smart, J., 50
Smith, J., 64, 178
Smith, T.B., 123, 178
Snowdon, D., 141, 176
Solomon, S., 69
Spilka, B., 147
Sprenger, J., 117
Stokes, C.E., 101
Stork, J., 113–14
Storr, A., 120–21, 125

Stroebe, W., 43
Swanson, G., 95, 98

Tamayo, A., 98
Teasdale, J., 154, 161
Terry, K., 59, 134
Tertullian, 99
Tipler, F., 25
Toews, J., 143
van de Port, M., 94, 120
van Lommel, P., 72

Vasconcelles, E.B., 150
Venerable Bede, 93
Venter, C., 26
Vergote, A., 98
Voas, D., 101
von Helmholtz, H., 38
Vossler, M.T., 125

Wallace, D., 125
Watts, F., 55
Weber, M., 4 120, 122
Wesley, J., 53
Western Shugden Society, 105
Whitcomb, J., 25
Williams, J.M.G., 161
Wirth, D., 147
Wohler, F., 26
Wolf, E., 93–2, 99
Woods, B., 125
Wright, R., 8, 17, 64

Zhang, J., 159

Subject Index

Abraham, 7, 15–17, 42, 50, 111
Acupuncture, 153
Afterlife, 10, 11, 17, 72–3, 178
Agrarian communities, 6–7, 9, 98, 170
Ahura Mazda, 13, 18, 50, 63
Akhenaten (Amenhotep IV), 11–16, 42, 170–71
Albigensians, 110
Alien abduction, 79–80
Allah, 81–82, 108
Alpha male, 98
Alzheimer's disease, 76
Amarna, 12, 14
Amen, 15
Amaterasu Omikami, 2
Ambivalent self, 63
Amnesia, 73
Amulets, 9
Amun, 11, 14–15
Andaman Islanders, 41–42
Anencephalia, 76–7
Anesthesia, 71
Angel, 20
Angel Gabriel, 63
Angel Moroni, 64
Angra Mainyu, 13, 18, 50, 63

Animal sacrifice, 95
Anorexia, 62
Anthropic Principle, 25–7
Anthropomorphism, 29, 50
Apocalypse, 129
Apostasy, 48–9
Archbishop Ussher, 21, 23, 163–64
Aristotle, 21–2
Asclepius, 151
Asherah (Athirat), 7–8, 96
Assumption of Mary, 100, 171
Astral projection, 70, 71
Aten, 12, 14–15, 170–1
Atheism, 20, 31, 38, 110–11, 160, 173–5, 178–9
Attachment theory, 98
Australian aborigines, 5–6, 41, 169
Autism, 40, 76
Automatic writing, 129
Aztec, 93, 99

Baal, 8, 30
Baptism, 53, 155–6
Belief systems, 25, 69, 101, 128, 142, 144, 161, 164, 172–74, 179
Bereavement, 43–4
Bhagwan Shree Rajneesh, 113–14, 122

Bible
  Acts, 75, 82
  Corinthians, 132
  Daniel, 127
  Exodus, 14–15, 91
  Ezekiel, 7
  Genesis, 16, 21, 24, 29, 42, 127
  Gospels, 84
  Isaiah, 17
  Literalism, 29
  Luke, 45, 75
  New Testament, 84, 127
  Old Testament, 16, 21, 50, 78, 84, 86,
    111, 127, 142
  Mark, 45, 155
  Matthew, 45–6
  Pentateuch, 16, 84
  Psalms, 14
  Vulgate, 153
Black widows, 158
Blasphemy, 130–33
Blue Mosque, 177
Book of Mormon, 64
Brahman, 19
Buddha, 19–20, 42–3, 123
Burial practices, 9
Burqa, 132
Bwa Kayiman ceremony, 74

Cardiac problems, 72–3, 109, 145–6
Carmelite nuns, 63
Castrati, 177
Causal explanations, 39–40
Celibacy, 58–60, 130, 133–6
Central executive system, 36
Charisma, 60, 120–23
Charismatic movement, 75–6, 156
Chiefdoms, 8
Child abuse, 48, 59–60, 79, 116–17,
    134–6, 164, 177
Child development, 39–40, 48–9
China, 39, 110–11, 159–60

Christmas, 91
Church attendance, 101, 143, 148–9,
    174–75
Chwal, 74
Collectivist cultures, 160
Columbia Miracle Study, 147
Computer, 35–6
Confession, 162
Consciousness, 21, 34–8, 43, 69–77,
    168, 171, 178
Contraception, 164
Conversion, 82–3, 156, 175
Cosmology, 21–3
Council of Nicaea, 18, 84–5, 92, 100
Creation myths (cosmogonies), 7–8, 72
Creationism, 25–8
Croesus, 126
Cronus, 98–9
Crusades, 109–10, 164

Dalai Lama, 1–2, 19, 27, 104–6
Darwinism, 23–5
David Koresh, 122–23
Death, 43–7, 148
Deception, 37
Deliverance ceremony, 155–6
Delusions, 170
Demeter, 96–7
Democracy, 106–7, 171
Depression, 46, 62, 143, 152, 154, 159,
    163
Deva, 20
Devil, 62, 75
Dinosaur, 24–5
Dissociative state, 35–6
Dominicans, 117
Doomsday cult, 129
Dreaming, 40–43, 67–8, 169
Dreamtime, 5–6, 41, 169
Dualism, 35, 38, 50, 77
Dyads, 95–8, 111
Dynastic race, 8–9

Easter, 91, 92–93
Ecstasy, 56–7, 170
Egocentrism, 39–40
Egyptians, 8–12, 16–17, 26, 42, 58, 90, 96, 133
Eid, 16
El, 8
Emergent property, 35–6
Emotion, 131, 178
Emperor Hirohito, 2, 27
Emperor Vespasian, 84
Enlightenment, 21
Eostre, 93
Ephesus, 96
Epilepsy, 63, 71, 83
Eschatology, 127
Espanto, 154–5
Evil, 49–54, 130, 154
Ewing's sarcoma, 85–6
Existential anxiety, 69–70, 162, 172
Exorcism, 155–6

Faith, 21
False memories, 79–82
Fatima, 65–6, 68, 85
Fatwa, 131
Feminism, 30
Fertility rites, 7, 9, 93
Fire worship, 13
Free will, 50
Freemasonry, 10, 136–8
Fugue state, 73–5

Gadarene swine, 155
Garden of Eden, 25
Generativity, 176–7
Geocentrism, 22–3
Geology, 23–4
Glastonbury Tor, 93
Glossolalia, 75–6, 104
God, 28–9, 30, 47–50, 81–82, 96–8, 111, 120, 150, 159, 164, 171

God-king, 28, 105, 171, 173
God-of-the-gaps, 26, 168
Grief, 43–7, 169, 172
Gurdjieff, 122
Guru, 120–21, 123, 125

Hadith, 106, 159
Hajj, 81, 157
Hale-Bopp comet, 128
Halloween, 90–91, 94
Hallucinations, 34, 43–5, 61–68, 169–70
Happiness, 176–7
Harry Potter, 5, 90
Health behaviors, 143–44, 148, 163, 172, 177
Heliocentrism, 22–3, 26
Hell, 30–31, 62
Hijab, 132
Hijra, 106
Hiram Abif, 137
Holy Fool, 77–9
Holy Ghost (Holy Spirit), 75–6, 100, 104
Horoscopes, 126
Horus, 10, 96, 98
Hunter gatherers, 5–6, 115, 170
Hypnosis, 79–80

Illusions, 44–5
Imhotep, 10, 137
Immaculate Conception, 65, 100, 171
Immortality illusion, 35, 37–8, 69, 77, 168
Incubation, 151
Inquisition, 22–3, 47, 117
Isis, 9–10, 96, 98, 133
Israelites, 7, 8, 15, 17, 56
Ivan the Terrible, 78

Jacobin clubs, 137–8
Jayavarman II, 28

Jehovah, 15, 128
Jesus Christ, 10, 12, 17–18, 44–6, 74–5,
    84–5, 100, 123, 133, 137, 155,
    169
Jihad, 106, 110
Jim Jones, 122–23, 128
Jivaro tribe, 64
Joseph Smith, 64, 178
Juan Diego, 93, 99

Kaaba, 16, 17–18, 81, 157
Karma, 20
Karnak, 11
Knights Templar, 137
Koan, 20
Koran, 18, 81–82, 159
Korea, 103–4
Kosher (kashrut), 52, 57, 130

Last Judgment, 127
Limbo, 52
Loa, 74
Longevity, 3, 141–42, 163, 176
Lourdes, 65, 85–6, 100, 152, 157
Lunar calendar, 99
Lying, 37

MacTaggart, 134
Magical thinking, 40
Mana, 8
Mantra, 108
Marshall Applewhite, 128
Martin Luther King, 102
Martyrdom, 159, 163
Mary Magdalene, 45–6, 169
Masturbation, 133, 136
Mayotte people, 73–4
Meaning, 38–40, 46, 68–70, 164,
    172–74
Mecca, 12, 16–7, 63, 81, 106
Meditation, 20–21, 161–2, 178
Mediums, 44

Mega-church, 102–104, 111
Mesopotamia, 9
Metonic cycle, 92
Min, 9
Mind, 35, 77
Miracles, 68, 83–6, 152
Misogyny, 67, 97, 114–20, 132, 177
Monastic movements, 175
Moral development, 51–52
Moses, 14–16, 81
Mother goddess, 96, 170
Mount Athos, 115–16
Muhammad, 12–13, 17–18, 30, 63–4,
    81–82, 106, 132
Mystical experience, 55–6, 73, 169

Narcissism, 121, 125, 163
Natural disasters, 68–9, 147
Near-death experiences (NDEs), 71–73
Neolithic period, 6–8, 9, 96–8, 115,
    119, 138, 167–8
Neuroscience, 71–72
Neurosis, 4
Neurotheology, 144
New Religious Movements (NRMs),
    83, 103, 124–5, 175
Nicene Creed, 100
Nihilism, 173, 179
Nile, 9–10
Nirvana, 20
Nun Study, 141–2, 176

Object relations, 48
Oceanic feeling, 55–6
Orgasm, 56
Olympus, 99
Oracle at Delphi, 126
Original (ancestral) sin, 53–4, 100
Orisha, 94
Osiris, 9–11, 96, 98
Out-of-body-experiences (OBEs),
    70–72

Paleolithic period, 5–6, 29
Paleontology, 23–4
Papal infallibility, 100
Paradise, 11, 17, 171, 178
Pascal's Wager, 30–31
Paschal moon, 93
Passover, 86, 92
Patriarchy, 97, 114, 118–19, 137, 164, 170–1, 173
Pax Romana, 106
Penis envy, 97
Pentecost, 75
Pentecostal movement, 75–6, 104
Perception, 36
Phantom limb, 46–7
Pharaoh, 10–12, 14, 28, 90, 137
Phosphenes, 68
Physical constants, 26
Pilgrimage, 156–8
Placebo effect, 145, 153, 156
Pope, 3, 177
  Benedict, XVI, 53
  John Paul II, 1
Possession, 73
Post-traumatic stress disorder (PTSD), 69, 168
Prayer, 101, 108–9, 145–7, 178
Prayer liturgies, 108
Prayer wheel, 108
Priest-shaman, 6, 40, 64, 150, 153–54, 161–62
Primates, 37, 168
Primitive mind, 4
Prophecy, 126–30
Prostitution, 116
Protestant reformation, 91, 110, 127, 134
Psychic, 130
Psychopathy, 53–4, 178
Psychotherapy, 150–51, 153–54, 158, 161–2, 178

Ptolemy, 22
Pyramids, 10–11, 137

Quakers, 127
Quality of life, 176–7

Ra, 9, 11, 14
Ramadan, 64
Reductionism, 35, 55
Regeneration cycles, 5, 7, 96, 168
Reincarnation, 20
Religions
  Animism, 3–6, 13, 39–40, 173
  Assemblies of God, 103–4
  Branch Davidians, 100, 123
  Buddhism, 19–21, 36, 38, 58, 104–6, 133, 156, 160, 175, 177
  Candomble, 94–5, 119–20
  Cargo cults, 123
  Catholicism, 22–3, 49, 58–60, 67–8, 90, 94, 98, 100, 124, 134, 136, 160–61, 164, 171, 177
  Christianity, 13–16, 18, 21, 28, 53, 78, 90–91, 96, 110, 131, 134, 171, 175
  Church of Jesus Christ of Latter-Day Saints, 65
  Deism, 18, 20–21, 26
  Evangelical Protestantism, 102–103
  Heaven's Gate, 128
  Hinduism, 18–20, 156–8, 160
  Islam, 15–16, 30, 49, 52–3, 63–4, 95, 106, 110–11, 131–32, 156–8, 160, 171, 175
  Jediism, 125–6
  Jehovah's Witnesses, 127–8, 164
  Judaism, 13–14, 52–3, 57, 90, 92, 111, 130, 143, 143, 156, 171
  Macumba, 94–5, 119–20
  Manichaeism, 13
  Millenialism, 126–7
  Monotheism, 3, 7, 12–18, 42, 50, 58, 96–7, 149, 170, 173, 176

Religions (*Continued*)
Moonies, 78–9, 83
Mormonism, 49, 64–5, 127, 178
Orthodox, 77–8
Pagan, 91
Parsis, 12
Polytheism, 3, 15–18, 42, 98, 170, 173
Protestantism, 22–3, 49, 53, 136, 148,
  160, 161
Scientology, 124–5, 129
Scottish Free Presbyterianism, 57, 91
Seventh Day Adventists, 127
Shaking Quakers, 58–9
Shinto, 2, 177
Southern Baptist Convention, 100
Theism, 18, 31
Zoroastrian, 12–13, 18, 50
Religiosity, 83, 101–102, 111–12,
  142–44, 148–9, 159, 162
Religious extremism, 149, 158–9
Religious (faith) healing, 150–52, 154
Repressed memories, 25, 82
Resurrection, 17, 44–6, 92, 96, 169
Rhea, 98–9
Ritual, 107–9, 150–51
Rosary, 108

St. Basil, 77–8
St. Bernadette, 65, 100
St. Jerome, 153
St. John the Apostle, 127
St. John the Evangelist, 115
St. Paul, 63, 82–3
St. Simeon, 78
St. Stephen, 82
St. Teresa of Avila, 107, 169–70
Sagrada Familia Church, 177
Samhain, 90
Sannyasim, 113–14
Santa Claus, 174
Satan, 50
Saturnalia, 91

Science, 21–7
Scopes Trial, 24–5
Second Lateran Council, 58, 133–4
Seth, 9–10
Sexual revolution, 60
Sharia law, 131–32
Simulacra, 66
Sin, 116–17, 130–36
Slavery, 94–5, 119, 170
Sneezing, 156
Social capital, 112, 163, 174
Social structure, 89–90, 95, 98, 111,
  114, 116–17, 170–71, 173
Sol invictus, 91
Soul, 24, 35, 47, 77
Sovereignty, 95, 98, 101
Soviet Union, 38–9, 110–11, 160, 174
Speaking in tongues, 75–6, 104
Spirit walking, 70
Spirituality, 33, 89, 118
Stress, 68–70, 147–50
Subha, 108
Suicide, 122–23, 128, 158–61, 163
Sulis-Minerva, 151
Supernatural, 60, 63, 68, 71, 87, 95,
  124, 167, 169, 173
Superstition, 4–5, 149
Swearing, 130–33
Syncretism, 90–91, 96, 151

Taboo, 8, 131
Temple of Solomon, 137
Templeton Foundation, 109, 146
Temporal lobe, 71
Ten Commandments, 57, 142
Terreiro, 94, 119
Terror management theory, 69–70
Tertullian, 99–100
Tetragrammaton, 128
Theocracy, 19–20, 49, 104–7, 111, 174
Theodicy, 50–51
Theory of mind, 40

Thetans, 124–5
Tonantzin, 93–4, 99
Trance, 67, 73–4
Transportation, 63–4
Traumatic memories, 79–81
Trinitarianism, 95–6, 99–100, 111
Tutankhamun, 15, 170

Umbanda, 119
Unconscious, 38, 40, 67, 124
Universe, 25–6, 29, 34, 50, 163–64,
    168
Untouchable (dalit), 20, 163
Urbanization, 97, 115–16, 118

Vatican, 66, 90, 92, 104, 136
Vedas, 19
Venerable Bede, 93
Venus of Willendorf, 96
Vernal equinox, 92–93
Vestal virgin, 133
Virgin of Guadalupe, 93–4, 99
Virgin Mary, 65–8, 99–100, 111, 115,
    169, 171
Virgin mother, 28
Visions, 54, 61–68, 100
Visual afterimages, 68, 85
Vitalism, 26–7

Vohu Manah, 63
Volunteering, 175
Voodoo, 74

War, 109–11, 164, 175–6
Way of St. James (Camino), 157
Well-being, 176–8
Western Shugden Society, 105–6
Whitsunday, 75
Wiccaphobia, 117–18
Witchcraft, 94, 117–18
Witches, 90, 117–18
Wizards, 90
Womb envy, 97

Xenoglossia, 76

Yahweh, 14–17, 30, 128, 171
Yoido Church, 103–4
Yoruba people, 94–5
Yuletide, 91
Yurodivy, 77–8

Zamzam well, 157
Zen, 20
Zeus, 98–9
Zombie, 74
Zoroaster, 12–13, 63, 123